REVELATION
Three Viewpoints

REVELATION: Three Viewpoints

G. R. Beasley-Murray

Herschel H. Hobbs

Ray Frank Robbins

Summary by David C. George

BROADMAN PRESS
Nashville, Tennessee

© Copyright 1977 • Broadman Press
All rights reserved

4213-63
ISBN: 0-8054-1363-4

Dewey Decimal Classification: 228
Subject headings: BIBLE, NEW TESTAMENT//REVELATION
Library of Congress Catalog Card Number: 77-74512
Printed in the United States of America

Preface

Revelation is probably the most disputed and difficult book in the New Testament. Although it was recognized early as Scripture by some Christian leaders, others found it quite difficult to interpret and hesitated to acknowledge its authority. But the appeal of the book persisted, and eventually it was recognized as inspired Scripture. Through the centuries, however, Revelation has continued as an enigma to many interpreters. Luther rejected it because he felt that it did not present the message of Christ. Calvin omitted it from his commentary on the Bible. On the other hand, the book has frequently suffered at the hands of allegorical, literal, and schematic interpreters with easy answers to difficult questions. In recent years both popular and scholarly interest in the book has grown, evidenced in conferences and publications.

In May, 1976, the Sunday School Department of the Sunday School Board, Southern Baptist Convention, sponsored a five-day Revelation Bible Conference at the Ridgecrest Baptist Conference Center in North Carolina. It was attended by about one hundred pastors and lay persons. Three speakers were invited to interpret in five hours each the book of Revelation from their personal points of view. The sessions were so arranged that each interpreter could speak to the whole conference in small enough groups to allow for questions and answers. A panel discussion on the last day brought the three speakers together for queries and comparisons.

From the beginning there was no intention to present all the interpretations of Revelation. The three views considered had already been published by the speakers. Dr. George R. Beasley-Murray is professor of New Testament interpretation at Southern Baptist Theological Seminary and has written a number of books, including *Highlights of the Book of Revelation* (Broadman, 1972). Dr. Herschel H. Hobbs is pastor emeritus of the First Baptist Church, Oklahoma City, and among his many books is *Studies in Revelation* (Convention, 1974). Dr. Ray Frank Robbins is professor of New Testament interpretation at New Orleans Baptist Theological Seminary and has published *The Revelation of Jesus Christ* (Broadman, 1976). Those who planned the conference wanted to provide an overview of the book from three perspectives that would help participants arrive at their own approach to Revelation. The climate of the study was earnest, open, and constructive. The result was a fresh appreciation of an exciting book and a growing confidence in comprehending it.

Believing that such an approach to Revelation could be useful in book form, Broadman Press secured permission to transcribe the three sets of lectures and asked each speaker to revise the rough drafts. Dr. Beasley-Murray preferred to write three chapters based on his lectures and discussion sessions. Dr. Hobbs and Dr. Robbins condensed and edited their material for easy reading. Of course, the chapters herein cannot be considered adequate for weighing the whole view of any of the three men; for that purpose the reader should refer to their books. But this symposium can be a helpful guide through a fascinating book of the Bible.

Dr. David C. George, pastor, Immanuel Baptist Church, Nashville, Tennessee, attended the conference and talked at length with all three lecturers. He was asked to read their material and write a summary chapter on the context of the conference, the similarities and differences among the speakers, and some insights gained from the study.

BROADMAN PRESS

Contents

Contents

Part I

Premillennialism

George R. Beasley-Murray

1
An Approach Toward Understanding the Book of Revelation

It was a tall order to give an interpretation of the Book of Revelation in three lectures. There is such a lot of teaching crammed in its pages, so many difficulties that cry for explanation, and so many lessons that call for application, it is hard to make up one's mind what to leave out and what must be included. We are concerned here to consider distinctive approaches to the Revelation, so that we may understand precisely what people do believe about the book, and why they believe as they do. That helps us to determine the material we shall concentrate on. It seems to me that it will be most helpful to consider first how we should approach the book of Revelation, and to find out if there are any principles that enable us to understand the fundamental message of the book; and then we should go on to examine in greater detail two issues which we associate with this book more than with any other of the Bible, namely its teaching on the second coming of Christ and its teaching on the kingdom of God.

First a word about books written on the book of Revelation. Each of us lecturing at the conference was asked to submit three titles of books about the book. Now that's more difficult than you might think. If you go into a good theological library and look at the commentary section on the Bible, you will be surprised at the large number of books written about the last book of the Bible—and no library will attempt to gather together all the books that have been written on it. Many of them are magnificent, the fruit of years and years of study. And many of them differ to an extraordinary degree on the book they are writing about. When people ask me what commentary on the Revelation I would recommend for them, I sometimes say that if they want one which they will agree with completely they had better write one themselves. On the other hand, it is encouraging to see how writers of recent years, coming to the book from different angles, appear to be drawing closer together on many of its great issues. Let me tell you the three titles I gave and comment on them, for I think that each of them will stimulate you to fresh thinking, and each has a contribution of its own to make. I leave out, by the way, the commentaries which my two colleagues have written on the book, since attention will naturally have been drawn to them already.

The first book is not a commentary at all, but is written to give an idea of the fundamental message of the book. It is called *Time and History: A Study of the Revelation,* and was written by the Swiss scholar M. Rissi, now teaching in Richmond, Virginia, and it was published in 1966. This volume is written in a very concentrated manner, and though short, it has a great deal of information. I don't think I have read a better brief statement of the message and purpose of the book of Revelation than this.

The second is the commentary by George Caird, published in the Harper series of New Testament commentaries in the USA. Dr. Caird belongs to the United Reformed Church in England and is now professor of New Testament in Oxford. His commentary is in some respects the most brilliantly written on the Revelation that has appeared. Often commentaries are dull, but there's not a dull page in his book. You will not always agree with his positions, but you will always find them helpful, setting you thinking further, and what is more, Caird is concerned to understand the meaning of the book for people in the world today, and in this respect he is often highly successful.

The third is the commentary of George Ladd, independently published in 1972. Ladd is a Baptist, and during a long career of teaching (chiefly in Fuller Theological Seminary) he has taken a great interest in eschatology, notably with regard to the kingdom of God and the coming of Christ, and he has written a number of books on these themes. His commentary does something which few scholarly expositions of Revelation attempt to do: as a scholar of evangelical convictions Ladd constantly keeps an eye on what dispensationalist interpreters of the book say about it, and he explains why he has to take a different line at many points.

I will admit, by the way, that I added a fourth book to the list: it's my own commentary on the Revelation, which has been published in a series of commentaries little known this side of the Atlantic, *The New Century Bible*. It didn't appear in the USA till 1975, and consequently it has hardly come to be known yet. It provides a full-scale exposition of the kind of interpretation which was sketched in the little volume, *Highlights of the Book of Revelation*, and that will be enough to indicate its viewpoint to those of you who have read the latter book.

And now to business.

When people talk about ways of interpreting the book of Revelation, it is common for them to list the four classical types of understanding it, namely the *preterite*, which relates the book solely to the circumstances of the writer's age and discounts applications to future developments in history; the *futurist*, which sees the book as concerned solely with the last generation of history, when its prophecies will find fulfillment; the *historicist*, which views the Revelation as an outline of the history which unfolds between the incarnation of Christ and the end of the world; and the *symbolic* or *poetic*, which stresses the pictorial element in the book and declines to apply its prophecies to any one particular era. Most interpreters now recognize that each of the above approaches to the book has elements of truth which need to be taken into account for its right understanding, and at the same time that each taken by itself is seriously wanting. It seems to me helpful to get away from this kind of discussion and examine the relation of the work to other types of writing with which it has affinities, both within and outside the Bible. Interestingly enough we find in the opening verses of the book references to three different kinds of literary works with which it is linked. These are *apocalypse, prophecy,* and *epistle.* Let us look at these three in turn and see how the Revelation is related to them.

The first words of the book of Revelation are these: "*Revelation* of Jesus Christ which God gave him.*"* As you know, the book was written by John in the Greek language, and the word translated "revelation" is *apocalypsis,* which has passed over into our language as apocalypse. The word literally means the removal of the cover from something which is hidden, or the drawing back of a curtain to show what is behind it, and so it is naturally applied to the unveiling of what is concealed, a "revelation." Now the term has become a technical one for a whole class of writings, mainly Jewish, which were written during the two centuries before the birth of our Lord and the first century of our own era. These books are mainly concerned to reveal God's purpose in history, above all telling how he will bring his judgments on the wicked of earth who oppress his people, and how he will establish his kingdom for the righteous. The first complete book of this kind is in the Old Testament, the book of Daniel, and its style was imitated by a large number of writers. Most of them used the pen name of a great saint of earlier ages, and so we find that there is a book of Enoch (three of them in fact!), an Apocalypse of Abraham, the Testaments of the Twelve Patriarchs, the Assumption of Moses, an Apocalypse of Elijah, an Apocalypse of Ezra (in the Apocrypha), and so on. These books freely use the picture mode of setting out their messages such as we see in parts of Daniel and in the book of Revelation, though none of them do it to the extent that the book of Revelation does. This way of putting out a message has been likened to the political cartoons of our newspapers, and even the strip cartoons of comics, which some enterprising publishers are using to convey the story of the whole Bible. It's not irreverent to make comparisons of this sort; sometimes a picture can convey an idea more effectively than words, and when it uses caricatures it will often arrest the attention far more than a straightforward picture. God has many ways of communicating his truth, and the book of Revelation brings to a height of perfection this particular method.

One feature of apocalypses is their frequent use of earlier prophecies, both from the Old Testament and from later writings (which were almost always themselves dependent on the Old Testament). This did not come about through laziness or lack of originality on the part of the writers. Rather it was because of their conviction that God's Word in the early prophecies had yet to be fulfilled. Consequently the apocalyptists often combined earlier prophecies and rewrote them so as to apply them to the situations of their own times. This also is done by John, in that we find him using Old Testament prophecies at times in a quite new way, and applying prophecies of his contemporaries in a manner that they never dreamed of. We have to be on the lookout for this phenomenon, for it will often bring into being a picture in which, by a few deft additions, an old meaning has to be wholly subordinated to the new one that John makes it bear. Let me give just one example of this procedure. In chapter 11 of Revelation we read of the ministry of two witnesses, who powerfully bear their testimony in the last time, the period of tribulation when Antichrist appears. The witnesses have extraordinary powers—they can shut the sky that it shouldn't rain, turn the waters into blood, and smite the earth with every plague, and if any would harm them fire can come from their mouths to consume their enemies. Such a description is clearly intended to identify these two witnesses with Moses and Elijah. The return of Elijah is mentioned in the last paragraph of the Old Testament. A first-century rabbi stated that God said to Moses, "If I send the prophet Elijah, you must both come together." In the vision the two witnesses are killed, and their bodies lie in the city which is allegorically called "Sodom and Egypt, where their Lord was crucified"; but they are raised to life and ascend into heaven, and the city suffers an earthquake, after which the terrified citizens give God the glory. It is unlikely that John himself composed this prophecy from scratch, as it were; it is much more likely that it was a Jewish prophecy which literally looked for Moses and Elijah to return and preach in the last days; but John recognized in it a powerful picture of the witness of the church in the last times, and so by a slight change at the beginning he spoke of these two witnesses as *the two olive trees* of Zechariah's vision (in Zech. 6) and the *two lampstands* which stand before the Lord. Zechariah had spoken only of the *one* lampstand, which stood in the Temple; John had already symbolized the seven churches as seven lampstands, but here he made them two in number to correspond to the two witnesses. Hence the picture in Revelation 11 is made to show how the church of the last times will witness in the world like the two mighty and fearless prophets of ancient times, who led the people of God against the tyrant rulers of their day and whose witness was vindicated by the God at work with them.

In the introduction to his book John pronounces a blessing on those who read the words of *the prophecy,* and who keep it. He, therefore, speaks of his book as a prophecy, just as he also refers to himself later as a prophet. We are familiar with the works of the Old Testament prophets. These men gave God's people God's word for their times, and in so doing they ministered to God's people of all times. It is important to recognize that in the first instance the ministry of the prophets was directed to the needs of their contemporaries. Indeed the uniqueness of the prophets lay in the manner in which they set their own people in the context of God's dealings with them in the past, especially in relation to the covenant he had made with them in the desert, and also in the light of God's revealed purpose for them in the future. For those who rejected God's revelation in the past and his call in the present there could be only judgment in the future, but the burden of the prophets was a call to repentance precisely in order that God's people might have a part in the glorious kingdom of the future.

We recall that part of the result of the redemption of the Lord and the outpouring of the Spirit was the rebirth of prophecy. Apart from the gift of prophecy imparted to many an unknown believer, we read of specially gifted prophets in the church, like Agabus in Jerusalem, the prophets and teachers of Antioch, and Philip's four daughters. John, the writer of the book of Revelation, was such a man. Someone who carefully examined the use of the term *prophecy* in the New Testament defined its meaning as "speech borne from the inspiration of charismatic preachers, through which God's plan of salvation with the world and the Church is made known, as also the will of God in the life of the individual Christian" (Gerhard Friedrich in a *Theological Dictionary of the New Testament*, vol. 6, pp. 849 ff.). More simply that could be stated as denoting *God's purpose for the world* and *God's will for man*, and it is a fair description of the content of the book of Revelation. The great message this book has had for Christians of the first century, and of every subsequent century, is an assurance that the opposition of men and of all powers of evil cannot frustrate God's purpose for the world he has made, and in the light of this truth the call goes out for persistence in faith and obedience to the Lord on the part of his people.

Prophecy never has the purpose of satisfying the curiosity of men about the future. It is given always in order to call forth repentance, and faith, and obedience in living. Accordingly, the first of the seven Beatitudes which occur in the book of Revelation pronounces the blessedness of those who "*keep* the things written in it" (1:3).

I would draw attention to the third type of writing to which the book of Revelation belongs, because it is not so commonly recognized as it ought to be, though it should be obvious enough. The term *epistle* does not appear in the opening paragraph of the Revelation, any more than it does in the introductions to Paul's letters; but just as Paul addresses by name the churches to which he writes, so does John: "John to the seven churches that are in Asia: Grace to you and peace." Observe that it is not simply the case that John includes in his book seven separate letters to seven local churches (chaps. 2 and 3), but rather that the *whole* work is addressed to the seven churches; this the greeting makes plain, and we note that the book finishes up like any other letter of the New Testament. The book of Revelation therefore is undoubtedly an apocalypse, and it is a prophecy, but it is also a letter to churches for whom John had a responsibility and a great deal of concern.

Now the implication of this simple fact is of great importance. This book was as truly addressed to the situation and to meet the needs of the churches mentioned in its greeting as, say, the letter of Paul to the church at Colosse, which was in the neighborhood of the seven churches, or the letter to the Galatians, who lived not far to the east of them. We all recognize that in the providence of God the letters to the Colossians and the Galatians and the Romans convey God's word to us as truly as to the Christians to whom those letters were originally addressed; but we also surely acknowledge that we grasp that word most truly, and can apply it to our own situations with confidence, when we understand what its message was for the Christians to whom it was first addressed. That means that we have to take a bit of trouble to discover what called forth those letters, and how they met the needs of the churches concerned. There isn't a single epistle of the New Testament which is not illuminated when we approach it in this way, and indeed some of them (like that to the Colossians) cannot really be understood if we do not make such an effort. Similarly it is as we relate the pictures of the book of Revelation to the situation of the seven churches of Asia Minor that we come to understand the nature of its message to us today, and to the church of the last generation.

Accordingly we must add a brief statement about the setting of the book of Revelation, and what called it forth, so far as we can discern it. From very early times (from the second century, in fact), it was the belief of the teachers and leaders of the churches that John wrote his book almost at the end of the first century, in the closing days of the rule of the emperor Domitian. To what extent a persecution of the church had actually set in is disputed, but the fact that John is banished to a penal island, Patmos, shows that a beginning of active opposition to the church on the part of civil authorities had set in. Right through the century the emperors of Rome had laid claim to divinity, and they had used the titles "Lord" and "Savior," both of them in a sense which belonged to gods. Nobody, however, who confessed at his baptism "Jesus is Lord" (Rom. 10:9), could also declare publicly, "Caesar is Lord." Some of the emperors did not press this, but Domitian did more than any of his predecessors. A favorite title of his was *"Dominus et Deus noster"*—"our Lord and God"; and he especially liked to preface his condemnations of subjects whom he put to death with the words, "It has pleased the Lord our God in his grace . . . ." When a man with power arrogates to himself claims of this sort he can always find men ready to follow him. And it is astonishing, and all but incredible to us moderns, to learn the extent to which men carried this out. The poets of Domitian's court vied with one another in their exaggerated expressions of adulation. "May I gaze upon thee, Hope of mankind and Favourite of the gods," said one. Another wrote of the emperor:

> See, there is God,
>> there he is established with supreme power
> By the Father in heaven,
>> to rule the fortunate earth.

Ethelbert Stauffer, in his account of the struggle between the Caesars and the church of the Lord, gives a whole stream of acclamations with which Domitian was greeted, like "Lord of the earth," "Invincible," "Holy," "Blessed," "Worthy art Thou," "Worthy is he to inherit the kingdom," and so on. He added, "An ingenious organization, whose essential elements were established in the reign of Nero, ensured that these spontaneous acclamations took on a rhythmic quality, which was given emphasis and order by liturgical gestures of every kind. So the circus became a temple, the people's festival became worship of the emperor, and the festival meal became the Holy Meal of the Lord" (*Christ and the Caesars*, p. 155).

These things happened at Rome. But more sinister than the court poets were the promoters of the worship of the emperor in the cities of Asia Minor where temples were built for this purpose. There were officials ready to curry favor by their support of the cult, and priests anxious to extend their influence by persuading the populace to participate in the worship. There were, in addition to regular festivals in the temples, all manner of special festivals in the city, with mass proclamations of the emperor's deity and glory, of processions through streets with holy images and chanting of songs in praise of the lord emperor, and above all games in his honor, which concluded with holy meals and orgies such as befitted that kind of worship. It was difficult for Christians to get away from this sort of thing, but even more difficult for them to avoid was handling the money through which the propaganda of the emperor's cult was furthered. For the authorities were given permission to issue coins proclaiming the emperor's divine glory and victories and achievements, and on some of them the emperor was portrayed as Zeus, the chief of the gods. One could hardly refuse to use the money, either to accept it and give it, for that would put one out of business and lead to starvation. There's no doubt that the net was tightening for the Christians in Asia Minor in John's day. When one remembers the cruelty of Domitian and his evil ways—it was a Roman governor, Pliny, who called Domitian the beast from hell, sitting in its den and licking blood—it is not surprising that later Christians used his characteristics of bald head, heavy paunch, and thin legs as the model for Antichrist. (Stauffer has a fascinating account of all this in chapter 11 of his book.)

But there's another aspect of the relation of the Roman rulers to the world and the church which needs to be mentioned at this point. Domitian had a close rival in cruelty, vanity, and self-exaltation, namely in his predecessor Nero. The latter came to the throne at the age of seventeen when his mother had his own father Claudius stabbed to death. Five years later Nero gave his mother the same treatment, and had her murdered. He had his young wife Octavia executed after accusing her of adultery, and married his mistress Poppaea; in due time he personally kicked her to death. When Rome burned, he stood on the stage of his palace and sang a song about the burning of Troy. When he heard of whispers going around Rome that he had caused the fire of Rome, he instituted the persecution of Christians as the alleged culprits of the deed, and then he had them subjected to all sorts of sickening tortures and deaths. Rome was delivered from his reign of terror through a revolt of his army, and in the end he committed suicide before he could be captured. We know, however, from writings which came from subsequent decades of the first century that the fear of this degraded creature remained alive long after his death. At first it was disbelieved that he was really dead, and there was a fear that he would return at the head of an army to take vengeance on his enemies. That made it possible for impostors to claim that they were actually Nero still alive—we know of no less than three such men, one leading a rebellion against Rome in A.D. 69, and two others gaining a welcome among the Parthians east of the Euphrates in the years A.D. 80 and 88. At length it was realized, by the mere passing of time, that Nero must really be dead. But then a strange and terrifying notion spread about the world, that Nero would rise from the dead and lead his armies against Rome. There is a reference to this belief in the Sibylline Oracles (book III, lines 28 ff.), which were written two generations after Nero's death. So deeply did this fear of Nero become ingrained among many peoples of that time, in one language at least (the Armenian) the name Nero became and remains to this day the equivalent for Antichrist.

Now John was a Christian prophet, and he knew that there was only one Lord of the dead and living, and that is Jesus Christ, the risen Son of God, raised by God the almighty Lord, and I do not for one minute believe that he gave any credence to this notion about Nero that was circulating in the world of his day. But the combined wickedness of Nero and the blasphemous claims to deity of the monster Domitian enabled John to see with clear eyes just what it was that was going on in the world wherein he lived: this emperor worship was a devilish imitation of the true Christ sent from God for the salvation of the world. It was indeed the spirit of Antichrist at work already in the earth. Not that Domitian was the real Antichrist of the last days. John saw that he must pass from the scene, but that another would arise of the same fundamental type as Domitian, only even more terrible and successful in promoting his image as savior of the world; and that would be *another Nero*, the devil's "Anti-christ," both an imitation of the real Christ and his fierce opponent in the world. This seems to be what John would tell us in his visions of chapters 13 and 17. In both chapters the Antichrist is depicted as a seven-headed monster rising out of the sea. That was an ancient picture of the god of the sea, who rose in rebellion against the powers of heaven but was itself overcome by the Lord of heaven, and it came to be a caricature for antigod political powers, both empires and rulers, which attempted to repress God's people and true religion in the earth (that's why it is used in the book of Daniel, chap. 7). In Revelation 13:3 we read that one of its heads seemed to have a mortal wound, but its wound was healed, and the earth followed the beast and worshiped both the beast and the dragon (Satan) who had given the beast its power. It is easy to recognize in this picture the features of an emperor of the world like Nero, whom men thought dead, and who is to arise and claim the worship of men as Domitian did. Not only so, but another beast also appeared on the scene, who exercised authority and made men worship the Antichrist; here again we see the kind of thing that was at work in the very area where the seven churches were set: promoters of the cult of the emperor, men who called on their fellows to give religious allegiance to the emperor of the world.

Here then is the clue to the famous number of the beast, which is mentioned at the end of chapter 13: "Let him who has under-standing reckon the number of the beast, for it is a human number, its number is six hundred and sixty-six" (v. 18). The number of a name is the total gained by adding the numbers represented by each letter in the name, something that was possible in languages (such as Hebrew and Greek) where there were no separate signs for numbers and only letters were used for them. As may be imagined, all kinds of names have been put forward in the course of history to solve the puzzle presented by John. In reality it is likely that most Christians knew it already, and one had but to mention the number to secure recognition: when *Nero Caesar* is put into Hebrew from Greek (the language of Revelation) it makes the desired 666; oddly enough when it is put into Hebrew from Latin it makes the total of 616, which is read by some ancient copies of the Revelation of John. But should the name be in Hebrew? Because almost certainly the name was first recognized in Palestine among Jews. Its fitness as a symbol for Antichrist was seen in its failure to reach 777, the symbol for perfection, and Christians will have early known that the name Jesus in Greek totals 888 (this fact is mentioned in one early Christian work). The contrast between 666 with its failure to reach the goal on the one hand and the superabundance of 888 in Jesus is a striking illustration of the difference between the devil's christ and God's Christ.

My concern in mentioning these things is not to get a discussion going about ancient lore, but to draw our attention to the real issue with which John faces us. The glorifying of political power by making claims which belong to God alone is of the devil, and can lead only to destruction. And Antichrist in the book of Revelation is drawn from just such a model, which appeared in history in John's day, and has done so more than once since, and can be expected again in the future till the ultimate fulfillment comes. For Protestants to identify the Antichrist with the Pope of Rome, or Catholics to identify him with Luther (as some did), or for modern Evangelicals to make him the future leader of the World Council of Churches is to miss the mark completely, for it is to fail to take into account the relation of the symbols John uses to the world of his day. It is, in fact, to trivialize the Word of God and to make one blind to the real enemies of God and man as revealed in this book. Whoever witnessed the frenzy which Adolf Hitler was capable of inducing in normally reasonable men and has contemplated the devilry which he persuaded men to engage in, or has thought on the like influence of Mussolini on the Italians, and the appalling evil in the world inspired by Stalin, will come much closer to what John was talking about in the book of Revelation. Here are genuine approximations to the principles embodied in the inspired symbolism of the book of Revelation, and the events of our times show how truly they need to be taken with seriousness.

From this point of view the book of Revelation can be regarded as an unveiling of the nature of the forces at work in this world: God the Creator in his glory and majesty, sovereignly working his will in the world, over against the beast from hell, the dragon who would bring the world down to hell with him; the Christ of God, who alone is the Redeemer, giving himself for the life of the world and coming again to rule it with the power and grace of God over against the Antichrist who seeks to enslave the world in wickedness and bring it to destruction; and the City of God, represented by one who is called the Bride, the Wife of the Lamb, wherein redeemed mankind finds the fulfillment of creation in a new existence provided by the almighty love of God, over against the City of this world, represented by a glitteringly arrayed harlot, drunk with the blood of the righteous but destined to perish at the hands of the power it serves—the Antichrist himself. Such are the forces portrayed in this book, but never are they represented in such a manner as to suggest that they are equal forces, locked as it were in a mortal combat, which mankind looks on with bated breath to see which side wins. The entire book, from its first line to its last, makes it clear who is the real Lord of this world. The end of the story cannot be in doubt for any who know that Lord and have experienced his power in their lives.

It is our special task in the next two lectures to examine the teaching of the book of Revelation on the nature of the end which God through Christ will bring to pass. We shall therefore have to ignore a great deal of what the book says about the present. It would be helpful therefore to take a brief look at the beginning of the book, to ensure that we are set right for the rest of the course we are to follow. In so doing we shall discover that in the very opening statements of the Revelation the issues which have occupied us come to expression.

The customary greeting with which any letter of the ancient world begins is for John an elaborate one; it is a trinitarian one, in fact, which embodies a full-blooded faith, and is rooted in the Old Testament, is centered in the redemptive work of Christ, and anticipates the ultimate triumph of God. "Grace to you and peace from him who is and who was and who is to come." Here is an invocation of the blessing of God the eternal Father. It echoes one of the best known passages of the Old Testament, the revelation of God to Moses at the burning bush, and theoretically could have been uttered by any Jew, but it never was—till Jesus came. When Moses asked God his name, that he might tell his fellow Jews who it was who sent him, the reply was given, "I am that I am," or in more modern English, "I am who I am." Hebrew tenses however are much freer and wider in application than ours, and that name could as well be rendered: "I will be who I will be." Consequently, we find among the Jews a variety of ways of understanding its meaning. It was put in the Greek translation of the Old Testament as, "I am he who is," so asserting God's timelessness. A Jewish paraphrase (the Jerusalem Targum) expanded it to read, "I am he who is and who will be"; but in another place it explained it as, "I am he who is, and who was, and I am who will be." By these means the name was understood as signifying that God is the Lord who exists through all ages. But it will be observed that John makes a small but vital change in the name: God not only was and is and will be, but he is the one who *is to come*. That indicates that it is of the very nature of God that he should come from the future and work his gracious will. He did so in the past, he does so in the present, and he will do it in the future. And that is important, because so many forces in the world are ranged against God and his cause and his people right now, it is essential to know that God himself will act to bring that cause to triumph and vindicate his people. In a sense this is not new, for it is wholly in accord with the teaching of the Old Testament prophets; but there is no doubt that the teaching of the prophets has been underscored, vivified, and clarified through the knowledge that Jesus Christ our Lord is to come, for it is in his coming that God will come and fulfill his ancient promises. And there is no power in the world that can prevent *that!*

With God the Father there is joined in the greeting "the seven spirits who are before his throne." Coming between the name of the Father and the Son there can be no doubt that this is a designation of the Holy Spirit. Why then does John speak of seven spirits? He must have in view the vision of Zechariah chapter 4, where we read of a golden lampstand with seven branches which stands in the Temple ("before the Lord"), along with a statement, "Not by might, nor by power, but by my Spirit, says the Lord of hosts," which affirms that it is by the mighty Spirit of God that his people will achieve the task God has given them; and the seven lights are identified with the seven eyes of the Lord which range through the whole earth, that is, by which he sees all that goes on in the world. The link John observes between lampstand, mighty Spirit, and God's all-knowing scrutiny of what is happening in the world enables him to link the Spirit with the seven churches, which he himself represents as lampstands: the blessing of the sevenfold Spirit thus is invoked on the churches, since he is the almighty power of God at work in the world, and is sufficient to enable God's people to meet every challenge that can come to them and fulfill every task committed to them.

And the blessing of the Lord Jesus Christ is added: "from Jesus Christ the faithful witness, the first-born of the dead, and the ruler of the kings on earth." Jesus was the supreme *witness* of God of all time, and faithfully bore that witness to the end of his trials (see the use of this thought in 1 Tim. 6:13), a fact which afforded a silent encouragement to walk in his steps by his grace. As *the first-born of the dead* he has the privilege of the first-born, that is, of occupying the first place, and so in his case of exercising lordship over all the generations of man in the past; but as Lord of the dead Jesus also opens the path of life for the dead, and so gives promise of resurrection from death. And as for the living, he is *ruler of the kings of earth*—all of them!—including the man on the throne of Rome, who vaunts his rule to the skies, and boasts of his divinity but is a liar, and every successor to that tyrant as generations pass, and including the last impostor who will come as the servant of Satan. Jesus is Lord today! His coming will reveal who he is today, and who he ever will be.

Thus the revelation of the name of God in his triune majesty is both a blessing and a promise of all the blessings that are to be. No wonder that John utters a doxology of praise to the Redeemer (vv. 5*b*–6)! For by his death he has brought about another exodus, and brought to fulfillment the promise of God declared to the old Israel at the Exodus (Ex. 19:6), making his new Israel kings and priests with the Lord who is King and Priest for all. That leads to a statement which could serve as the motto of the book: "Behold, he is coming with the clouds." The language echoes that of Daniel 7:13, where the clouds with which "one like a son of man" comes indicate his origin from heaven and his divine power. When the Old Testament talks about God coming on the wings of the wind and with thick clouds, the language is intended to convey the thought of the subjugation of all creation before him, as he comes to rescue his people in need (see Ps. 18:4-19 for an instructive example of this). So again in this introduction to the Revelation we are reminded of the intention of the Savior to come and exercise the authority and power which belong to God for the subjugation of all evil and the deliverance of his people. Then will be fulfilled the words spoken through the prophet Zechariah (12:10) of the mourning for one whom men have pierced.

The prologue concludes with a final assertion of the unlimited sovereignty of almighty God: "I am the Alpha and the Omega," says the Lord God. *Alpha* is the first letter of the Greek alphabet, *omega* is the last one. It is the same as if one should say in English, "I am the *A* and the *Z*," and it suggests that God is the beginning and the end of the alphabet of life and all things, especially in relation to history. God began it, he will end it. He began it as he willed, and he will end it as he intends. And because that is so, he is Lord not only of the beginning and of the end, but of all that falls between—the Lord of the whole alphabet! We who stand between the *A* and the *Z* of time need to remember that, whatever the point of history we happen to occupy, we're under the hand of "the Lord God . . . *the Almighty!*"

We should not be surprised that this symbolic name of *Alpha* and *Omega* is applied to Jesus (Rev. 22:13). We should not be surprised, because Jesus is God's representative to man and to the universe as a whole, and moreover we see this name embodied in his story of redemption. When the risen Christ tells John who he is (in 1:17 f.), he declares, "I am the first and last and the living one." That is the meaning of *Alpha* and *Omega:* the Lord initiates God's purpose, he ends it, and as one who is above the limitations of time he is the Lord of the period between. He goes on to add, "I died, and behold I am alive for evermore, and I have the keys of Death and Hades." He who is the beginning and end of the alphabet of history is the beginning and end of the alphabet of salvation. He began it in his dying for us. He is the Lord who lives and exercises his grace for us in the present, and as the holder of the keys of Death and Hades, he will unlock those doors through which we pass at death and give us entrance into the everlasting life of God's kingdom.

Yet one final word is added before the letters are given to the churches. The Lord who walks amidst the lampstands and holds the stars in his right hand tells what this symbolism means: the lampstands are the churches set in the seven cities named—he is ever present with them. And the stars in his right hand are the "angels" of the churches. Are they then literally angels in heaven, which guard or represent the churches on earth? Or are they by chance the leaders or pastors of the churches? Some have maintained these views through the years, but both are difficult in view of the way the following letters are addressed to the angels of the churches, but in all cases it is the members who are spoken to in the letters themselves. In any case it is difficult to think that the Lord wrote letters to angels in heaven via John on earth. It is likely therefore that the angels of the churches mean the churches "in Jesus"; living inconspicuous lives on earth, they are nevertheless saints of God, priests and kings with Christ, who already belong to God's sovereign rule. Those so related to their all-powerful Lord are assured that they are held in his right hand. They are safe evermore! But more than safe. They are upheld in their endeavors to serve the Lord. Here it is to be remembered that the churches are compared to "the seven stars." In the ancient world the seven stars recalled the seven planets. And because men commonly believed that the planets exercised a powerful influence in the world, they became a symbol of power exercised in the world. Quite frequently the coins issued by the Roman emperors had the seven stars stamped on them as a symbol of the rule which they (the emperors) bore over the whole world. The symbolism of this statement accordingly is quite startling: when John states that the seven stars are the churches in Jesus, held by his right hand, he is declaring that the sovereignty of this world does not belong to those lords of the nations who sit on the throne of Rome and elsewhere, but to the Christ of God and his people. The King of kings and Lord of lords alone has all power over the universe, and he is pleased to associate with himself the group despised and persecuted by men, but dear to him since they look to him and walk with him. The future of the world is with Christ and his people! The rest of the book of Revelation explains how that will come to pass.

2
The Coming of Christ in the Book of Revelation

The last book of the Bible, as everyone knows, is a book about the last things of time and history. It gives a large amount of space to describing judgments which will occur at the end of the age on a rebellious world, and a fuller account of the kingdom than any which may be found elsewhere in the Bible. Curiously, however, it gives comparatively little space to describing the coming of Christ as an event, and there are surprisingly few references to it in the body of the book. The one unmistakable description of the second advent occurs in chapter 19, where the returning Lord is depicted as the mighty leader of the hosts of heaven. The sole interest of the vision, however, is to show what the coming will mean for those elements among the nations which have set themselves against Christ and his people and have followed the Antichrist. How the vision is to be related to the church on earth is not stated, or how it affects those on the earth who have not joined the forces of Antichrist—and various passages in the book indicate that there will be many such. Admittedly John has not left us without hints about these matters, but it remains that there is no picture in the Revelation which tells of what happens to the church at the coming of Christ comparable to that given by Paul in 1 Thessalonians 4:15 ff., nor does John provide an exposition of the resurrection like that in 1 Corinthians 15. On reflection, perhaps that should not surprise us unduly, for after all it is also true that Paul does not say a word

about the relation of unbelievers to the Lord at his coming in 1
Thessalonians 4 (unlike 2 Thess. 1—2), nor does he discuss the
meaning of resurrection for mankind outside the church in 1
Corinthians 15. And the reason for the limitations which Paul
imposed on himself in the Thessalonian and Corinthian letters is
almost certainly the same as that which led John to restrict
himself in the scope of his own prophecies: neither Paul nor John
wrote to provide handbooks on the doctrines of the last things;
still less were they concerned to give descriptions of the judgment of God and the kingdom of God which unbelievers could
examine with a view to comparing Christian ideas with scientific
and philosophical prognostications of the future of man and the
universe. The apostles, like the prophets of the Old Testament,
were concerned to meet the spiritual needs of the people to
whom they ministered, to encourage them to live in such a
manner as to be ready for the Lord when he comes and to be
worthy of the blessings of the kingdom. As was earlier mentioned, prophetic declarations in the Bible about the future of
mankind were not intended to satisfy the curiosity of God's
people but to stir them to repentance and faith, to hope and love,
to obedience in living and endurance in testimony, to adoration
and to service.

There is, in addition to this, another factor which would have
affected John in his representations of the second coming of
Christ, and it is a theological one of great importance. I think it is
a fact of bedrock certainty that while the book of Revelation is
concerned with the end of history, its teaching about the end is
determined by the revelation of God in Christ which has been
given in the life, death, and resurrection of Christ. The second
coming is not an isolated event which arbitrarily brings the
curtain down on the story of man; rather it is the last link in a
chain of acts of God in Christ through which his will is wrought in
the earth. Fundamentally the doctrine of Christ's coming at the

end is the outworking of the doctrine of the God who in Christ was reconciling the world to himself. It is the end of *that* story which John writes about, and we do wrong to look for the last advent without holding firmly its relation to the redemptive acts of the first. The kingdom comes through the total work of Christ, not through the last act alone. Indeed the last act can come about only because of the supreme importance of the first act.

The rightness of this conclusion may be illustrated from the central vision in chapters 4—5, which I am accustomed to describe as the fulcrum of the book of Revelation. Admittedly this "fulcrum" stands nearer the beginning of the book than its end; but the previous chapters lead up to its revelation of God in his glory and Christ in his exaltation, and the visions which follow (concerning the judgments of the Lord and the kingdom to which they lead) flow out of this central one. The two chapters may be viewed as an exposition of the biblical doctrine that the God of creation is the God of redemption. The vision is separated into two parts. First it represents God in his transcendent majesty, exalted high above the storms and confusion of this small planet; its picture is reminiscent of some of the visions of God in the Old Testament prophetic books, such as those of Isaiah 6 and Ezekiel 1; then there is given a visionary description of the Lamb through whom God makes his saving sovereignty effective in the universe (chap. 5). The separation of the vision into two parts throws emphasis on the second one, and so on the salvation already accomplished by Christ and its effects on the future. It is thereby made clear that the eternal intention of God to give to his creatures his kingdom of grace and glory is put into effect through "the Lamb"; by his death and resurrection he has brought about a redemption for mankind, and through this victory he has won the right to set in motion the events which will end this age and bring in the kingdom which belongs to the next. The scroll which is handed to the Lamb appears to symbolize the promise of God to give the kingdom; the handing of it to the Lamb evidently signifies that to him has been given the authority to reign in that kingdom, and so the hosts of heaven and all creation offer worship to God and the Lamb, who are jointly enthroned on the throne of the universe. In all this there is no mention of the passage of time. We are told that the Lamb who had been slain "stands," and therefore is risen from the dead; but there is no reference to any subsequent coming in glory, nor, since the scene of the vision is in heaven, is there a hint of his going forth to manifest his victory and establish his reign. Yet, the ascribing of glory to God and the Lamb by every creature in heaven and earth and the realm of the dead shows that the vision looks on to the end of the age, when all rebellion is ended and all acknowledge the one Lord of the universe. In reality the rest of the book is written to show what acts of divine sovereignty, in judgment and deliverance through Christ, must take place before all creation acclaims its Lord, and that is the burden of the prophecies from chapter 6 on. Nevertheless it is plain that all those deeds are the outworking of the central action of the vision.

The point which we labor to make clear is that the process of salvation, and the establishment of the divine sovereignty which we call the kingdom of God, is an indivisible whole. The work of God in Christ from the incarnation to the final advent is one unbroken action. The dual event of Good Friday and Easter Sunday calls for the coming in glory as its complement and completion, and together they constitute one great victory of almighty love.

Since these things are so, and having recognized their importance, we may be prepared to find that in the earlier part of the Revelation, namely in the letters to the churches, the thought of Christ's great coming is applied to his work among his people in the sense of preliminary "comings" to them, alike in discipline and in blessing.

The first of the letters is addressed to the church in Ephesus, the oldest, largest, and best known of all the churches of Asia Minor. By this time, indeed, the Ephesian church could conceivably have become the largest Christian church in the world, for the church of Jerusalem had been scattered a generation earlier, and only the church at Rome could have been larger. Yet this church which had been founded by the apostle Paul, and had had the benefit of the ministry of the apostle John, is charged with the grave sin of having abandoned its first love (Rev. 2:4). From the context it looks as though we are to understand that this applies alike to love to God and love to man. A church which has ceased to love God and man is a living repudiation of the first command of the old covenant (see Mark 12:28–30), and a denial of the revelation of God in Christ which constitutes the heart of the new covenant. Such a group, however great it may be in the eyes of men, has ceased to be a true church of the Lord. The risen Savior therefore demands of them, "Remember from what you have fallen, repent and do the works you did at first. If not, *I will come to you and remove your lampstand from its place*" (Rev. 2:5). That seems to clearly mean that if the congregation does not repent, the Lord will "come" to it in judgment, just as one day he will come to the world in judgment, and by the removal of its lampstand end its existence as a church of the Lord. It will no longer be owned by the Head of the Church as belonging to him. The situation is similar as when Ezekiel once declared that the Temple was forsaken of the glory of God when his word of judgment was pronounced upon it (Ezek. 11:22–25), and when Jesus stated that the time was coming when the Temple would be empty of God—a shell without meaning (Matt. 23:38). These are words calculated to shock any congregation, but they would not have been uttered if they had not been meant. They do not state that the sentence of judgment had already been passed, but they do warn of its possibility. The church therefore is called to repent and recover the love it once had, in order that such a judgment might be averted. We observe again that the word of the risen Christ to this church does not state what will happen to it at his coming in glory, but it compares his work of discipline among them in the present to the effect of his final coming. It is evident that the acts of the Lord among his people are as powerful now as they will be in the day of his appearing before the world.

In the light of this message to the Ephesian church we have to reckon seriously with the fact that the presence of the Lord with a particular congregation can never be taken for granted, as though it may be assumed that he will be with them whatever the church may do in the future. There are many churches of former centuries which died through walking in ways comparable to the Ephesian congregation. We need to be alert that the congregation to which we belong does not permit itself to develop in the same way. It may further be remarked that it is precisely the book of Revelation, with its stark emphasis on the reality of judgment, which also lays the strongest possible emphasis on the importance of love in the church. Concern for maintaining truth in the face of those who perverted it was the Ephesians' strong point (Rev. 2:2). But truth maintained without love has lost the most important truth. John doesn't often repeat the point in the remainder of his work, nor was it to be necessary. A church without love is a spurious church. And if the greatest of churches needs to take heed lest it fall, how much more the rest?

Two other churches have words addressed to them in a similar vein to those sent to the church of Ephesus, namely the church at Pergamum (Rev. 2:13 ff.) and that at Sardis (Rev. 3:1 ff.). The former is said to have among them "some who hold the teaching of Balaam, who taught Balak to put a stumblingblock before the sons of Israel, that they might eat food sacrificed to idols and practice immorality." From that we gather that there were some leaders in that congregation who held "advanced" ideas on religion and morality. Since meat was meat, whether sacrificed in honor of idols or not, they would have urged, why hesitate to take it, even in pagan temples and on festival occasions when the patron gods of the city or trade guilds were honored and worshiped? And in the pagan world of the first century immorality was very much taken for granted—to consort with a harlot was every young man's right, and the older men included themselves in that freedom. It is strange that there could have arisen teachers in the church who deduced from the proposition that the Spirit alone was supreme in life that it did not matter what you did in the flesh; so the more spiritual you were, the more freedom in the flesh you allowed! That was Balaam's way of destroying Israel (Num. 25:1 ff.), and that's a highly effective way of destroying a church. The Lord therefore says: "Repent. If not, I will come to you soon and war against them with the sword of my mouth" (Rev. 2:16). What a fearful possibility! But note that in this case the Lord does not warn that he will come to judge the whole congregation, but that he will take action against the offenders who are spoiling it. It is a call for *self*-discipline, for personal repentance, and genuine faith, that they may be on the Lord's side and not have him against them.

The word of Jesus to the church at Sardis, the church which had a name that it was alive but was dead (Rev. 3:1), is a little uncertain of interpretation. He says: "Remember what you received and heard; keep that, and repent. If you will not awake, I will come like a thief, and you will not know at what hour I will come upon you" (v. 3). The language echoes the parable of the burglar at night, spoken by Jesus in his ministry (Matt. 24:43 f.), wherein he warns of the possibility of being unprepared for the coming at the end of the age. Could he mean the same in this passage, and is he warning the church at Sardis that if its members do not repent they may be caught off their guard by his advent and suffer loss in that day? It could be so, but in view of the similar warnings in the earlier letters it is more likely that language relating to the second coming of the Lord is here used in relation to his work of disciplining his people in the present.

In each of the three instances in which the imagery of the second coming is applied to the Lord's work among his churches in the present, the aspect of coming in judgment has been foremost. There is one instance where the coming to bestow the blessings of the kingdom is in view, and that, most surprisingly, is addressed to the least deserving church of all, the church in Laodicea. The strong words of condemnation spoke to this most satisfied of churches are followed by the well known call: "Behold, I stand at the door and knock; if any one hears my voice and opens the door I will come in to him and eat with him, and he with me" (Rev. 3:20). No longer is the whole church in view, for this is a word to each individual hearer. The Lord declares that as one day he will come and welcome his people to the feast of his kingdom (see the rich imagery about this in Isa. 25:6, and also Rev. 19:9), so he will "come" to any who open their lives to him; and he will hold the kind of fellowship with them that one has at a dinner, and to which one day he will invite them at his table. It is a beautiful picture. Quite understandably it is often quoted in church at the Lord's table, where his people hold fellowship with him as once he did with his disciples, and as he will do again in a new way, in his Father's kingdom (Mark 14:25). There is nothing more wonderful in all the world than to know its truth in one's own life.

As to John's teaching on the coming of the Lord at the end of the age, we do well to recall the significance of the name of God as defined in the introductory greeting of the Revelation: God is he who is and who was and who is to come (Rev. 1:4). It belongs to the nature of God that he "comes" to perform those things which are needful for the establishing of his will on earth. We pointed out that this modification of the traditional Jewish understanding of the name of God revealed to Moses was a direct consequence of the knowledge that Christ himself is to come at the end of the age. The allusion to that doctrine in the divine name has the effect of saying that God comes to achieve his will in and through the Christ, the Son of God. And that is a very important bit of biblical theology.

The teaching that God "comes" to set right the wrongs of this world, through judging the evildoers and delivering the righteous, is a theme which runs right through the Old Testament. One of the earliest pieces of poetry in the Old Testament is the Song of Deborah, sung in jubilation at the defeat of Sisera, commander of the Canaanite army. The prophetess recalls an earlier occasion when God "came" for the rescue of Israel, namely at the Exodus (Judg. 5:4–5, RSV):

> Lord, when thou didst go forth from Seir,
>> when thou didst march from the region of Edom.
> the earth trembled,
>> and the heavens dropped,
>> yea, the clouds dropped water.
> The mountains quaked before the Lord,
>> yon Sinai before the Lord, the God of Israel.

It is instructive to see how this song is elaborated in the last chapter of the prophecy of Habakkuk, some of which we will cite:

> God came from Teman,
>> and the Holy One from Mount Paran.
> His glory covered the heavens,
>> and the earth was full of his praise.
> His brightness was like the light,
>> rays flashed from his hand;
>> and there he veiled his power (vv. 3–4, RSV).
>
> He stood and measured the earth;
>> he looked and shook the nations;
> then the eternal mountains were scattered,
>> the everlasting hills sank low (v. 6, RSV).
>
> Was thy wrath against the rivers, O Lord?

> Was thy anger against the rivers,
>> or thy indignation against the sea,
> when thou didst ride upon thy horses,
>> upon thy chariot of victory? (v. 8, RSV).
>
> The mountains saw thee, and writhed;
>> the raging waters swept on;
> the deep gave forth its voice,
>> it lifted its hands on high.
> The sun and moon stood still in their habitation
>> at the light of thine arrows as they sped,
>> at the flash of thy glittering spear.
> Thou didst bestride the earth in fury,
>> thou didst trample the nations in anger.
> Thou wentest forth for the salvation of thy people,
>> for the salvation of thy anointed (vv. 10–13, RSV).

The important feature of this poem is its representation of the terror of creation before the coming of the Lord. It is a typical Oriental way of setting forth the incomparable majesty of the Creator, whose power all elements in creation acknowledge and at whose appearance they all tremble. Observe that it is when the Lord *comes* for judgment and deliverance, that the powers of nature go into confusion.

This kind of imagery is both employed and even extended in passages of Old Testament prophecy which describe the Day of the Lord, which is a day when God acts to judge nations, whether on occasions that cry out for God's rebuke for particular evils or at the climax of history, when God calls a halt to all the wickedness of men. This is understandable, inasmuch as the Day of the Lord is the day when God himself "comes" to intervene in the affairs of men, and puts forth his almighty power to overthrow the oppressors of the earth and set right its wrongs. If the earth shook when God stepped forth to rescue his people from the hand of Pharaoh, how much more when he appears to put a stop to all the evils of earth and to change the course of history? Accordingly, Isaiah tells how the Lord himself will come on his fearful day:

> Behold the name of the Lord comes from far,
>> burning with his anger, and in thick rising smoke;
> his lips are full of indignation,
>> and his tongue is like a devouring fire (Isa. 30:27, RSV).

And here is a typical description of nature's reaction on that day:

> I will make the heavens tremble,
>> and the earth will be shaken out of its place,
> at the wrath of the Lord of hosts
>> in the day of his fierce anger (Isa. 13:13, RSV).

For this reason it is further stated:

> The stars of the heavens and their constellations
>> will not give their light;
> the sun will be dark at its rising
>> and the moon will not shed its light (Isa. 13:10, RSV).

The elements of the universe are in confusion when almighty God performs his great deeds of power.

In an altogether happier vein it is described in many Old Testament passages how God comes to bring salvation to his people and to the world.

> Behold, your God
>> will come with vengeance,
> with the recompense of God.
>> He will come and save you (Isa. 35:4, RSV).

And what happens then?

> The wilderness and the dry land shall be glad,
>> the desert shall rejoice and blossom;
> like the crocus it shall blossom abundantly,
>> and rejoice with joy and singing.
> The glory of Lebanon shall be given to it,
>> the majesty of Carmel and Sharon.
> They shall see the glory of the Lord,
>> the majesty of our God (vv. 1–2, RSV).

The pertinence of all this to the book of Revelation should be clear. As the Old Testament prophets emphasize the prospect of the coming of God to the world, so does John, only even more so, for it is the controlling theme of his book. There is, however, an important difference between his perspective and that of the Old Testament prophets: John knows that the God whose nature it is to come has already come in Christ, the incarnate Son, and in him wrought a judgment and a deliverance of a different order from that which most of the early prophets were given to see. But that judgment was crucial, and the kingdom is among men, in a hidden manner. From chapter 6 onward John is to show how God is to come in the Lord Jesus Christ in a new way, to unveil the glory that was present but hidden in the first coming and to bring to victory the kingdom which is among men now.

John, however, is in no hurry to depict the final coming itself. In the Old Testament the Day of the Lord was the precursor of the kingdom, the bridge, as it were, from the old age to the new. So John depicts that day, and does it as no other prophet before him. He elaborates the judgments that are to be in the earth in the great Day of the Lord into three series, under the symbolism of the effects of unsealing God's covenant-will for the world, the sounding out of trumpets, and the pouring out of cups of wrath. These are not stretched out through vast reaches of history but are the immediate precursors of the kingdom; nor do the three follow in succession, but they are three representations of the judgments of God at the end. Moreover these events are the acts of God almighty in and through the almighty Christ: hence all nature trembles and shudders and flees at this unprecedented intervention of God in the earth. This is why we read of the cosmic upheavals near the end of the first descriptions of judgments, at the opening of the sixth seal:

> There was a great earthquake; and the sun became black as sackcloth, the full moon became like blood, and the stars of the sky fell to the earth as the fig tree sheds its winter fruit when shaken by a gale; the sky vanished like a scroll that is rolled up, and every mountain and island was removed from its place (6:12–14, RSV).

This does not, as is often affirmed, portray the break-up of the universe and the end of this world. It is the old prophetic tradition of the accompaniments of the Day of the Lord, when the Creator steps forth in his majesty and wrath to judge the nations (note v. 17: "the great day of their wrath has come—of God and the Lamb—and who can stand before it?"). In addition to this we read that at the end of each series of seven judgments there occur thunder, loud noises, lightning flashes, and earthquake (see 8:5; 11:19; 16:18 ff.); these are brief allusions to the same basic response of nature to the coming of the Lord, and they confirm what on other grounds we are led to deduce, that *each series of judgments issues in the last advent.* That is to say, the outcome of each of them is that majestic vision of the returning Lord in Revelation 19:11 ff. Accordingly we should recognize that insofar as the judgments narrated in chapters 6—19 are to be viewed as acts of the Lord Christ himself (some sections contain explanatory interludes and are to be excepted from this), and inasmuch as his appearing brings about the revelation of the kingdom described in chapters 20—22, the entire book from chapter 6 to chapter 22 is one great exposition of what the coming of Christ means.

We have referred several times to the description of the coming of the Lord in chapter 19, but before we consider it we should take note of a briefer portrayal of the Lord's coming which occurs in chapter 14 (vv. 14–19, RSV). The paragraph likens the judgment which the Lord executes at his return to a reaping of a harvest of grain, and it is followed by a similar paragraph which tells of the gathering of the harvest of grapes by an angel.

> I looked, and lo, a white cloud, and seated on the cloud one like a son of man, with a golden crown on his head, and a sharp sickle in his hand. And another angel came out of the temple, calling with a loud voice to him who sat upon the cloud, "Put in your sickle, and reap, for the hour to reap has come, for the harvest of the earth is fully ripe." So he who sat upon the cloud swung his sickle on the earth, and the earth was reaped.

And another angel came out of the temple in heaven, and he too had a sharp sickle. Then another angel came out from the altar . . . and he called with a loud voice to him who had the sharp sickle, "Put in your sickle, and gather the clusters of the vine of the earth, for its grapes are ripe." So the angel swung his sickle on the earth and gathered the vintage of the earth, and threw it into the great wine press of the wrath of God.

Now these two paragraphs put in visionary form a single short statement in the prophecy of Joel (3:13, RSV):

> Put in the sickle,
>> for the harvest is ripe.
> Go in, tread,
>> for the wine press is full.

Joel's double picture of judgment under the figure of the grain and grape harvest is filled out in the vision of John 14:14 ff. Why is it set at this point in his book? It is due to its relation to the section, chapters 12—14, which give an exposition of what lies behind the conflict between the state and the Christian church, and what it will eventually lead to: it is part of that age-long spiritual warfare between the forces of darkness and the Lord of heaven. Chapter 14 brings this section of Revelation to a conclusion by a series of seven short prophetic oracles, to which the two paragraphs on the messianic judgment form the conclusion. So the coming of the Lord is seen to form the end of *that* story. It is not depicted on the grand scale of chapter 19, yet its meaning is plain: the Christ appears as "one like a son of man," seated on a cloud, as in the vision of Daniel 7:13, but in contrast to the Danielic vision, its purpose is not for his coronation as king but for judgment—the coronation comes later. Curiously there is no clear statement in John's picture that the one like a son of man *comes* on the cloud; he is simply seated on it, as though stationary. Nevertheless, every reader of John's vision in the early church would recognize the picture, and would realize that the cloud is not to serve as a throne or a halo, still less to hide the

Lord from earth's view (as at the ascension, Acts 1:9), but that it serves as a means of coming from heaven to earth. To come on the clouds in the Old Testament is constantly represented as God's way of coming to the world to act mightily in judgment and salvation; for the Son of man so to come shows that he comes from God and that he shares the nature of God. Hence he waits to hear the divine word intimating the arrival of the hour before he sets forth: the angel who bids him put in the sickle comes out of the Temple, and so carries the word of the Father to the Christ that the moment has arrived. That is in accord with the Lord's teaching given before and after his death (Mark 13:32; Acts 1:7).

The harvest of earth's judgment sets forth under one symbol what in chapter 19 is depicted under the image of a battle, and to that passage we now turn. Its essential content is contained in verses 11–16:

> Then I saw heaven opened, and behold, a white horse! He who sat upon it is called Faithful and True, and in righteousness he judges and makes war. His eyes are like a flame of fire, and on his head are many diadems; and he has a name inscribed which no one knows but himself. He is clad in a robe dipped in blood, and the name by which he is called is The Word of God. And the armies of heaven, arrayed in fine linen, white and pure, followed him on white horses. From his mouth issues a sharp sword with which to smite the nations, and he will rule them with a rod of iron; he will tread the wine press of the fury of the wrath of God the Almighty. On his robe and on his thigh he has a name inscribed, King of kings and Lord of lords (RSV).

This description of the Lord at his coming is reminiscent of a number of earlier representations of him which are scattered through the Revelation. The interesting feature of their appearance here is that they are brought together with no attempt to make them form a single and consistent picture. For example, the Lord is depicted as the Field Marshal of the armies of heaven: he rides forth on a white horse, followed by the armies of heaven also riding on white horses. Yet, it is said that he treads the wine press of God's wrath—alone. The two pictures are imaginative and symbolic ways of setting forth a single idea, that of the execution of judgment upon rebellious and reprobate members of mankind, but their very nature makes them widely different; a Commander of the forces of heaven must come with a great multitude, whereas, he who treads a wine press does it on his own—there's no room for a crowd! Again the Lord is said to have a name inscribed which no one knows but himself (v. 12); yet his name is inscribed on his robe, so that all can read it (v. 16), and it is openly said that his name is the Word of God (v. 13). There is a reason for these apparently contradictory statements; in the world of the Bible a name revealed the nature of a person (hence a change of a person's character or status could be accompanied by a change of name, like those of Abram and Jacob); the unknown name of Christ fittingly symbolizes the fact that the mystery of his nature eludes the understanding of man, as he himself once said (Matt. 11:27). Yet, one must admit that these statements about the name of Christ are paradoxical and certainly set one thinking! The robe of Christ is said to be blood stained (v. 13), but the battle has not yet taken place, and the winepress has not been trodden, this too is unexpected, but in fact it simply denotes the function of the Lord to be the agent of the divine judgment.

This diversity of pictures points to something of great importance, namely that every element of this description of the coming of the Lord is pictorial. The horses in heaven on which the Lord and the angels ride, the winepress of God's wrath, the great supper of God wherein the birds of the air gorge themselves with the flesh of the great and small of humanity, all these are as elements in a surrealist picture of the end of history. They portray ideas, not things. The really extraordinary feature of this picture is that although it sets the stage for the greatest battle of all time—the armies of heaven led by the Christ of God *versus* the armies of earth under the command of the Antichrist and his

master the devil—*there is no battle*. The trinity of leaders of the
revolt against God are seized; the beast (the Antichrist) and
the false prophet are thrown into the "lake of fire" (v. 20), and the
dragon (the devil) is chained in the bottomless pit (20:1–3). It is
then said that "the rest," the armies in revolt, are "slain by the
sword of him who sits upon the horse" (19:21), that is, the sword
which issues from his mouth (19:15). It would appear that although the stage is set for a fearful conflict, it turns out to be a
judgment uttered by the Word of God. What exact reality corresponds to that we are not entirely sure. There are those who
remember what Hebrews 4:12 says about the power of the divine
Word to reveal the nature of men's hearts, and so to lead men
either to repentance and renewal or to condemnation; on this
basis the great commentator H. B. Swete interprets this passage
as implying the *conversions* of multitudes to obedience to Christ.
That would be a happy ending to the story, but it hardly fits the
picture of the birds, which is drawn from Ezekiel's prophecy of
the subjugation of Gog and Magog in their attempt to overwhelm
Israel (39:17 ff.); while Ezekiel sets that at a later point in the
story of the kingdom (and John does the same, Rev. 20:7 ff.) the
imagery seems to point to a judgment of condemnation rather
than a blessing of the invaders. However we interpret the details,
the intention of the picture is not in doubt: the Lord at his
coming is revealed in majesty and illimitable power to fulfill his
promise of deliverance from all evil and to bring about the
overthrow of all evil. When he appears, the powers of hell and all
who follow them are helpless to resist, and earth has to submit to
his judgment.

The positive result of the Lord's coming, namely the triumph
of his kingdom, will be the subject of our next lecture; but we
mention it even now as a reminder that we must never think of
the coming of the Lord solely in terms of judgment. However
important the judgments of the Lord may be, they are not the

end but the precursor of the end. Just as Jesus in his incarnate ministry came not to judge the world but to save the world (John 3:17), so the ultimate purpose of the Lord's coming is the completion of God's good purpose in creating man and the world, yes and even the creation. The real goal of the book of Revelation is to tell of the city of God which comes down from heaven to earth.

One final observation, however, should be made at this juncture with regard to the coming of the Lord. We have briefly referred to it already, but it deserves to be underlined. The fullest description in the New Testament of the coming of the Lord, that of Revelation 19, is entirely and frankly pictorial. Not even in this book of highly imaginative symbolic representations of events, involving beasts with seven heads, horses that breathe out fire and smoke and sulphur, and stars which fall from heaven and can open the shaft of the bottomless pit, nowhere, we repeat, do we have a greater concentration of symbolic descriptions of a single event than here. When John attempts to describe the coming of the Lord, he resorts to a series of pictures, cheerfully unconcerned whether they fit one another or not. And this he does because he is aware that this event, which brings all history to its climax, transcends the thought and imagination of man. It is greater than our powers of thought also. But this need not provoke in us frustration; on the contrary, it should awaken adoration. We are as incapable of describing in advance the appearance of the Lord in the great unveiling as we are of painting a portrait of God in his transcendent majesty, seated on a great white throne, judging the universe (Rev. 20:11). We are equally unable to give detailed accounts as to how the Lord will separate the righteous from the unrighteous on the earth in the days of judgment, how he raises the dead, what a resurrection body is and will look like, what the relation of the city of God is to history, what the new creation itself will be and its relation to this world, and so on; if these things are beyond our knowledge, how much more are we incapable of reducing to words of our contrivance the glory of the Lord at his coming?

The important issue here, alike for John in the Revelation and for the New Testament writers as a whole, is that hope is focused not on man's development or supposed laws of history but on a person, on *the* Person who has power to meet the needs of man. The Christ of God, in whom God almighty works in this world, alone can redeem man from the powers which destroy this world, and call a halt to the agents of destruction. This assurance the church of John's time needed for its encouragement in faith and obedience. The church of all ages needs it, and ours no less than any other. In some respects the work of God is being challenged on a broader front in our time than in any previous generation, and the prospects ahead, humanly speaking, are wholly unpredictable. But the scene on earth takes on a different aspect when viewed in the light of the coming of the Lord. If the glory of that event has power to transform present living and inspire continuance in well-doing to the end, the church can afford to wait to learn the nature of the great unveiling. We shall know it when we see Him!

3
The Kingdom of God in the Book of Revelation

We do well to remember that although the unveiling of the kingdom of God is the obvious goal of the book of Revelation, and the description of the kingdom is the content of the final vision in chapters 20—22, the theme of the kingdom is not left until the end of the book, but rather it runs right through the book from beginning to end.

This is seen in the doxology to the name of Christ, which follows on the greeting at the beginning of the book (vv. 5–6, RSV): "To him who loves us and has freed us from our sins by his blood and made us a kingdom, priests to his God and Father, to him be glory and dominion for ever and ever. Amen."

In referring to Christ's death as a means of setting us free from our sins there is little doubt that John has in view an idea which is fundamental to the entire prophecy which follows, namely that in Christ God brings about a new exodus of his people. Here praise is given to the Lord for a greater redemption, of which the first exodus is an anticipation. As Moses led the Israelites to Sinai, where they received the covenant which made them "a kingdom of priests and a holy nation" (Ex. 19:6), so here John celebrates the fact that the redemption of Christ has made us "a kingdom, priests to his God and Father." There is no difference in meaning between this language and that of the Old Testament, for it simply echoes current Greek rendering among Jews of the phrase in Exodus. Jewish teachers understood it as meaning not "a kingdom consisting of priests," but "kings and priests" who made up the holy nation. It is evident that this is how John intended it to be read, and that what was laid down under the terms of the old covenant has been transcended in the new. The Lord Christ in the new exodus has given his people to become kings and priests with him.

The same understanding of the effect of Christ's redeeming work lies at the root of the central vision of the book, chapters 4—5. There all emphasis falls on the accession to sovereignty by Jesus Christ as a result of his "conquest" through an all-prevailing death and resurrection. It is often thought that the form of the vision in chapter 5 reflects the ancient enthronement ceremony of kings in the Near East. The steps of the ceremony are defined as exaltation, presentation, and enthronement. Something like this is to be seen in John's description of what took place.

The *exaltation* corresponds to the declaration of the elder in 5:5, RSV: "Lo, the Lion of the tribe of Judah, the Root of David, has conquered, so that he can open the scroll and its seven seals."

The *presentation* is reflected in verse 6: "Between the throne and the four living creatures and among the elders, I saw a Lamb standing, as though it had been slain." Here the Christ is not on the throne with God, but in the close circle immediately about the throne, and he is about to move forward to the throne itself. This step, which entails *enthronement*, is described in verse 7: "He went and took the scroll from the right hand of him who was seated on the throne." By this is symbolized a delivery of authority from God to carry out the terms of the deed by which the kingdom of God is established in the earth, and all heaven and the universe acclaims the glory and the sovereignty of the Christ. It is to be observed that while the deed of covenant, or however we are to describe the scroll, includes the judgments needed for the establishment of the kingdom in power, the songs of adoration recorded in verses 12 and 13 assume that the Christ has entered on his sovereign rule at once. Praise is given to the Lamb who is worthy to receive the "power and wealth and wisdom and might and honour and glory and blessing" of supreme kingship. Similarly the adoration given to God and the Lamb assumes that the Lamb shares the glory of divine sovereignty with the Father, as is explicitly stated in Revelation 3:21.

But what of the "kings and priests" in all this? They are referred to in verses 9–10, RSV, in terms which are highly significant: "Worthy art thou to take the scroll and to open its seals, for thou wast slain and by thy blood didst ransom men for God from every tribe and tongue and people and nation, and hast made them a kingdom and priests to our God, and they shall reign on earth." The redeemed have been constituted by the saving acts of Christ a kingdom of priests. Since the exaltation of the Lamb has initiated the new age, the privilege of being kingly priests for God belongs to the emancipated people even now; nevertheless, as the revelation of the Lord in his kingdom takes place at the future coming, after his judgments have been in the earth, so the full exercise of their royal priesthood belongs to the time of his triumph: *They shall reign on earth.*

In the interest of full understanding about that last statement, it should be noted that there are a few ancient manuscripts of the book of Revelation which read a present tense of the verb here: "they *reign*," instead of the future "they *shall reign*." Some expositors draw attention to this fact, and suggest that the present tense was that which John originally wrote, for he desired to make it clear that the church was given the rule with Christ in this age, not simply in the world to come. It is an instance of the necessity to exercise care that we do not adopt a reading of the text which suits our own views best. Undoubtedly the present tense would favor the position of those who see no millennial rule in the book of Revelation. If it was the correct reading we should have no hesitation in adopting it; apart from other considerations, it is sound New Testament theology to affirm that there is a sense in which the church is seated with Christ in a position of sovereignty now (Eph. 2:6). Nevertheless it remains that the great majority of textual experts on the New Testament agree that the future reading in verse 10 is the original reading, and all modern translations of the New Testament so understand it.

In this connection it is noteworthy that the letters to the seven churches all conclude with a promise to "him who conquers," that is to him who persists in faithful obedience to Christ to the end. These promises all relate to blessings which are to be bestowed in the kingdom of our Lord, as described in the final vision of the kingdom. So we see that they include eating the fruit of the tree of life in the paradise of God (Rev. 2:7); escape from the second death (2:10); the gift of the hidden manna, and a white stone with a new name (2:17); rule with Christ over the nations, and the morning star (2:26 ff.); white garments, the inclusion of one's name in the roll of the living, and an acknowledgment by Christ in the judgment (3:5); becoming a pillar in God's temple, and bearing the name of God and the city of God and Christ's new name (3:12); and finally a place with Christ on his throne (3:21). An examination of these promises will give a good idea of what it means to inherit the kingdom of God. In connection with our theme, however, we should especially note the promise in 2:26–28, RSV:

He who conquers and who keeps my works until the end, I will give him power over the nations, and he shall rule them with a rod of iron, as when earthen pots are broken in pieces, even as I myself have received power from my father; and I will give him the morning star.

The language echoes that of Psalm 2:8–9, words addressed to the king at his coronation and which find supreme fulfillment in the rule of Christ. The parallelism is very close between the word to the king and that to the believer who, in grace, is associated with Christ in his rule: the king as adopted son of God is promised the nations as his inheritance, and that he will shatter all opposition within them; so also the conqueror is promised authority over the nations, and power to overcome all resistance to the will of God in the world. John probably has in mind in the first instance the opposition and resistance to God shown by the Antichrist and his followers, but it is clear that he extends his view to sharing with Christ in his rule over the nations of the world.

That leads us to consider the passage which has become the crux of the discussion about the kingdom of God in the book of Revelation, namely chapter 20. I am inclined to think that the chief cause of students and scholars misunderstanding what John has written is the unfortunate placing of a chapter division in the midst of John's narrative of events which takes place at Christ's coming. In Revelation 19:11–15 a description of *the Lord in his coming is given.* In 19:17 to 20:3 we read of *what takes place at the coming:* the "beast" and the "false prophet" are taken prisoner and thrown into the fiery lake; the "rest" are slain by the sword which issues from Christ's mouth; and the dragon is seized and thrown into the abyss, which is shut over him and sealed for a thousand years. It is quite incomprehensible to me how it should have come about that this last item has been separated from the others in editions of the Bible by making it to begin a fresh chapter, as though it belonged to a different context. Let it be clearly understood, however, that these chapter divisions have no authority and have been made purely for convenience; they go back to Stephen Langton, Archbishop of Canterbury in the eleventh century, and in this instance he simply made a blunder. That John intended us to read his description of the fate of the three ringleaders of revolt in 19:19 to 20:3 as a continuous whole is evident from chapter 16; there we read how the dragon and the beast and the false prophet send out demonic spirits to go abroad to the kings of the earth, and assemble them for battle on the great day of God the Almighty (vv. 13 ff.); the earlier passage thus tells of the evil trinity massing forces against God, and the later one (19:19 ff.) describes the scene after they have done it, and what happens to the leaders; two are banished to hell, and the third is securely locked away for a thousand years. Immediately thereafter (in vv. 4 ff.) John states that the first resurrection takes place and the thousand year kingdom begins. "Blessed and holy is he who shares in the first resurrection! Over such the second death has no power, but they shall be priests of God and of Christ, and they shall reign with him a thousand years" (v. 6, RSV).

The simplicity of John's account is such that it is puzzling why it should ever be questioned. To no small degree the opposition to the plain interpretation of his words is due to the extravagant, not to say crude, application that has often been made of them through the centuries, as can be illustrated from the time of Dionysius, bishop of Alexandria in the third century, to the present day. Dionysius was disturbed by the spread of millennial teaching among the churches of his diocese, and it led him to combat it in a treatise; this he did by maintaining first that the book of Revelation is not to be interpreted literally, and secondly by demonstrating that in any case the book was not written by John the apostle, the author of the Fourth Gospel. The latter was a subtle point, for in his time if a book in the New Testatment was thought not to be written by an apostle it had no place in the Bible. And so it came about that doubt was spread as to whether the Revelation should be included in the New Testament. We owe our knowledge of Dionysius' work through Eusebius, who cited it because he too disliked the millennial teaching of the Revelation and would have gladly seen the book excluded from the Bible. And so it has happened through the centuries; the opposition of Catholics, Lutherans, and Calvinists to the millennium has made it difficult to approach the book of Revelation, and above all this particular passage, without the noise of battle

in our ears, and we have to make an effort to read it dispassion-
ately.

Some expositors have maintained that the binding of Satan
described in chapter 20 puts in another way the victory over the
"dragon" described in chapter 12, where the latter is said to have
been defeated through Michael and his angels and thrown down
to the earth; the statement in 12:11 shows that in this case John
wishes us to understand that his vision represents the victory of
Christ's atonement, and it is urged that this is how the imagery of
20:1–3 should be interpreted.

That the ejection of Satan from heaven in chapter 12 is to be
interpreted of Christ's redemptive death and resurrection is not
to be doubted; but the equation of that vision with the binding of
Satan in 20:1 ff, is wholly improbable. In 12:9 it is said that the
dragon is thrown out of heaven to the earth. Thereupon a woe is
pronounced on earth's inhabitants: "Woe to you, O earth and sea,
for the devil has come down to you in great wrath, because he
knows that his time is short!" Accordingly the dragon pursues the
woman who had borne the male child, and he tries to overwhelm
her, but in vain. He therefore embarks on an all out war: "The
dragon was angry with the woman, and went off to make war on
the rest of her offspring, on those who keep the commandments
of God and bear testimony to Jesus." The next chapter describes
how he intensifies this "war" against the saints by the agency of
the Antichrist and the false prophet. In 20:1 ff. however a wholly
different idea is in mind: the dragon is on earth and has incited
the nations to fight against the Lord; he is now bound with a
chain, put into the abyss, locked up, and his place sealed, so that
he should not deceive the nations again until the thousand years
are finished. Let us fully recognize that both representations are
highly symbolic and obviously are not to be taken literally.
Nevertheless the picture of the evil one being thrown out of
heaven down to the earth, where he proceeds to wreak mischief

among men, in wrath because his time is short, is vastly different from that in which he is said to be seized while leading mankind against God on the earth, and then is packed off to the "abyss," the realm of the demons, where he is imprisoned and made safe so that he cannot deceive the nations any more for a thousand years. There is no question here of our interpreting the book of Revelation *literally;* but it is equally true that we are not free to interpret its symbolic pictures *arbitrarily.* Revelation 12 provides an apocalyptic picture of the powerful efficacy of the death and resurrection of Christ, to free men from the guilt of sin and initiate God's saving rule in Christ; Revelation 19 is an apocalyptic picture of the might of Christ in his future coming, to free the world from Satan's grip and to bring God's saving rule to victory. The confusion which reigns in the discussion about John's meaning in Revelation 20 should not be attributed to John himself, for he uses his pictures with remarkable consistency.

One further observation should be made about the interpretation of chapter 20: from its first paragraph to its last the Book of Revelation is written in the conviction that the end is "near," in accordance with the perspective shared by prophets of both the Old and New Testaments (see 1:3; 22:20). It is part and parcel of the prophetic consciousness to reckon seriously with the possibility that the end may come shortly. But if John had believed that before the parousia of the Lord the contemporary empire would be overthrown, and would then be followed by the millennial kingdom of Christ on earth, he could never have represented the coming of the Lord "at hand." No writer in the New Testament ever held such a view, nor did John.

We take it, therefore, as reasonably certain that John's vision is intended to teach that the coming of Christ will usher in the kingdom of God in history, and that at the last the kingdom in history will give place to the kingdom in the new creation.

It is not without interest that the great majority of critical writers on the New Testament agree that such is the teaching of the book of Revelation; many of them do not accept this teaching as authoritative, but neither are they conditioned by the teaching of their own particular confession, and so they feel quite free to state their convictions on the matter. As an example of this I may adduce the verdict of Paul Althaus, the well-known German Lutheran theologian. Althaus wrote one of the most profound expositions that has appeared in modern times of the doctrine of the last things. He recognized freely that the Old Testament prophets set their hope on a kingdom of God which would be established in this world, and that the author of the book of Revelation similarly taught that the kingdom of God would be realized in this world after Christ's coming, prior to the final consummation of the new creation. But Althaus believed this to be inconsistent with the principles of the gospel of Christ, and so he declared that in the name of the word of God the millennial teaching of the book of Revelation must be rejected. Now I believe that Althaus was wrong in thinking that John's vision of the triumphant earthly kingdom of Christ is inconsistent with the gospel, as I hope this lecture will show, but I respect the honesty of this theologian, and believe that his candor is itself a testimony as to the real teaching of the book. The first requisite to understanding the Scriptures is to sit down and listen to what they have to say, whether they fit our own ideas of truth or not. Only so can we hope to fashion our own thinking by the truth of the Bible.

Before we proceed another step in our discussion of the kingdom in its earthly manifestation, let us look again at John's statement about it in Revelation 20:4, RSV:

I saw thrones, and seated on them were those to whom judgment was committed. Also I saw the souls of those who had been beheaded for their testimony to Jesus and for the word of God, and who had not worshiped the beast or its image and had not received its mark on their foreheads or their hands. They came to life, and reigned with Christ a thousand years.

Who are these who "came to life, and reigned with Christ a thousand years"? The popular view is that two groups of people are here in mind, the martyrs of Jesus who had paid the supreme price for their witness to him, and the rest of his faithful people who had not bowed the knee to Antichrist but had not been called to tread the martyr's way; this describes the church which has remained faithful to its Lord. Recent expositors, however, have tended to stress the identity of the believers described in the two clauses of the second sentence: these, it is maintained, had been beheaded for their fearless testimony *and* they had rejected the demand to acknowledge Antichrist; the millennium, accordingly, is for the martyrs only, and these alone are raised in the first resurrection. There is nevertheless a third understanding of John's statement, which has not been considered as it should have been. The first sentence is an allusion to Daniel 7:9 ff.; there the coming of the Ancient of Days to execute judgment on the antigod power is described, and it is said: "As I looked, thrones were placed and one that was ancient of days took his seat." Who the occupants of the thrones are is not stated in the vision, though they will be viewed as assessors who assist the Judge when the court sat. The court decides to give the kingdom to "one like a son of man," and in the later exposition of the vision it is declared: "The kingdom and the dominion and the greatness of the kingdoms under the whole heaven shall be given to the people of the saints of the Most High" (v. 27).

Clearly John has interpreted in the teaching of Daniel as meaning that the kingdom in the last days will be given to the Son of man, who will rule with *his* saints, and this he expresses by citing the words of Daniel. The prophet had further stated (Dan. 7:22) that when the Ancient of Days came "judgment was given for the saints . . . and the time came when the saints received the kingdom"; that is their cause was vindicated in the court and the rule was given to them.

John's statement therefore would appear to mean that the rule with Christ was given to his people, and that without limitation. But among his people who have the privilege of so reigning he then singles out the martyrs and confessors of Jesus, for encouragement to all who may be called to tread that path. It is understandable that he should give such consolation, writing as he is for a church which is already experiencing pressure, and which can see the end of the policies against them as a conflict between Christ and Antichrist. We recall, however, that this encouragement is precisely the content of John's doxology at the beginning of the book, and of the song which celebrates the redemption achieved by the risen Savior: "They shall reign on earth" (5:10). That statement manifestly relates to the whole church of the Lord, not a part of it.

"They came to life" (20:4), or more simply, "they *lived*," is a way of describing resurrection from the dead. It is not to be referred to the gift of spiritual life or eternal life when one comes to faith in Christ. The same use of the word for resurrection appears in various books of the New Testament in relation to resurrection; see especially Romans 14:9: "To this end Christ died and *lived* again, that he might be Lord both of the dead and of the living." For other instances note also the important passages John 11:25–26 and Revelation 2:8.

The brief statement about the millennial rule of Christ and his saints is followed by another, which has puzzled many readers of the Revelation. John writes that at the conclusion of the thousand years Satan will be released and will deceive the nations, that is Gog and Magog, to gather them for a final battle against God (Rev. 20:7 ff). The rebellion of course proves to be a vain resistance, but inevitably the question arises why the devil is allowed to be free, and how it is that the earthly rule of Christ should end in disaster. However unexpected and perplexing this may be, its cause is undoubtedly to be found in the Old Testament Scriptures. If John had been asked about this, he would have simply stated, "It is so written." He has meditated on the prophecy about Gog and Magog in Ezekiel 38—39, and has observed something that has escaped the notice of many who speak about that prophecy, namely its relation to the saving acts of God. The prophet tells of God's gathering his people from the countries, of his cleansing them and giving them a new heart and a new spirit, and of the restoration of the land so that it shall be as the garden of Eden (chap. 36); he repeats and enforces this teaching by his vision of the valley of dry bones, wherein Israel is represented to be as a resurrected people, made to live by the Spirit; God will set his servant "David" (i.e., the Messiah) over them as king, and God will raise his sanctuary in their midst and so be with them for evermore (chap. 37). Then it is that the prophecy of the invasion of Gog is described; it is represented as an attack on the people of God after they had been gathered from the nations and dwell securely—the language of Ezekiel 38:8 echoes that of chapter 36, which describes God's restoration of his people for the kingdom. Hence John interprets the attack of Gog to take place "after many days" *within* the kingdom of God, not *prior to* its establishment (Ezek. 38:8).

We further observe that the early chapters of the book of Genesis feature in John's vision of the kingdom of God in chapter 21—22; he shows how the blessings of the lost paradise are restored in the kingdom to come. It is more than possible that John's reflections on Genesis 1—3 led him to the thought that as Satan was allowed to enter the first paradise to expose the nature of man's heart, in the restoration of paradise he will be permitted to do so again. On this Austin Farrer commented, "All enmity must come out into the open and be annihilated before God's reign is made absolute."

It should also be recalled that John shared with the apocalyptists of his time, who, like him, had thought much on the Old

Testament teaching about the kingdom of God, an insight of some importance relating to the rule of God: namely, that the fullness of God's kingdom cannot be attained within the limitations of life in this world, not even in restored paradaisical conditions, in light of the unceasing possibilities for evil which exist in the world. This is often regarded as an expression of the apocalyptists' pessimism. One might think that it is better viewed as an expression of their realism. If we permit our gaze to go beyond the confines of history, when human existence as we know it can survive no longer, we have to recognize that it will be the grace of God, transfiguring men into his likeness through resurrection, which alone will enable man to reach the goal of his creation. Of this the last rebellion of redeemed history is the final demonstration.

One more point of exegesis regarding John's presentation of the earthly kingdom: the statement about the kingdom in Revelation 20:4–6 is so brief, it conveys hardly a hint as to the nature of that kingdom. Has John left any clue at all as to the conditions of the kingdom on earth? The answer may be surprising: "Yes, he has; it is likely that his description of the city of God in Revelation 21:9 to 22:5 is given as a revelation of the kingdom both in the millennial age and in the new creation." We must review the evidence for this statement.

First, it is noteworthy that the introductory sentence of the description of the city of God in Revelation 21:9 uses identical language with that in the introductory sentence of the description of the antichristian city in 17:1 (the latter reads, "Come, I will show you the judgment of the great harlot"; the former, "Come, I will show you the Bride, the Wife of the Lamb"). There is a deliberate contrast between the two cities: the one reposing on the Beast, partaking of the character of the devil, the other coming down out of heaven, partaking of the nature of God. But one thing they both have in common: they stand on the earth and invite humanity to come to them (if the city of God comes *down*, out of heaven, clearly that is to the earth, 21:10). The question arises: Which city rules in the earth between the destruction of the harlot-city and the bride-city in the new creation? If the rule of Antichrist is to be replaced by the rule of Christ, the likelihood is that the rule of the harlot-city under Antichrist will be followed by the establishment of the bride-city under God's Christ.

The correctness of this presumption is seen in two passages of the Revelation. In chapter 19 the overthrow of the harlot-city is celebrated in a series of Hallelujahs, the last of which reads:

> Hallelujah! For the Lord our God the Almighty reigns.
> Let us rejoice and exult and give him the glory,
> for the marriage of the Lamb has come,
> and his Bride has made herself ready; . . .
> Blessed are those who are invited to the marriage supper of the
> Lamb (vv. 6–7, 9).

The onset of the reign of "the Lord God Almighty," the marriage of the Lamb, and the marriage supper of the Lamb all take place at the coming of the Lord, which is immediately afterwards described. The "marriage supper of the Lamb" is another way of speaking of the kingdom of God as a feast, adapted to the centrality of the coming of Christ as the King. Similarly the bride and the city symbolize fundamentally the same thing: the people of God in holy fellowship with the Lord. This is why in 21:9 ff. the bride is identified with the city—they appear together. To say then that the saints rule with Christ in the kingdom and that the bride-city comes down from heaven to earth for the kingdom is to portray one reality. The city of God is revealed at the coming of Christ and is established in the earth in the kingdom of Christ.

The second passage which we have in mind is the difficult paragraph Revelation 20:7 ff. The rebellion of Gog and Magog is there described as an attack on "the camp of the saints and the beloved city" (v. 9). This is surely not intended to designate an onslaught on the city of Jerusalem in Palestine; the only prophecy in which Jerusalem features in John is in chapter 11, and there it is described as "the great city which is allegorically called Sodom and Egypt, where their Lord was crucified" (v. 8). If John had intended to relate his prophecy in chapter 20 to the Jerusalem of Palestine, he would have had to use different language from that which he has actually employed, if he was not to be misunderstood. The battle of 20:7 ff. is in fact allegorized, just as Armageddon is allegorized in 19:17 ff. Gog and Magog are no longer territories north of Palestine, but they represent "the nations which are at the four corners of the earth" (v. 8). Their enmity is directed to the Lord and his people. Consequently, "the camp of the saints and the beloved city" will represent the city of God which descends from heaven, the new Jerusalem. That means, however, that the city will stand revealed in the kingdom of Christ, its central feature in this world as in the next.

It has been pointed out that various elements in John's description of the city of God are more suitable to life in this world than to that in the new creation; for example it is said that the nations walk in its light, kings and the nations bring their glory into it, but nothing unclean passes through its gates (21:24 f.), and the leaves of the tree of life heal the nations (22:2). More generally it may be affirmed that the whole description of the city of God in 21:9 to 22:5 is appropriate to the kingdom of Christ in this world. Let the reader run through it again, and he will see that there's not a line of it which could not apply to the kingdom of God in this world. Naturally it is also to be acknowledged that the whole description is equally applicable to the city of God in the new creation, although it does involve a change in the application of some of the symbols (as in those mentioned above). It would appear then that the city of God is the context of the blessedness of the rule of God, in this world and in the new creation.

On this basis the book of Revelation presents a clear pattern of the events which bring God's purpose to its destined end. Chap-

ter 1 narrates the introductory vision of Christ; 2—3 the letters to
the churches; 4—5 the central vision, recounting the achieve-
ment of redemption through the Lamb of God and his authoriza-
tion to execute the purpose of God; 6—16 the judgments leading
up to the coming of Christ and his kingdom, with an appendix in
17—18 describing the overthrow of the antichristian city; 19:1 to
21:8 the coming of the Lord, his kingdom in history, the last
judgment, and the new creation, with an appendix in 21:9 to 22:5
describing the nature of the city of God; an epilogue, which
concludes the book in 22:6–21.

It is noteworthy that the teaching in the book of Revelation on
the kingdom of God is related both to the Old Testament's
prophetic works and to contemporary Jewish writings on the
kingdom; but on the other hand it has features which distinguish
it from all these. The Old Testament writers look for the kingdom
to be established in this world. Admittedly the concept of new
heavens and new earth does appear in Isaiah 65—66, but the
portrayal in those chapters of the kingdom of God is still given in
terms of life in this world (e.g., it is said that it will be but a child
in that time who dies at the age of a hundred years, 65:20). In the
later Jewish apocalyptic writings the concept of new heavens and
earth becomes increasingly dominant. A reconciliation of the two
expectations is sought in the expectation of a kingdom ruled by
the Messiah in this world, according to the promises of the Old
Testament prophets, followed by the eternal kingdom of the
world to come.

This was a widespread view among the rabbis in the Christian
era, and they indulged in much speculation as to the length of the
earthly kingdom of the Messiah. In this discussion two verses
came to be of great importance: Isaiah 63:4, "I resolved on a *day*
of vengeance; the *year* for ransoming my own had come"; and
Psalm 90:4, "A thousand years in thy sight are but as yesterday
when it is past." These led to the idea that in the kingdom of God

a day represents a year, and so that the messianic kingdom would last for 365 years, or perhaps 365,000 years! The speculations were considerable. But the thought of a day representing a thousand years was combined with the idea that the history would consist of a week of years, a kind of recapitulation of the week of creation. As the six days of creation were followed by God's sabbath, so the six days of history will be followed by the sabbath of Messiah's kingdom—the six thousands by the seventh thousand—and at the last the seventh will give place to the eighth day, which has no end, for it is the timeless age of the eternal kingdom. This interpretation is set forth in a Jewish apocalypse of uncertain date, 2 Enoch chapters 32—33, but it is also expounded in the Christian Epistle of Barnabas, chapter 15, written in the same era of the book of Revelation, as well as in some later Christian writers. This appears to be the context in which John's teaching on the millennium has to be set. The period of a thousand years is likely to indicate not its *length* but its *character:* it is the sabbath rest of history, an idea related to a concept expounded in the letter to the Hebrews (chap. 4), according to which the sabbath is a type of the kingdom of God.

Doubtless John would have been confirmed in this understanding of the kingdom of God by his reading of Ezekiel 36—48: Israel's restoration under the rule of the Messiah, the new David (chaps. 36—37) is followed by the rebellion of Gog (chaps. 38—39), and finally by the promise of a new Jerusalem with a new temple in an untroubled kingdom (chaps. 40—48). Moreover, the teaching of Jesus and of the apostles was naturally of immense importance to John. Not least he would have known the Lord's Prayer, with its clauses at the beginning:

> Hallowed by thy name,
> Thy kingdom come,
> Thy will be done,
> On earth as it is in heaven.

The Beatitudes would also surely have been learned by him:

> Blessed are the poor in spirit,
> for theirs is the kingdom of heaven.
> Blessed are the meek,
> for they shall inherit the earth.

With teachings such as these John would have meditated on the meaning of the gospel of Christ incarnate, giving his life a ransom for the many, raised from death by God, and coming in the glory of the Father. In all this process God's kingdom *was coming, is* here, and *shall come* in its fullness. Observe: *in all the redemptive process, not merely at the end.* This was made clear in Revelation 4—5, from which we learn that the turn of the ages occurred in the life, death, and resurrection of Christ. In his incarnate ministry the promised kingdom of God came among men. The kingdom which is to be revealed at Christ's coming therefore is not something new to this world, but the revelation of that kingdom which has been a power in the earth from Easter onwards. Jesus told Pilate in his trial that his kingdom was not of this world (John 18:36); by that he meant that it did not originate from this world and it has not the nature of this world's kingdoms—one has but to compare the Empire of Rome with the kingdom of Christ to see the point. But the kingdom of God was powerfully at work in the Lord during his ministry, and it was Pilate's blindness which prevented him from recognizing that it was there in the person of its King who stood before him. It has continued among men in the power of the Spirit since Easter and Pentecost, but at the coming of the King the Pilates of this world will know it—it will then be the *manifest* rule of God among men, and the Lord's sovereignty will be owned by them all.

Now this has one important corollary which those who look for the triumph of Christ's kingdom in the earth should steadfastly contemplate: if the kingdom that is to come is the kingdom over which Christ is Lord now, if it is one kingdom in two stages of revelation, as it were, then self-evidently it is a "Christian" kingdom of Christ for which we look. There is no question of a reversal to old covenant religion in the earth, or of imagining that in the city of God the cross of Christ dominates the worship while in the world Jewish sacrifices in the Temple of Jerusalem are central. All such ideas rest on a faulty understanding of the relation of Old Testament prophecy to New Testament fulfillment. The kingdom of Christ is not a kingdom of the Jewish nation, but of the saints of God of every nation, people, tribe, and tongue, to use John's language. It was the steadfast conviction of Paul that the ancient people of God's choice, which had rejected the Messiah sent to them, would not be excluded from the kingdom of Christ but would turn to the Lord and find their place in it (Rom. 9—11); but that is very different from viewing the kingdom to come as a kingdom above all for the Jews.

We are not at liberty, in interpreting the revelation of God given to us in the Bible, to read the Old Testament as though the New Testament did not exist. No single factor has prevented Christians from right thinking about the kingdom of Christ more than the endeavor to do that very thing; it has led to wrong expositions of the kingdom of God in the world on the one hand, and to unfounded rejection of the scriptural doctrine of the kingdom in the world on the other. It is more than time that fresh thinking was directed to this matter by all, not least by the teachers of the Bible and of Christian theology in our seminaries, colleges and universities. It is time that theologically-minded churchmen, that is to say members of the orthodox churches, recognized that the so-called millennium is not to be handed over as a happy hunting ground for Jehovah's Witnesses, Christadelphians, and the "fanatics"—a theological swear word from Luther on for Anabaptists and others who look for the kingdom of Christ in this world. If, as I believe, this doctrine is part of the revelation of God in Christ, we have erred in not giving it more careful attention, with a view to solving some of the problems which it presents. We have equally not recognized its importance in the proclamation of the gospel, above all to the Marxist world, which has taken the doctrine of the kingdom of God on earth and sundered it from faith in God, so producing a secular eschatology which cannot but lead to bitter disappointment and in the end to despair. There remains an unfinished task to do in this area for those capable of it.

Meanwhile for the church of God there is strong consolation in this doctrine. Salvation in the Bible is life in the kingdom of God. More explicitly, it is life eternal in the restored relation between God and man in Christ. Its context is the city of God. And in that city all the promises of God in the Bible, and the yearning hopes of mankind without the Bible, reach their true and complete fulfillment. The city comes down out of heaven, and so is from God. It is beyond the power of man to create it, and so it is the gift of the Father in and through our Savior, Jesus Christ the Lord. But it is also the bride of Christ—perhaps more specifically the sphere of her existence; but that means that it is the consummation of the fellowship which we know in the present, and which even now forms our life. It is thus the end of that which the Lord began in his living and dying and rising, and so the purpose of his coming in power and glory. It is therefore the end, the goal of faith.

With such consolation faith is well content.

Small wonder that the book of Revelation concludes with a final affirmation of the risen Lord:

Surely, I am coming soon.

We listen again to the Lord's renewal of his promise. And with the people of Christ through the ages we echo the ancient prayer:

Amen. Come, Lord Jesus.

Part II

Amillennialism

Herschel H. Hobbs

4
Understanding History from Heaven's Point of View

This is going to be a rather rapid tour of Revelation. Our first time to go to Europe and the Middle East was 1955 when all of "God's children" went to London to the Baptish World Congress. When we got home, someone asked if we went through the Louvre. I said, "Yes, we *galloped* through." About four years later my wife and I went back to Paris, and we spent most of one day there. If we are going to cover at least in part the book of Revelation in the time allotted, we are going to have to move rather rapidly.

First of all, I want to point out to you some books you may want to read. Three basic ones by the speakers of the conference are: *The Cosmic Drama*, which I wrote, *Highlights of the Book of Revelation* by Dr. George R. Beasley-Murray, and *The Revelation of Jesus Christ* by Dr. Ray Robbins. Others that would be helpful are: *Worthy Is the Lamb* by Dr. Ray Summers, *The Meaning and Message of the Book of Revelation* by Dr. Edward A. McDowell, and *What, Where, and When Is the Millennium?* by Dr. Russell Bradley Jones. These books are both scholarly and readable.

For these lectures I am using the King James Version. You use whatever version you wish. I like the King James Version. I've lived with it for all of my ministry. I have the other versions. I even dabble a little bit in the Hebrew and Greek now and then. When I refer to a Greek word or phrase, I'm not trying to demonstrate what little knowledge I have of Greek. But after all, the New Testament was written in Greek. I must tell you however, that I do know a little *Hebrew* and I know a little *Greek*. The little Hebrew is a tailor and the little Greek runs a restaurant. Having cleared that up, we'll go ahead with our study.

Introductory Matters

What do we mean by the book of Revelation or *The* Revelation? It is not "The Revelation of St. John the Divine" as the King James Version heads it. It is "The Revelation of Jesus Christ." Now scholars debate about whether the revelation is to Jesus Christ or from him. I think it is both. God gave it to him, and now he is giving it through an angel to John on the Isle of Patmos. I think the author John (1:9) is John the apostle. I also think that John the apostle wrote the books that bear his name, including Revelation.

Some scholars deny either that he wrote the Gosepl and the Epistles or that he wrote Revelation. They point out that in Revelation the Greek language is very rough while the language and grammar in the Gospel and Epistles are very smooth. So they insist that the same man could not have written both bodies of literature. Others who say that John did write them all say that he wrote Revelation first, and that he improved his Greek after that. Thus he was able to write the beautiful language of the Gospel, for instance. I don't agree that is the case either.

I hold John wrote all of these books. But that he wrote the Gospel and Epistles in Ephesus where someone, maybe one of the elders, helped him with his Greek. It may have been like the preacher who was asked if he ever used any of Dr. Truett's sermons. He said, "Yes, but I polish them up before I use them." Well, this helper polished up John's Greek. But Revelation was written on the Isle of Patmos where he had no one to help him. The Greek of Revelation gives the impression that the writer was one whose native tongue was Hebrew and yet he was writing in Greek. Someone suggests that the author may have had a speaking knowledge of Greek but not a writing knowledge. He thought in Hebrew and wrote in Greek.

This could explain in great measure the very roughness of the grammar in the Revelation. Dr. A. T. Robertson said he thought some of the roughness of grammar was deliberate to call attention to the message.

The word *revelation* means an unveiling. It is a Latin derivative from the Greek word *apokalupsis*. It came into English as *apocalypse*. Some of you are old enough to remember right after World War I they made a movie called "The Four Horsemen of the Apocalypse." Well, that is "The Four Horsemen of Revelation." So this is an unveiling.

Now Dr. Robbins is going to be teaching Revelation from the point of view of apocalyptic language. I will say only that it was a code language. It was used by the Jews in time of persecution or other trouble to communicate with one another in code language. When a nation is at war, it has a code. I'm told that one reason why we were able to defeat the Germans was because we broke their code and were able to tell in advance what they were going to do. Well, Revelation is in code language. The original readers understood that code; we understand some of it. Some of it we simply guess at.

Furthermore, the book of Revelation is a book of great drama. That's where the title of my book comes from, *The Cosmic Drama*. Dr. McDowell's book presents Revelation as a great drama. He says that it is the drama of the sovereignty of God and our Lord Jesus Christ. As we go through the book we will see that scene after scene unfolds like the action of a play or drama. To call it drama doesn't mean it isn't true. You can present truth in a drama. The book of Job is a drama. It has a prologue, the body of the message, and then the epilogue. So we are not saying that

Revelation isn't truth. We are saying that it is truth presented in the form of a drama. We do that in our churches in visual education. Dr. Robertson said that if you read the book of Revelation aloud to a child, the child understands it better than an adult, because he hasn't learned how to curb his imagination. He lets his imagination run loose.

The danger in studying Revelation is that you may get caught up in the scenery and miss the message in the drama that is being presented. In Revelation much of the apocalyptic element is stage setting. It is not the drama; it is the setting. Jesus used apocalyptic language. A good deal of Matthew 24 is this language. Paul used it in 1 Thessalonians 4 and in other places.

One element of the apocalyptic is disturbances in nature. These have a symbolic meaning as we will notice. Thunder, lightning, and so on symbolize God's judgment. But we must keep in mind that in studying a drama, we must focus upon the actors and the message. We are going to touch chapter 1 lightly and skip over chapters 2 and 3, the letters to the seven churches. We could spend a month studying those and not touch the hem of the garment. But in getting an overview, we will focus on chapter 4 where the drama begins.

Method of Interpretation

In chapter 1, after having pointed out "the Revelation of Jesus Christ," John says that God sent and "signified by his angel unto his servant John." The Jews thought of God's revelation as coming through angels. So the Lord *signified* his message. The Greek word *semeion* means "sign." In the Gospel of John, for instance, in the Greek text you don't find the word for "miracles." The King James Version has "miracles," but the Greek word in John is the word for *sign*. It was a sign of Jesus' deity. So "signified" or showed in signs may also read that he showed in *symbols*.

Now I think that this word is the key to the understanding of the book of Revelation. In other words, is it symbolic or is it literal? I don't know about you, but if I try to go literal I go crazy. So I vote for *symbolic*. You can't ride first one horse and then another just to suit your convenience. You can't go symbol, symbol, literal, symbol. You have to go all the way, one or the other. Just make up your mind which way you are going. And when you start to go literal all the way, if you are like I am, then make reservations at your state mental hospital because you'll need it later on. I think it is symbolic, as he tells us in the very first verse. So many people who try to interpret Revelation ignore this altogether. But as I see the word *signified,* you should draw a circle around it in your Bible so that you won't forget it.

John speaks of "things which must shortly come to pass." Now what things must come to pass? The word *must* is a verb meaning that it is morally and spiritually necessary. Jesus "must needs go through Samaria" (John 4:4). Well this is the same verb here. And it must come to pass "shortly." What does "shortly" mean? Some say it means *suddenly*. Others say that it means *certainly*. Some say it means both. I think it means that whatever is going to happen is *certainly* going to happen, and when it does happen it will be *suddenly*. As I wrote *The Cosmic Drama,* I asked myself what *did* happen shortly? After all, any meaning, any interpretation of the book of Revelation must have a word of comfort and encouragement for the persecuted Christians of the first century. If it did not speak to them, then I don't think it speaks the message that one might need at all. It did speak to the first-century Christians. But the principles laid down are applicable in any age anywhere, anytime, to any people of God who suffer for their faith.

What did happen shortly? Well, the book was written probably in A.D. 95 when Domitian was the Roman emperior. He reigned from A.D. 81 to 96. He claimed to be a god, and demanded that he be worshiped as a god. He even had bodies to enforce his worship, and even refused to accept correspondence that was not addressed to him in terms of deity. Now what happened shortly after John wrote this? Well one thing that happened was that Domitian died the next year, A.D. 96. And while there were persecutions even until the time of Constantine, there never was again a persecution of Christians on the scope and to the degree that we find in the Domitian persecution. So for whatever it is worth, I throw that out about this word *shortly*.

Revelation was written to seven churches in the Roman province of Asia. The word *seven* is a perfect number in Hebrew numerology. So we must recognize that this book was probably written to more than seven churches. While it names seven churches, I'm sure that churches all over that area read the letter. The province of Asia was the western part of Asia Minor, part of what is today Turkey. Ray Summers says persecution in that province seems to have been more severe than anywhere else in the Empire. So the Lord gave this message to John who wrote it down and sent it to these churches.

A Preliminary Vision

In Revelation 1:8–20 we have a preliminary vision prior to the beginning of the actual drama in chapter 4. We have God presented in verse 8. "I am Alpha and Omega." *Alpha* is the first letter in the Greek alphabet; *omega* is the last letter. He says that he which is to come is the Almighty. Domitian may be mighty, but God is almighty. Then John tells of his own experience of being on the Isle of Patmos. He heard a great voice as of a trumpet. This was Christ speaking to him. He told him to write this book and send it to the churches that are mentioned in verse 11. In verse 19 Christ told John to write about what he has seen, what is, and what will be. So here we have past, present, and future. Nevertheless there are various schools of thought as to the time element. Roman Catholics say that it is all in the past.

This is to get around the identity of the whore (chap. 17) as Rome, and the beast as the papacy (chap. 13). Others see all of Revelation as future. But Christ plainly says past, present, and future.

Then he mentions seven golden lamp stands (candlesticks). The lamp stands were the seven churches. Verse 16 mentions seven stars. They are the angels, perhaps the pastors, of these churches. Notice that he says that Christ is walking in the midst of his churches. He is aware of what is going on. And he holds these stars, these pastors, in his strong right hand.

When somebody jumps on the preacher, he ought to remember that. You are not just talking to a man; you are dealing with the Lord's anointed. When I am in a revival, I never fail to sound that note if I can work it in somewhere—that we ought to be careful how we treat the Lord's servants because he has them in his right hand.

An Explanatory Note

We three speakers are not here to debate issues. We are here to present three different views of interpreting Revelation. We have agreed that if we take out just a few differences, we could sign our name to the others' views on Revelation. There is not as much difference as you might think. We are not here to set dates as to the second coming. In Mark 13:32 Jesus said that no man, not the angels in heaven, nor even the Son, knows the time of the Lord's return. Well, I'm not going to claim to know something that Jesus did not know. He didn't know; I don't know. We could all quote Acts 1:8, "But ye shall receive power, after that the Holy Ghost [Spirit] is come upon you," and so on. Can you quote Acts 1:7? "It is not for you to know the times or the seasons [points and periods of fine details], which the Father hath put in his own power." In other words, the end of time is the business of God the Father. Jesus said that it is not given to you to know those things. They are hidden in the Father's heart, and when he is ready to reveal them he will.

So, in effect, Jesus said for us to leave to God what is God's business; and that we get on about our business of being a witness to the ends of the earth. One preacher said that because so many people haven't heard that the Lord came the first time, he was not trying to figure out when he's coming the second time. So there we are.

Now I think the Lord's return is near. The Lord is about to come. I think that is always true. Jesus said we don't know the day or the hour. He said that it might be at midnight or at noon. In other words, the whole content of what Jesus had to say is that we should stand on tiptoe, be on the alert every second, because we don't know when he's going to come. Paul said, "In a moment, in the twinkling of an eye" (1 Cor. 15:52). "Moment" translates the word from which we got *atom*. It means something so small it can't be divided. And "the twinkling of an eye" was also used as the buzzing of a gnat's wing. How quickly does the eye twinkle? That's how quickly the Lord will come. It may be before I utter the next syllable.

G. Campbell Morgan was once asked, "If you knew this was the last day of your life on earth, what would you do?" "Well," he said something like this, "I would get up in the morning, take a bath and shave, and eat my breakfast. Then I would read the paper, and go to my study and work a while. Then I would eat lunch, and take a nap. Then I would go to church. After that I would come back home and work in my garden a little while, take another bath, eat dinner, read the paper, and go to bed. Because, you see, I'm not looking for death, I'm looking for him." Well, we ought to be looking for him all the time.

People say that Paul thought Jesus was coming back in his own lifetime. Therefore when he didn't come, Paul didn't know what he was talking about. Paul knew exactly what he was talking about! He was doing exactly what Jesus told him to do. Paul said that we shall not all "sleep" or lie in a cemetery (1 Cor. 15:51). "Sleep" comes from the word whence we get our word *cemetery*. But *we* shall all be changed; note "we." Some generation will be alive when the Lord returns. Paul says that his is the only one alive. We ought to speak of his coming in the same terms today.

Jesus never spoke of his second coming in terms of time, always condition. "When the Son of man shall come in his glory" (Matt. 25:31). "When" translates a little Greek word *hotan* which refers primarily to *condition*. When the condition is right, that is the time. Jesus said that where the carcass is there will the buzzards be (Matt. 24:28). This condition is the *carcass;* the buzzards are the time. He always spoke of his return in terms of conditions, not time. Does he know now? Well, that gets us into another realm. I think in heaven he knows. But on earth in the conditions of his humanity which he had voluntarily assumed, he did not know. He said "when."

The Drama Begins

Now let us look at chapter 4 where the drama really begins. Christians were being persecuted because they refused to worship the emperor. In doing so they were required to say *Kurios Kaisaros* or "Lord Caesar." But the Christians wouldn't do it. They said *Kurios Iesous*, "Jesus is Lord," the Lord Jesus. When Paul said, "If thou shalt confess with thy mouth the Lord Jesus," really he was saying that the believer must declare "Jesus is Lord" (Rom. 10:9). Now we read this today and say glibly, "If you will confess with your mouth 'Lord Jesus.' " You say, well, I can do that: "Lord Jesus, Lord Jesus." And that is about as far as it goes. About like water off a duck's back. But in those days it could cost you your life to say that. Christians were giving their lives in the province of Asia for saying "Lord Jesus" instead of saying "Lord Caesar."

So you can well imagine as they were being persecuted and saw some of their people dying, they were asking the question, "Well, what is going on in the world? Has God been dethroned? Doesn't God know what is going on? Or doesn't God care what is happening to us? Or worse still, does he know and care, but he is powerless to do anything about it? What is going on? Is Satan on the throne? Is the universe in the control of Satan?"

So in that thought context Christ himself told John, "Come up hither" (v.1). Come closer, come here, and I'll show you. We know it is the voice of Christ because it speaks of the voice as a trumpet as seen in the first chapter. Jesus says, "Come, and I'll show you another view." They were looking about at what was happening to them on earth. Jesus said to look up to heaven. In other words, don't look *about* you, but look *up*.

Now notice in verse 2 he says that "a throne was set in heaven," and one was sitting on it. The word is not "sat" but "sitting." The verb means that it was set in heaven and it still is, with the idea that it will continue to be. It is what is called an imperfect tense expressing continuous action in past time. There never was a time when that throne wasn't there. And there never has been a time when it was not occupied by the one whom we immediately learn is God. He that sat upon the throne was "like a jasper and a sardine stone." A jasper was a brilliant stone, probably a diamond. Now this is symbolism. No man has seen God, for God is Spirit. You can't see him with the natural eye. But the symbol of God is a dazzling diamond and a red stone. A "sardine stone" is blood red, and perhaps the suggestion there is of the redemptive work and purpose of God in Christ. But as a dazzling diamond, expressing the glory, the holiness, and the righteousness of God.

Righteousness as presented in the Bible is, first, what God is in his nature, then what he demands in man but which man cannot achieve in his own effort, and what God in Christ bestows upon those who believe in Christ. The inclusive idea applies here.

Notice the rainbow round about the throne. "Round about" means in a circle. The Greek reads "in a circle." We see the rainbow while on earth as a half circle, people who have been out into space tell us that out there it is a complete circle. So we see here the heavenly view. We are getting a view from heaven, wherever heaven is. I don't know where heaven is. It is "a place." "I go to prepare a place for you" (John 14:2). It is where Jesus is, and that's heaven enough for me. But anyway, in heaven the rainbow is a complete circle.

In his treatment of Revelation in *The Broadman Bible Commentary,* Morris Ashcraft said that this has no relationship to the convenant rainbow God made with Noah, the rainbow he gave as assurance that he would never destroy the earth by water again. But I see all of this as symbolism. And in the book of Revelation we find John drawing on the Old Testament for ideas, but he uses them in his own way. So in this context I see a symbolic reference to the rainbow which God gave to Noah. John not only sees God on his throne, but he sees a rainbow encircling the throne, reminding the people on earth of God's promise that he would look after them.

Then round about the throne there were twenty-four other thrones, and on those thrones sat twenty-four elders (v. 4). People have various ideas as to who these elders are. But I think that they refer to a totality of God's redeemed people. Adding the twelve heads of the tribes of Israel and the twelve apostles makes twenty-four, symbolizing all of God's redeemed people.

In studying Revelation we have to keep Hebrew numerology in mind. To the ancients numbers had a value. In Hebrew numerology three was the symbol of deity. Four was the symbol of the world; note the four directions. Three plus four equals seven. That is a perfect number. Three times four equals twelve, another perfect number, and so on. So we have to keep that in mind. Twenty-four would be twice twelve, a perfect number. And these, as I see it, are the redeemed of God that are in heaven. Later on we are going to see the redeemed that are still on earth undergoing persecution. But these are the redeemed in heaven. They are wearing white garments symbolizing vindication, victory, and purity. But also that was the garment the priest wore when he served in the Temple. On their heads were crowns of gold, reward, but also suggesting kingship. So they are priests and kings unto our God, as we will see in chapter 5.

Now out of the throne proceeded lightning, thunder, and voices (v. 5). The word in Greek means voice or sound. So I think it means sounds like a thunderstorm. In other words, out of the throne of God is the thunderstorm of judgment. These things symbolized judgment to the ancients, and to the Hebrews especially. So the idea is that God's judgment is coming out of his throne on those who have opposed him and his people.

Now note the seven lamps, called the seven spirits of God, before the throne. Seven is a perfect number. Here it is the symbol of the Holy Spirit who is before the throne. In the next chapter we see the same figure as the spirits of God sent forth into all the earth. The Holy Spirit is God's Spirit sent forth to do his work. In Romans 8:9 we have the phrase "Spirit of God" and "Spirit of Christ" in one verse. So he is the Spirit of God and the Spirit of Christ.

Now then also before the throne was a sea of glass like unto crystal, transparent glass, or glittering glass (v. 6). Someone has interpreted it as like a sea of ice but transparent glass. Now a sea separates people. John was on the Isle of Patmos, and the sea separated him from his friends in Ephesus. "Sea" in some places in Revelation is used to refer to people, the restlessness of people. But here it suggests a separation. Even though the elders are in heaven there is a separation between them and God. God is with his people, but he is transcendent. He is above his people. We are not to get too familiar with God. He's not "the man upstairs." He is God on the throne. Later on we are going to see this sea two more times. We will notice them as we go along.

In the midst of the throne and around it in a circle there were four beasts. Now the word *beast* is not the word for a fierce animal as we find in chapter 13. It is the word for a "living creature." I think these symbolize a redeemed nature. In a way unknown to us when Adam and Eve fell, nature fell; Paul in Romans 8 says that the redemption of the created order is related to our redemption. And nature waits for our redemption, that it might also be redeemed. So here we have the redeemed saints in heaven, and we have a redeemed nature in heaven. "Full of eyes": The meaning for that could be great wisdom, but it could mean that they are watchful in guarding the sovereignty of God. Or they are guarding God's people. It could have a number of meanings, but that is not too important for our purpose. John describes these creatures: one like a lion refers to wild animal life; one is like a calf, domestic animal life; one has the face of a man, human life; and the other as a flying eagle, bird life (v. 7). So these are the four created orders of life on earth. The six wings in verse 8 suggest Isaiah 6. Following this theme, with two wings they covered their faces and with two covered their feet. With two wings they did fly. The Hebrew means that they stood standing, or hovered above the throne of God. All this suggests humility and obedience, reverence, and a readiness to fly to do God's will.

They are crying, without rest day or night, they are crying constantly (present participle), saying, "Holy, Holy, Holy, Lord God Almighty" (v. 8). But notice that they say Lord God Almighty. Domitian said that he was god. He said, "I am Lord of all I survey, and I am mighty." But the creatures say that the true God is Lord. He is almighty compared to Domitian's power. Notice also that Domitian is for a little while only. He reigned from A.D. 81 to 96, and died in 96. But notice that the creatures speak of God who is, who was, and who is to come. "Who is to come" translates a Greek word *ho erchomenos,* "the coming one," which was one name for the Messiah among the Jews.

I think that here the idea is that he is coming to the aid of his people. Now then as nature gives glory, honor, and thanks to God, the twenty-four elders fall down before the throne (vv. 9–10). And notice, they cast their crowns before the throne. They don't wear them around proudly, comparing them, and counting the number of stars each one has to see who has the most. They cast those crowns at the feet of God. E. Y. Mullins in his book *The Christian Religion in Its Doctrinal Expression* says that one element of heaven will be appreciation, appreciation for what God has done for us to redeem us. The chapter closes with them praising God for his creative work.

Now in chapter 5 John continues describing this vision. He said he saw the right hand of him that sat on the throne (note right hand again), the idea of his strong hand. There was a book written on both sides. Really it was a roll or scroll. They didn't have bound books in those days. The scroll was sealed with seven seals, seven being a perfect number. Thus, it was completely sealed.

Now to seal something is to conceal its message; to unseal it is to reveal its message. This message was sealed, and the question was asked by an angel, "Who is worthy to open the book, and to loose the seals thereof?" (v. 2). "And no man in heaven, nor in earth, neither under the earth, was able to open the book" (v. 3). Of course, we know about heaven, and we know about the earth. But "under the earth"; what does that mean? Does it mean the abode of the dead? Maybe, but I rather think that it means more than that. I think we have to think of this in terms of *hell.* You recall that the rich man was in *Hades* (Greek text) but he was also in punishment. If that be a correct interpretation, then no man that had died and gone to heaven, no man that is living on the earth today, and no man who has died and gone to hell can give us the meaning of that roll.

Now this immediately raises the question as to what is this roll. Some say it is God's book of justice. Others say it is God's book of destiny. Several other ideas are mentioned. So with all the different ideas, one more won't hurt. I see it as the roll of history. Somebody points out that in chapter 6 we see the seals being opened, and we view all the things which happen. Well, that is part of history. So I see it as the roll of history. And as we will see before we get through with this chapter, you cannot understand history apart from the redemptive purpose of God. You may read the surface of history, but you don't get to the real meaning of it. So you can't interpret the real meaning of history in terms of anybody that has died and gone to heaven, anybody that is living today, or anybody that has lived and died and gone to hell. No human being can furnish the basis for an understanding of history. If we overlook the redemptive will of God in history and his purpose, then Shakespeare was right when he said that history "is a tale told by an idiot, full of sound and fury, signifying nothing." But there is a deeper meaning to history than what we read on the surface. The historiographers give the surface events. A holy history, a history within history, gives the divine purpose in history.

John "wept much" (v. 4). That means he began to weep and kept on weeping profusely, maybe out loud. But an elder came over and told him to stop crying (v. 5). He said, "Behold, the Lion of the tribe of Juda, the Root of David hath prevailed to open the book, and to loose the seven seals thereof."

So then John looked up. He thought he was going to see a lion, but instead he saw a lamb. "A Lamb as it had been slain" (v. 6). The word for "had been slain" means to have your throat cut. That's the way they slew sacrificial lambs in the Temple. Now

Jesus didn't have his throat cut. We know his wounds were in his hands, feet, and side—and maybe from the thorns, we might count the wounds on his brow. But he didn't have his throat cut. This is symbolism. The idea is that of a sacrificial lamb. To us a lamb suggests meekness in the sense of weakness. But the lamb was often used in Hebrew thought for sacrifice and redemption. Isaiah 53 has it. John the Baptist said "Behold the Lamb of God" (John 1:29). And yet there is another thought behind this. Notice that John says that he had seven horns and seven eyes. Horns are the symbol of power, and seven is the perfect number. So, perfect or complete power. Some would say that "seven eyes" means that he is looking after his people. Maybe so. But I think it refers to wisdom, complete wisdom. He is not just a weak lamb as we think of a lamb on the altar. He is a strong lamb. You've seen pictures of Alexander the Great. He has a ram's horn on either side of his helmet, symbolic of his power. In the biblical period between the Old and New Testaments Judas Maccabeus was the George Washington of that era. He led the Jews to a freedom which lasted for 100 years. He was called the mighty lamb or the strong lamb. So this lamb that is a sacrificial lamb also has the strength of a lion. He is the Lion of the tribe of Judah. The seven spirits of God (v. 6) we've already noted. In other words, the Lamb is looking after his people. You don't see him, but he is there.

And so this Lamb came and took the book out of the right hand of him that sat upon the throne (v. 7). Let your imagination run riot. Oh, it is a majestic moment. Incidentally, the King James Version says that God has this roll in the right hand. The Greek text says *upon* the right hand. He holds it in his palm. And the Lamb came and took it out of his hand. As he did so, a redeemed universe and spiritual order both fell down before the lamb (v. 8). They had their harps for music and they had their golden vials or bowls full of odors, which are identified as the prayers of the saints. The saints had been praying for relief, and release was on the way. So they sang a new song (v. 9). It is the song of redemption. We read about the song of Moses and the Lamb. The song of Moses was sung after Israel's deliverance through the Red Sea. But here it is the song of redemption. "Thou art worthy to take the book, and to open the seals thereof: for thou wast slain [throat was cut], and hast redeemed us to God by thy blood out of every kindred, and tongue, and people, and nation; and hast made us unto our God kings and priests: and we shall reign on the earth" (vv. 9–10).

Now he has redeemed us. Every kindred, tongue, people, and nation means without regard to race, or color, or national origin. The universal Savior! He has made us kings and priests before our God. In 1 Peter 2:1–10, Peter in essence says that Christians are the true Israel of God. In the Old Testament the nation Israel as such never was called the chosen people of God. Israel was not chosen for privilege but for responsibility. If you will do certain things (Ex. 19:5–6), then you will be unto me a kingdom of priests, and so on. A kingdom of priests was a priest-nation that should bring the rest of the nations to worship Jehovah. That was the "if," that along with keeping his law. Israel didn't keep the law; Israel didn't bring other nations to worship God. In 1 Samuel 8, the leaders of the tribes came to Samuel and said that they wanted a king like the other nations. Thus instead of being a separate priest-nation they wanted to be like the other nations.

Isn't that one of the things wrong with our nation today? We want to be like the other nations. I don't think we are the Israel nation of God in that sense. But I think that God has a role for our nation to play in his spiritual purpose for mankind, his redemptive purpose. I don't think the Federal Government ought to go into the missionary business. But I do think that we as a people have a special relationship to God. Palestine was located in the center of the ancient world. The United States is the crossroads of the present world. We have the ability, we have the know-how, we have the money; if we would give it, we could send missionaries in hordes to the rest of the world. But we want to be like all the other nations. We want pomp, splendor, and power, and so on. We've largely forgotten as a nation our spiritual purpose. Southern Baptists have more missionaries than any other non-Catholic group in America. And yet as a nation we have forgotten that mission.

But here John says that we are the true Israel. In the Old Testament the true Israel was the faithful remnant. Paul in Romans 9 says they are not all Israel that are of Israel. Only those that were faithful to the covenant were the true Israel. And the same is true of us. Not all Americans are Christians, therefore, all of our nation is not a part of the true Israel. But every Christian, regardless of his color or race, is a part of it.

Later on in Romans 11:26 Paul said, "And so all Israel shall be saved." He's not talking about a nation. He's talking about all the people that believe in Christ, Jews and Gentiles alike. God just has one plan of salvation, not two. In Acts 15:11 Peter said, "But we believe that through the grace of the Lord Jesus Christ we [Jew] shall be saved even as they [Gentiles]." The Judaizers were saying that Gentiles had to become Jews, then believe in Christ and be saved. Peter said they had it just backwards. We must be saved the same way they are.

Now let's return to our text. When that happened, John heard the voice of many angels that joined in with a redeemed nature and redeemed humanity (v. 11). But the angels did not sing of redemption. Angels do not know anything about sin, suffering, and redemption. Peter says that they long to look into such things; they wonder about all of this (1 Pet. 1:12). That is why God didn't give to angels the job of preaching the gospel. They can't understand the gospel as do you and I, sinners saved by grace. They are neither moral or immoral; they are amoral. I'm talking about the righteous angels of course. But notice they did not join in singing the song of redemption in verse 9. However, they did join praising the Lamb as worthy to receive riches and blessings (v. 12).

And then every creature, every created being, which is in heaven, on the earth, under the earth, and in the sea joined in the song (v. 13). "Blessing, and honour, and glory, and power, be unto him that sitteth upon the throne [God the Father], and unto the Lamb [Son] for ever and ever"—unto the ages of the ages. That is the strongest expression in the Greek language for expressing eternity. Every creature, every created being, means all the people; it means all the redeemed people; it means a redeemed nature. It places them in heaven, on earth, and under the earth. If our idea of *under the earth* carries over that it refers to hell, then we even see those in hell joining in this song. Why not? Doesn't Paul say in Philippians 2 that at the name of Jesus every knee shall bow, not just the Christians, but every knee should bow? Even those under the earth. Every tongue should confess that he is Christ and Lord to the glory of God the Father. I see "under the earth" in both places to mean this. Those in hell, by the power of God's might, will be forced to admit that the one they rejected was truly Jesus Christ the Lord, *Jehovah in flesh* for the purpose of saving people. But for them it is too late!

Now in 1 Corinthians 15:24—28 Paul pictured Christ as subduing the universe. Well, Christ is in that business now. He's reigning in his mediatorial kingdom, and subduing all that oppose God. The word *subdue* means to line up as troops under a commander. And when he has done so, he will march the whole of a redeemed universe, natural and spiritual, into the presence of God. Then he himself will become subject to God, that God may be all in all. God reveals himself to us as Father, Son, and Holy Spirit. I think that they are still God, the Father, and Son, and the Holy Spirit. But we're not worshiping three Gods; we are worshiping one God. We see him in these three ways. But in heaven we shall fully know as we are fully known, as Paul said in 1 Corinthians 13.

So here we have this view of heaven. God on his throne, all is right with the world. God is watching over his own. He hasn't been overcome. And the redeeming Lamb—in the light of the redemptive purpose of God—through him we have a proper understanding of history. In spite of what men are doing on earth, God is guiding history. Now this doesn't mean that he's responsible for everything men on earth do. But it does mean that he is guiding history toward the accomplishment of his purpose. Colossians 1:16 says that Christ is the sphere in which creation took place, he is the intermediate agent by which it took place, and he is the goal toward which all of creation is moving. So we see the climax. But keep in mind that the theme of the book is the sovereignty of God and of our Lord Jesus Christ. That is another way of saying that in spite of what happens to us on earth, Christ is going to be victorious, and we are victorious in him.

God doesn't seal his people in plastic bags that have been sterilized from sin. He leaves us out in the world to be tempted, to undergo the things that are necessary for developing us into the kind of people God wants us to be.

Mrs. Hobbs and I moved from Mobile, Alabama, called the azalea capital of the world, to Oklahoma City. We love azaleas. And people knowing that would bring us potted plants, most of the time they would be azalea plants. Well, as soon as one began to wilt in the house we would take it out in the yard and plant it, hoping it would live. But none of them did. Why? Because they had been grown in a hothouse. A lady went down to Mississippi where she was born and reared. She went out into the wild, had a man to dig up some azalea plants, put them in her car, and brought them home. She had her yardman come and put them out in our yard. Everyone of them lived. The most beautiful blossoms you ever saw anywhere! Why? Because they had grown up out in the wild. They had withstood the heat, wind, rain, and storms of life. That is the kind of thing God is doing with us. He is letting us endure all of this, but he is with us in it. "I know not where his islands lift their fronded palms in air; I only know I cannot drift beyond his love and care." Truth forever on the scaffold? Yes, "But that scaffold sways the future, and behind the dim unknown standeth God within the shadows, keeping watch above his own." Isn't that a glorious assurance? "Blessed assurance, Jesus is mine, oh, what a foretaste of glory divine!"

5

Reviewing Judgments Coming Against Christ's Enemies

Opening of the Seals

Now in chapter 6 the Lamb begins opening the seals. Here we find three series of sevens: seals, trumpets, and vials. I see each series beginning at a low level and rising to a climax. After the first series the second drops back and starts at a low level, and then rises to a higher climax. The third one starts at a lower level and reaches the top climax. These all have to do with the judgment of God upon a wicked world. And each series presents a greater judgment. In the first series of seven we see one fourth of the earth and man was affected. In the second series, one third, and in the last series *all the earth and all men are affected,* that is the unredeemed.

So with that in mind, let us look for a moment at the four horsemen. Revelation 6:1 in the King James Version says that one of the four living creatures says, "Come and see." Well, scratch out "and see." That is not in the Greek text. That sounds like he is saying to John, come and see. Well John has already come, and he's already seen it. Keep in mind now this is a drama. We've had this glorious vision of heaven, and now we see the drama begin to move. The living creature simply said, "Come." That is true in all four cases. "Come" is a command, as if from the director of the drama. That would be Christ ultimately, but he is saying it through these creatures. Anyway, he says "Come," and when he says it, a horse with a rider gallops out of one wing, rides across the stage, and disappears (v. 2). You don't see him anymore. At the opening of the second seal, he says, "Come," and another horse with a rider does the same; also the third and fourth.

Now the first horse was white. Some say that the rider is Christ. Later on we find Christ riding on a white horse. But this is not Christ. In the later picture we have Christ with a sword coming out of his mouth. Here he has a bow in his hand and he wears a crown. From this we know this was not a Roman rider. Romans used a short sword, and they did not wear crowns. People wouldn't let them do so. But coins have been found of Parthian soldiers having bows, being on horses, and having a crown. That most likely explains the symbolism here. The one people that the Roman Empire never did conquer in their part of the world was the Parthians. The Romans had a dread that someday the Parthians would invade the Empire and destroy it. This idea comes through several times as we go through the book. The fact that Rome was not destroyed by the Parthians doesn't lessen the threat. The point is that Rome is going to fall. This first rider "went forth conquering, and to conquer." This symbolizes *conquest*. Rome was built on conquest, and by conquest Rome was going to fall. The whole idea of these four horsemen is that built into the Roman system is its own destruction. They built their empire by the sword, by conquest, and they are going to die by it.

When a nation tries conquest, it runs into war when the other nation resists. The second seal was opened, the call was heard again. "Come." Then a red horse came across the stage (v. 4). On it was a rider who could take peace from earth so that men killed one another. That is *war*. Answering the third "Come" (v. 5) was a black horse with a rider. He had a pair of scales in his hand, and was crying the price of wheat and barley. Barley was a grain used by the poor. Reduced to our own coinage, the prices would be something about $4.60 bushel for wheat and $2.50 for barley

(v. 6). These are famine prices, and this rider symbolizes *famine*. With the fourth "Come," a pale horse rides across the stage. It was followed by *hell* as it reads in the King James Version. The rider had the name "death" (v. 8). Really it is *Hades,* the abode of the dead. Death is followed by Hades; it was ever swallowing down those that death took. Power was given to them over the *fourth* part of the earth. Later on we will see a third part of the earth affected.

Historians say that the things that brought on the destruction of the Roman Empire were internal decay, natural disasters such as earthquakes, floods, and volcanic eruptions like at Pompeii, and outside invasion. Here we find conquest, we find hunger, we find war, we find famine, and then we find death. So these emphasize the fact that built into the Roman system is its own destruction. A nation built on conquest will end the same way. The fact of the matter is that the nation fell eventually from an invasion from the north. Those strong people living up there were hearty and hungry. The Romans had been eating the fat of the land all those years. The wealth of the world flowed into Rome. There were more slaves in Rome than free men. The Romans wanted to enjoy their bounties, the fruits of their conquest. They even hired soldiers to guard the frontiers and man the army. But the people grew soft. And when those people came in from the north the Romans were a hollow shell of what they once were.

When I look at our own nation and the things that have happened to us, I tell you, I tremble in my boots. We are at the very same place. We want to enjoy our prosperity, but we don't want to defend it. Let somebody else defend it, we just want to enjoy it. Hostile powers have already invaded us under the cover of night in their infiltration. I'm not so much afraid of a military attack from Russia, for instance, but I fear the termites that are eating out the foundations. If we don't turn around, we are going to go the way that Rome went. We are going to go the way that Egypt, Persia, Greece, Rome, and Germany went. It can happen here! And yet in the midst of it all, the Christian can be concerned about his world and his country. But within himself he can know that God is still on his throne, and God is still working out his redemptive purpose.

When the fifth seal was opened, under the altar were the souls of the martyrs (vv. 9–11). They were crying with a loud voice, "How long, O Lord," or literally, "until when." They were calling for judgment upon the persecutors. Some see that and say it proves that Revelation is not a Christian document. They were asking how long the Lord was going to wait before he avenged their death and the suffering of his people on earth. Don't we say, "Why doesn't God do something? Why doesn't he destroy the Communists?" Some people nitpick and miss the whole message. The Lord told them to be patient, that judgment was working. You see, 1,000 years are as a day in God's sight (2 Pet. 3:8). We want God to operate by our calendar instead of his. He's never in a hurry. Israel rebelled at Kadesh-barnea. We would have pulled our hair out while the chance of a lifetime was lost. God waited forty years. He said, "You just lost your opportunity, but I can wait. You can't, I can." We need God more than he needs us. So he says, "Just wait, be patient."

When the sixth seal was opened, there was a great earthquake, the sun became black, and the moon became as blood (vv. 12–14). These are apocalyptic figures. Since Dr. Robbins will go into that more in his chapters, I won't spend time on it, except to point out that we have come to the opening of the sixth seal. I did not say earlier that after the opening of the sixth seal and the blowing of the sixth trumpet there is an interlude. This is not true in the pouring out in the vials of wrath. So here we reach the first climax in the first series of seven. Notice that the disturbance in the heavenly bodies is a part of apocalyptic expressing God's invasion of history. Heaven was just rolled back as a parchment. Mountains and islands moved out of their places. Kings of the earth, and the great and rich men began to pray for the rocks to fall on them to hide them "from the face of him that sitteth on the throne, and from the wrath of the Lamb: For the great day of his wrath is come; and who shall be able to stand?" (vv. 16–17). That is the first climax. In other words, this refers to the end of the age, the return of the Lord. Now we come back to that idea again. Some say that there is a whole lot left in the book. But keep in mind these three series of seven. Each reaches a higher climax than the one before it. So here is one. The unsaved, the wicked, are facing the wrath of the Lamb. So they are calling to the rocks and hills to hide them from the wrath of the Lamb. Better to be crushed than to have to face his judgment.

The word for "wrath" in verse 17 is *orgé*. There were two Greek words used in the New Testament for wrath. One was *thumos*. This word is used in the book of Revelation more than the other. It expressed the idea of setting fire to dry grass which burns furiously for a moment and then goes out. I like to think of it as the eruption of a volcano. It erupts and subsides. *Thumos* was God's wrath at Sodom. The other word is *orgé* with two syllables, *org-é*. That word refers to abiding, deep-seated, general universal wrath. In the Christian context it refers to God's abiding, universal opposition to evil. It is the word that John the Baptist used when he said, "Who hath warned you to flee from the wrath to come?" (Matt. 3:7). At Sodom Lot was a few miles away when the fire and brimstone came down. He and his daughters were safe. But John uses the figure of a desert or prairie fire, with rats, snakes, and other things running ahead of the fire. How can one flee from this wrath to come? It is everywhere. You can't run from this fire. Where is the only place of safety in a forest fire or a prairie fire? Where the fire has already burned. And the only safe place from God's abiding, universal opposition to evil is at Calvary where the fire has already burned. God's wrath has been poured out upon his Son as our substitute.

So we have here in the first climax a picture of the second coming of Christ and the disturbances in nature and man. In spite of all that had happened, these people had not repented; therefore, they were crying out to be hidden from wrath, which of course is impossible. In the second series of seven again we shall see suffering through which man went but which did not cause him to repent. To me one of the best arguments against purgatory is the series of pictures we have here in Revelation. Our suffering doesn't remove sin. If it did, then all the world would have been saved according to the book of Revelation, but they did not repent.

First Interlude

In chapter 7 we come to the first interlude. Verse 1 depicts four angels standing on the four corners of the earth, holding back the four winds to prevent their blowing on earth, sea, and trees. *Corner* winds were evil or contrary winds. They symbolize evil or judgment. This is for the purpose of the sealing of a certain group. This interlude shows the sealing of the 144,000 with the seal of the living God (vv. 2–8). Now the 144,000 are described here as the tribes of Israel, and they are named. That would be 12,000 from each tribe. Go back to your numerology idea. Three plus four equals seven, three times four equals twelve and that was a perfect number. Raised to the 1,000th degree, it would be 144,000. So the idea is that it is a number signifying a great number, a great, perfect, complete number. Now who are they? Well, some say they are the Jews, Christian Jews that will be saved during the period of the millennium. They hold that Jews are going to go out and be the missionaries for the world while Christ and his people reign in Jerusalem. Well, frankly, I don't find that in the New Testament. But in order to save time you can read books if you want to know about the various views on this.

I think the 144,000 that are to be sealed are the Christians who are still on earth undergoing persecution. Now in verse 9 we find a multitude so great that no man could number it (vv. 10–12). I think those are the redeemed of God in heaven. They don't need any seal of protection. The seal is to protect those during the persecution; so those in heaven don't need any seals to protect them. But those on earth do. Now later on in chapter 14 we are going to find this 144,000 in heaven. But right here I think that is the idea. Those in heaven need no seal; those that are on earth do. So they are sealed for protection.

In verse 14 when asked about these that are in heaven praising the Lord, John was told that these are the ones who "came out of great tribulation, and have washed their robes, and made them white in the blood of the Lamb" (v. 14). Victory! Some see in the word *tribulation* a great tribulation at the end of the age or just before the end of the age, a seven-year period of tribulation. But again I just don't find it. In Matthew 24 Jesus said that at the destruction of Jerusalem the suffering there will be so great that there has never been any tribulation like it before; there will never be any like it afterwards. He is definitely talking about the destruction of Jerusalem. You only have to read Josephus' account of the fall of Jerusalem to the Romans in A.D. 70 to get the point. He said that blood ran up to the horse's bridle. Well, of course, Josephus had a tendency to exaggerate. But you see the idea. When those Romans finally broke through the siege of Jerusalem after all those years, they went wild; they went mad. They were burning and killing everything in their path. Titus didn't intend to destroy the Temple which was one of the great wonders of the ancient world. He was crying, "Save the Temple!" But Roman soldiers threw a torch in it and set it afire.

The word for "tribulation" simply means to be in a tight place.

Like grapes in a winepress, in a tight place with seemingly no way out. And by using that word and building up a system, it has evolved into a period of seven years. I think we are in the tribulation now. I think the tribulation began when the Lord went back to heaven or when he rose from the dead. But I think the tribulation is the suffering that the people of Christ are going to endure until the Lord returns again as they preach the gospel. Paul said in Colossians 1:24 that he was to "fill up that which is behind of the afflictions of Christ in my flesh." That doesn't mean that Christ didn't suffer enough to save people. Only Christ could suffer redemptively. Paul is talking about Christ's suffering as he revealed God to man before he went to the cross. Dr. A. T. Robertson put it in baseball terminology. Christ had his turn at bat; now it is Paul's turn at bat. Each suffered at his time.

The Seven Trumpets

In chapter 8 we have the opening of the seventh seal. "There was silence in heaven about the space of half an hour" (v. 1). Somebody said that this proves there won't be any women in heaven. I might say that could also include preachers. No, this is purely for dramatic effect. Now remember that this is a drama. If, for instance, in a drama the actors never stop talking, it diminishes the dramatic effect. I've seen a few people in my lifetime who could talk on *intake* as well as *exhaust*. If you just go on like that, it doesn't mean anything. We preachers ought to learn that it is just as necessary, if not more, to pause occasionally or lower the voice as it is to shout. You can emphasize an idea more effectively by lowering your voice than you can by raising it. We yell to high heaven and think we've really done it. An old preacher had in the margin of his notes, "Yell here." But you can stress a thought with a pause or a whisper. I had to get on the "Baptist Hour" before I really learned that. Really, we need both loud and soft preaching. We have soft music and loud music. But the change of tone, the change of pace in speaking, teaching, and preaching is effective. Silence in heaven. Dramatic effect. Something tremendous was about to happen, and for a space of half an hour there was silence in heaven. That could be symbolism, a brief but undetermined amount of time. But anyway there was a pause. There was silence.

And then seven angels came and brought with them seven trumpets. Trumpets that they were to blow at stated times. Another angel came having a golden censer and incense symbolizing the prayers of the saints (v. 3). And the smoke of the incense came up before God out of the angel's hand, and the angel took the censer filled with fire of the altar and cast it into the earth (vv. 4–5). In other words, the prayers of the saints were being answered. Then came thunder, earthquake, and lightning—again symbolic of judgment—and the seven angels prepared to blow their trumpets. The Greek word *trumpet* or *to blow a trumpet* has in it the very sound of a trumpet as you pronounce it. Now notice in the second series of seven there is judgment again. But it is on a greater part of the earth and man. First it was a fourth, now it is a *third*.

When the first angel sounded, there followed hail and fire mingled with blood (v. 7). Some say it was clotted blood. When this mixture was cast upon the earth, the third part of the trees was burned up, and all green grass was burned up. The third part of the vegetation. At the second angel's sounding (v. 8), a great mountain as it were burning with fire was cast into the sea, and the third part of the sea (salt water) became blood. Now the sea was important to Roman life, as would be the vegetation. They were farmers, but they also depended upon the sea for fish to eat and for commerce to bring their riches of their empire to Rome. So a third part of the sea become blood. A third part of the creatures in the sea that had life died, and a third part of the ships was destroyed (v. 9). Notice the third part.

Then the third angel sounded (vv. 10–11), and a great star from heaven as a burning lamp fell upon the third part of the rivers and the fountains. Now the curse was upon fresh water, the water necessary not only for the growth of vegetation but for the people to drink. And it says the name of the star is "Wormwood," maybe a poison. Those who drank the water died. The fourth angel sounded, and a third part of the sun, moon, and stars were smitten (v. 12). The sun was the source of all life on earth. And the sun was smitten. Now, of course, we can compare some of these with the plagues in Egypt. The Holy Spirit drew from these to give John the message.

Then at the time John heard an angel crying, "Woe, woe, woe" (v. 13). This was because of the other three trumpets that are yet to sound. When the fifth angel sounded, a star fell from heaven to earth (9:1). "To him [as a person] was given the key of the bottomless pit" (v. 2). As he opened the bottomless pit, smoke rose out of it, and out of the smoke came locusts. In that part of the world locusts were common.

I remember that in Louisville at Southern Baptist Theological Seminary we had a seven-year locust plague. Those things nearly ran us crazy day and night with their shrill sound. Millions and millions of them! When they died, they would fill in about those big tree roots. It took a big truck and men with shovels to scoop them up and haul them away.

To these locusts was given power as scorpions on the earth have power (v. 3). Now if you don't live in the western part of the United States, you may not know about scorpions. Only those men were to be hurt who did not have the seal on their forehead. You see, God had sealed his own for protection. It was given that they should not kill men, but they should be tormented five months (vv. 5–6). Five months is the life span of a locust. Those stung would seek death and not find it, try to die but death would flee from them. The sting of a scorpion's tail causes pain so terrible that you wish you could die, but you can't. Now some people die from it as some people die from bee stings; they are unusually allergic to that kind of poison. But normally a scorpion sting will not kill you, but it will make you wish you could die.

The shape of the locusts was like horses prepared for battle. On their heads were golden crowns; they had faces like men with hair as women; their teeth were as lion's teeth. They also wore breastplates. The sound of their wings was as the sound of chariots and horses, and they had tails like scorpions (v. 10). They were given power to hurt men for five months. This is symbolic of great suffering.

These locusts had a king over them, and he is identified as *Abaddon* (Hebrew) or *Apollyon* (Greek). The word means destroyer (v. 11). In John 3:16 the verb is "not perish." Now John says that one woe is past, and two more are to come (v. 12).

When the sixth angel sounded his trumpet, John heard a voice saying, "Loose the four angels which are bound in the great river Euphrates" (v. 14). We saw these bound angels in the four winds (7:1). In the idea of wind there is that of evil power. Now here the sixth angel says to loose the four angels which are bound in the great river. This has to do with the idea of that fear of outside invasion. The fact that such never took place doesn't alter the meaning of the book. It simply is using the events of that time or what the people themselves thought and believed to express truth for all times. "The four angels were loosed, which were prepared for an hour, and a day, and a month, and a year, for to slay the third part of men." Notice again the *third* part.

The number of this army like the locusts was two hundred thousand thousand (v. 16). Figure it up—two hundred million men. Now some say that only the Chinese could furnish that size army. Perhaps India could, but again, this is symbolism. By then a third part of the men were killed (vv. 17–19). There's your increased part—one fourth, now a third. But the rest of the men which were not killed by these plagues repented not (v. 20).

We come again to a climax, you see, the end of the age in this series of seven. They did not repent. They had greater suffering than we find in the first seven. In the first seven there was more or less the ordinary day-to-day events of history, with wars and rumors of wars, pestilence and famines, and plagues. But in the second series we have these definite forms of suffering described. But that did not cause the pagan people to repent. They "repented not of the works of their hands, that they should not worship devils." In other words, worship of the emperor is called devil worship here. These images of Domitian and other idols can't see, hear, or walk. But the worshipers didn't repent of any of their sins (v. 21).

The Second Interlude

Now then in 10:1 through 11:14 we come to the second interlude before the seventh trumpet is sounded. Even after this trumpet is sounded there is considerable material before the next series of seven. John says that he saw a mighty angel come down from heaven (v. 1). The description of him is simply to show how big he is. He had in this hand a little book open, a little piece of parchment (v. 2). So large is he that his right foot is upon the sea, and his left foot is on the earth. The idea of putting a foot on the sea and one on the land shows the idea of universalism in the sense of the whole earth. His voice came in seven thunders representing judgment again (v. 4). Before John could write down what the thunders said, he was told to seal up those things and not write them. In other words, God says, "I've given my warning, no more warning will be given." Verse 6 says time shall be no longer. In other words, the destruction is now going to come without a warning. Even God's patience has run out (v. 7). John was told to take the book and eat it (vv. 8–11). Although it tasted sweet in his mouth, it was bitter in his stomach. It would be sweet as the message of God is to any preacher knowing that he was declaring the word, but the contents would be bitter when he had swallowed it because they had to do with the terrible judgment to come.

In chapter 11 John was told to measure the Temple. The word for "temple" here is *naos*, which refers to the holy of holies, not for the whole Temple area. The holy of holies was where God was said to dwell in mercy with his people. Measurement in the Bible is used sometimes of destruction and also of defense or security. I think the latter is true here. The Temple represents the people of God, the *naos* where God dwelt. But the court of the Gentiles is not to be measured.

The Temple area had several courts. The first court, outside the building itself, was the court of Gentiles. All people could go in there, but a Gentile could not go beyond it. Archaeologists have found a stone sign warning Gentiles on pain of death against going further into the Temple. It was at an entrance to the court of women, and the writing was in Greek, Aramaic, and Hebrew. I saw it years ago in a museum in Istanbul. The other courts were those of Israel and of the priests. There were also the holy place of sacrifice and the holy of holies.

The thing that started the riot when Paul was arrested in Jerusalem was that his enemies claimed he had taken a Gentile beyond the court of Gentiles. He didn't do it, but they claimed he did. Male Jews could go into the court of the women, but women could go no further than that in the Temple. Only priests could go into the court of priests. We know that Jesus was in the court of Gentiles and the court of women, but as a Jewish man and not a priest he could not go beyond the court of Israel. Well, anyway this is the court of Gentiles. Now remember that this is symbolism. Actually, the court of Gentiles could include the whole city of Jerusalem.

We have read Jesus' warnings about the destruction of the city, which did come in A.D. 70. He said in Luke 21:20 that when you see Jerusalem circled by armies, get out because you know the end is nigh. This is not the end of time but the end of the city of Jerusalem. And in Matthew Jesus quoted from Daniel, "When ye therefore shall see the abomination of desolation" (24:15). An abomination simply means something with a bad smell, something that smells bad in the nostrils of God.

The abomination of desolation, or destruction, referred to in Daniel has been interpreted in several ways. Some say that it refers to Antiochus Epiphanes defiling the Temple. He sacrified a hog on the Jewish altar, letting hog blood run down over the altar and into the chamber below. He boiled the meat in water. And taking the water, as Dr. Robertson used to say, "he sprinkled sow juice all over the walls of the Temple." He so defiled it that this action kicked off the rebellion of the Jews against Antiochus Epiphanes who ruled over the Selucid kingdom in Antioch. This was one of the five divisions made of the Greek empire when Alexander died. The leader of this rebellion was Judas Maccabeus.

Others say that this "abomination" had to do with Caligula who gave the order that his statue be placed in the holy of holies. But before it could be carried out he died; fortunately it was never carried out. During Pilate's time as procurator of Judaea he brought Roman troops into the city of Jerusalem bearing the Roman standards with images of eagles on them. The Jews said that was an image, an idol, and they raised such a row he had to take those eagles out. This shows how sensitive Jews were even about the city itself.

So the fact that Gentiles would be besieging the entire city fits the idea of verse 2. They would walk over it for forty-two months. Now forty-two months is three and a half years, and three and a half is half of seven. Since seven is a perfect number, three and a half would be an imperfect number. In Revelation it is used many times referring to a brief but indefinite period of time.

Chapter 11 then introduces two witnesses (vv. 3–11), whose description reminds us of Elijah and Moses, who had the power to shut up the heavens so that it wouldn't rain and to smite the earth with plagues and turn water into blood. There have been various interpretations of them. Some say there will be two great witnesses near the end of time who will bear witness to the Jews. I see them as symbolic of the law and the prophets, the Old Testament Scriptures.

Do you remember Jesus talking with them during the transfiguration on Mount Hermon? Incidentally, note that there are two of them. Two is stronger than one in numerology. Jesus, you remember, sent his disciples out two by two. Even today when we send people out on visitation we try to send them two by two. They strengthen one another. In the figure here these two witnesses were killed and they lay dead for three days in a city called "Sodom and Egypt." Dr. McDowell thinks it was Jerusalem, but I don't think so. If it refers to any particular place, it seems that it would be Rome. But the idea is that the pagan world rejoiced because the two witnesses were dead. It thought it had triumphed over Christianity. But then after three and a half days—after a brief but indefinite period of time—they were brought back to life and taken up to heaven. The idea as I see it is that Moses and Elijah symbolize the proclamation of the gospel in that time as well as through the ages. The pagan world tries to destroy the proclamation of the gospel. The Romans thought they had done it.

Earlier, Saul of Tarsus, a Jew, started out with the idea that he was going to destroy the very name of Jesus, going to erase it from history. But he met Jesus on the Damascus road and became his greatest apostle. To me he is the greatest single human argument in favor of the bodily resurrection of Jesus that I know about. What changes were wrought in his life! So Rome thought she had conquered, she had won. The gospel was destroyed. But then the witnesses were raised up and taken up into heaven. In other words, God is going to look after his own, and the proclamation of the gospel is not going to cease. This would certainly encourage the suffering saints in Asia.

We have to apply these things to our own day. We read articles about how the gospel has failed, that we live in the post-Christian age, and that the gospel has nothing to say to this age. We don't live in a post-Christian age, beloved. We still live in a pre-Christian age. We haven't come *up* to Christ yet! We haven't come up to the gospel yet! But still some people say that the gospel is dead, Christianity has failed. Even good church people swallow that sort of thing. They join some social reform group or other earthly effort. But when Jesus said that the gates of Hades will not have strength against his church, he was saying that his church will live. The abode of the dead will not overcome it. So if you want to be where the action is, then you get busy in your church. Long before these fly-by-night things came along, and long after they're forgotten, if the Lord delays his coming, the church will still be in business until the Lord says, "It is enough."

Now notice in verse 13 that the tenth part of the city fell. John is talking about Rome. Later on we're going to see it divided into three parts, which means divine judgment, three being the symbol of deity. But here we see partial judgment upon it.

In verse 15 we have the blowing of the seventh trumpet. Revelation 11:15 is the climax of the book. It means that God's sovereignty over the universe is true. Satan falsely claimed this. But here we see that it belongs to "our Lord [Jehovah], and . . . his Christ [the Son]." This fact results in further worship from the elders or the redeemed in heaven (vv. 16–18).

Now when the seventh angel sounded in verse 19, we see the Temple of God "opened in heaven, and there was seen in his temple the ark of his testament." Since the Babylonians destroyed Jerusalem, nobody had seen or known what happened to the ark of the covenant. It wasn't in Herod's temple. But John looked into the heavenly temple and the ark is still there. The ravings of mad men on earth haven't destroyed it; they haven't defeated God's purpose. His ark is still in heaven. Now the earthly counterpart is not there, but John saw the heavenly ark still in the *naos,* in the holy of holies. This chapter closes with the symbol of judgment (v. 19*b*).

Wonder in Heaven

Chapter 12 tells us about John seeing a great wonder in heaven. A woman was clothed with the sun. The description of her in verse 1 is window dressing or stage scenery. She is with child and suffering to give birth (v. 2).

Now who is this woman? Some say that she is the nation of Israel, and she could be. It was out of Israel that the Messiah was born. Some say it's the church, meaning of course the Old Testament church, but if so you have the idea here that the church produced Jesus when really Jesus produced the church. Whatever meaning you may put on it, I think we must accept the fact that this is a reference to the incarnation of God in Jesus Christ. In fact, I think that idea runs through this chapter. Some say that she's the virgin Mary, but I don't see that. She certainly is not seen here as the "Queen of Heaven" as some would have her to be. But you can't get around the idea that she's involved, because she was the virgin mother of our Savior. However, it is symbolism. I think in this chapter the Holy Spirit is telling John that the devil has already tried to destroy Jesus. Through the first eleven chapters we find the devil fighting against the people of Christ. Now from chapter 12 through chapter 20, we find the devil fighting against Christ himself. It's that cosmic struggle of which we see only the earthly aspect. But in chapter 12 the events seem to refer to the past but with a flavor of the present and future. It refers to Jesus' birth and subsequent events.

And notice the second wonder in heaven: a great red dragon (Satan) with seven heads and ten horns symbolizing perfect wisdom, perfect power, that is, great wisdom and great power (v. 3). Perfection belongs only to God. He had seven crowns on his heads as one ruling over a great portion of the earth. Jesus called him "the prince of this world" in John 12. "His tail drew the third part of the stars of heaven." This is symbolism, showing how large the dragon was. The idea that he's trying to devour the child as soon as it's born suggests Herod the Great's efforts to destroy Jesus when he was born. But the woman brought forth her child, and the child was caught up unto God into his glory (v. 5).

Satan tried to destroy Jesus more than once while he was on earth. He tried at his birth. He tried to destroy him in storms at sea. He tried to destroy him when he had the people try to throw him over a cliff in Nazareth. He tried to bleed him to death in the garden of Gethsemane; he tried to beat him to death in Pilate's hall. Satan wanted Jesus dead, but he didn't want him to die on the cross because that was the way God was going to redeem man. His last effort to keep Jesus from dying on the cross was to have the people say, "Come down from the cross and we'll believe." Now I think evil itself got out of Satan's control when they nailed Jesus to the cross. He didn't want him to die on the cross. That was God's redemptive plan. But he wanted him dead. Jesus was finally killed, but he was put in a grave which somebody described as just a wayside inn on the way back to the Father's house. Then Jesus was caught up to God at his ascension, and to his throne seated at the right hand of God, as we're told in Hebrews.

The woman fled into the wilderness where a place had been prepared for her, and she was fed 1,260 days (v. 6.) That's about three and a half years. There's your three and a half again, a short but indefinite period of time. This reference reminds us of Elijah going into the wilderness and being fed by the ravens.

"And there was war in heaven: Michael and his angels fought against the dragon: and the dragon and his angels fought and prevailed not, neither was their place found any more in heaven" (vv. 7–8). He was cast out of heaven, that old serpent, the devil, Satan—all these names are given for him. He has deceived the whole world. Now Michael was the warrior angel. Some see this as referring to the expulsion of Satan from heaven before the foundation of the world. Satan rebelled against God and tried to take over heaven, and Michael and his angels fought against him and drove him out. He was driven into the earth, and we've had to entertain him ever since.

But I don't see that. If it is true, then the sequence is all out of order. Here we have what quite obviously to me is a reference to the birth and the earthly ministry of Jesus. Then we suddenly switch back to a time before the beginning of time before the creation. I see the whole point here beginning in this chapter as Satan's fighting against Christ to try to destroy him. He tried to destroy him on earth and couldn't. When he saw him back in heaven and seated at the right hand of power, he and his forces stormed heaven itself to try to get to him to destroy him. But the forces of God drove them back. They couldn't get into heaven, and were cast into the earth. Thus we see redeemed people in heaven rejoice because they knew by then that they were safe. The devil can never get to them in heaven. John said that the martyrs in heaven overcame with "the word of their testimony, and they loved not their lives unto death" (vv. 10–11). They could rejoice, but "woe to the inhabiters of the earth and of the sea! for the devil is come down unto you, having great wrath, because he knoweth that he hath but a short time." In other words, Satan tried to kill Jesus on earth at his birth, and he failed. He tried to storm heaven and failed after Jesus went back to the Father. Now he's trying to destroy the work of Christ by persecuting his church. And that leads us right up to this present time. It was very much true at the time this book was written. It has been true through the ages, it is true now. Satan is all the more ferocious because he knows that he "hath but a short time" (v. 12).

We must not figure "time" here by our calendar. Indeed, the Greek word used for "time" is not the one for chronological time. It means "opportune time." When Satan failed to destroy Jesus on earth, and also failed in his attempt to storm heaven, he knew that he had failed completely insofar as Jesus was concerned. His one remaining "opportune time" was to persecute the people of Christ and try to defeat the Christian movement. When the allied armies made a successful landing in Europe in June 1944, Hitler had lost World War II. Much fighting remained to be done, but the issue was decided. So it is with Satan. He continues to oppose Christ and his people. But his final fate is already made certain.

And so he persecuted the woman (vv. 13–17). Here the woman is obviously the church, whether you think of it as the Old or New Testament idea of the church. Given two wings of a great eagle, she was taken into the wilderness and protected for "a time and times and half a time" from the serpent. Here also "time" is the opportune time as in verse 17. This evidently means throughout the persecution by the devil. *Three and one half* seems to be indicated in *time, times,* and *half a time*. This numerical figure is used repeatedly in Revelation for a short but indefinite period. The eagle's wings depict strength and speed as to how God rescued her. "And the serpent cast out of his mouth water as a flood after the woman, . . . and the earth opened her mouth, and swallowed up the flood" (vv. 15–16). Near Colossae the Lycus river went underground, and that may be involved in this symbolism. The people in the province of Asia would know about that condition. Anyway, the Lord protected his people, "and the dragon was wroth with the woman, and went to make war with the remnant of her seed" (v. 17), trying to destroy her. That's still going on.

The Two Beasts

Now in chapter 13 we see two beasts. These beasts are ferocious animals, unlike the living creatures (beasts) in chapters 4 and 5. But the word for beast here means a wild beast. While standing on the sand of the seashore, John saw a beast rise up out of the sea (v. 1). Dr. Beasley-Murray goes into this matter in his book on Revelation in a scholarly manner. But for our present purpose we shall confine the discussion to what they represent in this context.

This first beast had seven heads and ten horns. Now seven heads would mean great wisdom and the ten horns great power—seven and ten would both be considered as perfect numbers. And he bore the name of blasphemy. The emperor was trying to get the Christians to blaspheme Christ by saying, "Caesar is lord." This beast had the speed of a leopard, the strength of a bear, and the ferocity of a lion (v. 2). His power and his great authority came from the dragon, which is Satan. When Jesus refused to accept Satan's bait, Satan gave his authority to the Roman Empire, hoping to use it to destroy Christianity. He's been trying to do it ever since through those that have opposed Christianity. He's trying to do it today with communism and materialism and other "isms!"

Now this beast is seen coming up out of the sea. When the Romans invaded Asia Minor, they came across the Mediterranean. So the people in the province of Asia thought of the power of the Roman authority coming across from another land and up out of the sea. Obviously this refers to imperial Rome. Domitian himself as the emperor was the personification of the empire.

John said, "I saw one of his heads as it were wounded to death; and his deadly wound was healed: and all the world wondered after the beast" (v. 3). It was a marvel to them. This definitely points to Domitian as the beast coming up out of the sea, as representing the Roman Empire, and we will say more about this later.

John says, "They worshiped the dragon which gave power unto the beast" (v. 4). That's saying that emperor worship is devil worship. "And there was given unto him a mouth speaking great things and blasphemies" (v. 5), making great claims for himself of deity. He has the power to continue forty and two months, that's three and a half years (a time, time, and half a time)—a brief but indefinite period of time.

Another beast appears in verse 11. Coming up out of the earth suggests the idea of local power, resident in the Roman province of Asia. It had two horns like a lamb. A lamb, of course, is related to religion, and horns relate to power. So, it had religious power, but it had the devil's vocabulary. Now whatever this is, it had to do with emperor worship. In the provinces they had what they called the "concilia," the group that was charged with enforcing emperor worship. Ray Summers, in his book *Worthy Is the Lamb*, says the group in the province of Asia seems to have been more active than in any other part of the empire. "And he exerciseth all the power of the first beast before him" (v. 12). Now this beast operates under the power of the empire. This beast did great wonders, making fire come down from heaven and making the image talk; so life seemed to be given unto the beast (v. 15). All of this was done with magic, trickery, ventriloquism, to make the image of Domitian appear to be alive. "He causeth all, both small and great, rich and poor, free and bond, to receive a mark in their right hand, or in their foreheads" (v. 16). No man could buy or sell unless he had that mark. And that mark was the number of his name (v. 17). Now I remember before World War

II that there was a lot of preaching done about that mark of the beast being NRA, the blue eagle, the symbol of the New Deal.

This mark of the beast evidently has reference to the fact that back then if you worshiped the emperor you received a certain mark or evidence of that fact. You've already seen the 144,000 marked for protection. Now we see another mark. Without it you could neither buy or sell. John says that the name of the beast was the number of his name. At least John uses a *number* to identify him (v. 17).

Revelation 13:18 is a mysterious verse. This idea is anticipated in the words "Here is wisdom." It suggests that there is something coming that you're going to have to think about. "Let him that hath understanding count the number of the beast [that is, the emperor]: for it is the number of a man; and his number is Six hundred threescore and six" or 666. John was identifying this beast without naming him.

If he had said this beast was Emperor Domitian, he would have only hastened more trouble and maybe death for himself and others. But he camouflaged it by using numerology. Various writers have tried to figure out what this means. Remember that in ancient numerology a number had a value, an alphabetical value, maybe as illustrated with the Roman numerals. And so using various languages—Greek, Aramaic, Hebrew—people have come up with various names. One comes out Nero Caesar. Another comes out Latinus, and from that comes the idea of the Pope or the Roman Catholic Church. Ray Summers told me that one of his students figured out a system where it came out Hitler. Well these things, whatever value they may or may not have, tell us that it is impossible to figure out the meaning of this number in that way. You come up with so many different answers.

But if we go back to numerology I think we find help. Remember that seven is a perfect number. One less than seven (six) would be an imperfect number. The Sibylline oracles used "888" to refer to Christ. Seven being perfect, and they expressed infinity by raising 777 to 888!

In Kyoto, Japan, there is a *temple of a thousand and one goddesses*. It contains a thousand statues of a goddess with many arms, showing that she is able to help in many ways. To the Japanese mind a thousand is a perfect number; it is completeness. Then one statue was added to the one thousand to express infinity. We talk about the infinite God; they simply made another image to express this idea.

Well, one less than seven is six. It's an imperfect number. Three is a perfect number, so three sixes gives us a perfect number of imperfections or complete imperfection. That may not say much to us, but to the mind of the original readers that was an awful thing to say. And since it is the number of a man, we assume that 666 refers to Domitian.

Now here's another possible thought. As I was writing *The Cosmic Drama* another thought hit me. I put it in the book, and I'll throw it out here. *Three* is the number of deity, *six* is the number of a man. In other words three sixes suggest a man making himself God. Which again would come back to Domitian. But I think the perfect number of imperfections is the better idea.

6
Envisioning God's Ultimate Victory over Evil

Glory and Wrath

Chapter 14 opens with a Lamb standing on Mount Sion, and with him are 144,000 who have been redeemed from the earth. We saw them sealed with the seal of God's protection during the persecution; now we see them in heaven.

The Lamb stood on Mount Sion. What Mount Sion? Well, of course, those who claim that Jesus is coming back to earth and set up an earthly kingdom, and reign for a thousand years on earth with his capital in Jerusalem, would naturally say that it's Mount Sion in Jerusalem. But keep in mind the symbolic nature of the book. The fact is that this 144,000 are with Christ and were redeemed *from* [away from, *apo*] the earth. I realize that one could say that they came back to earth. But that seems to be stretching the point. Hebrews 12:22 talks about his readers not having come to Mount Sion on earth but to the heavenly Mount Sion. In the light of that and in the light of the overall message of the Revelation, which focuses not on earth but on heaven, I see this as the heavenly Mount Sion.

After seeing one angel "in heaven, having the everlasting gospel to preach unto them that dwell on the earth," John saw another angel and heard him proclaim: "Babylon is fallen, is fallen, that great city, because she made all nations drink of the wine of the wrath of her fornication" (v. 8.) Wrath here is the word *thumos*. Shall we call it "boiling rage"? "Babylon is fallen" or "Babylon fell." While the idea apparently is in the future, it's so certain that it is spoken of as already having taken place. She is to drink of the "wrath of her fornication." Fornication, or adultery, is a figure of idolatry. In the Old Testament God was pictured as the husband, and Israel was the wife. And infidelity on her part through pagan worship was regarded as adultery. We see it in the book of Hosea as well as other places. Corresponding to it is the New Testament idea that Christ is the Bridegroom, and the church is his bride. Fornication is a term used generally in the New Testament period for all types of illicit sex. The worship of idols was regarded as illicit sex that deserves the wrath of God. In verse 10 the angel says that the same shall drink of the wine of the *thumos*—the boiling rage—of God which is poured out unadulterated, "without mixture into the cup of his [God's] indignation." "Indignation" is *orgē*. Anyone worshiping the emperor is going to drink of the wine of the boiling rage of God, which is poured out unadulterated into the cup of his *universal, abiding opposition* to evil (see v. 11).

Now in verse 12 let's look at the word *patience*. To us the word *patience* suggests the idea of resignation. "I can't do anything about it, so I'll just endure it. I guess I'll have to be patient." Well, that isn't what the Greek word means. It means "an abiding under," from the verb *menō* "abide" and *hupo* "under," abiding under, or enduring. The word is used of an athlete or a soldier who could take all his opponent gave him and yet have reserve strength with which to countercharge to victory. This word in Greek was a masculine, a virile word. This is the thing that enables the Christian to take all that the devil and his forces can throw against him, stand up under it, and have enough reserve strength with which to counterattack and charge to victory.

Later in this chapter, beginning in verse 14, we have the figure of two reapings. John says that one being is wearing a golden

crown and is like unto the Son of man. In his hand he has a sharp
sickle. Another angel said, "Thrust in thy sickle, and reap: for the
time is come for thee to reap; for the harvest of the earth is ripe"
(v. 15). Then another angel appeared "out of the temple which is
in heaven," and was commanded: "Thrust in thy sharp sickle, and
gather the clusters of the vine of the earth; for her grapes are fully
ripe" (v. 18).

Some interpreters see these as two pictures of the same thing
and refer them unto judgment. Personally, I see the first one as
referring to Christ reaping out of the earth those who are his.
Here I'm not thinking so much in terms of the classical ideas of
the rapture as I'm thinking of evangelism. We sing about gathering the harvest; the field is white unto harvest, Jesus said. Now
the second, I think, has to do with wrath. The fact that they're
not the same thing is seen in that they're not harvesting the same
things—one was wheat and the other was grapes. So I think the
second one refers to wrath.

We think of the gospel of Christ as "good news," which is right.
But note that in Romans 1:16–18 Paul speaks of the gospel as
twofold. In it is revealed God's righteousness. But he also says
"the wrath of God is revealed." And that's the word *orgē*, God's
abiding opposition to evil. In other words the gospel is not only
the good news about salvation from sin; it is also in a sense the
bad news about the judgment of God upon the unbeliever. We
don't preach a whole gospel unless we preach both. Dr. J. W.
Storer wrote a book of sermons containing one on hell. He said a
preacher should never preach on hell unless he does it with a
broken heart. I agree with him. But at the same time we cannot
preach the whole gospel and only preach on love.

Every heresy that I know anything about started because
somebody emphasized one facet of truth, maybe one facet of
God's nature, and built a whole system of theology around it, like
"God is love." Yes, but he's more than love. His love is a holy and

righteous love. He loves the sinner, but he hates his sin. He can't be holy and righteous still and love or condone sin. So the old idea that "a God of love would not create a soul and then send it to hell" is born of sentiment, not sense.

In the first place God is a God of love, but he is also a God of righteousness. Everything he does is qualified by his love. A parent can punish a child in love. If you don't punish him in love, you ought not to punish him. You ought to wait until you get your temper down, and then punish him. I recall the last time my mother whipped me. I'd been involved with some boys in stealing a watermelon. I didn't steal it; they stole it. But I helped eat it and was as guilty as they were. By the time we reached the home of two of my friends their daddy had found it out. The owner of the watermelon patch had called, and the father had whipped them. I knew I'd get one when I got home. But my mother didn't say a word for two whole weeks. I was beginning to think that I was home free. But one morning I had to go over to a neighbor's house and borrow a singletree. And she said as I started to leave, "On the way back, bring me a switch." I knew what was coming. Well, when I got back, she held me to her bosom and wept aloud as she whipped me. I'd have to say she wailed as she whipped me across my back with that switch. I never forgot it, I'll never forget it! She never had to whip me again. If she had just gotten mad and whipped, we'd have both been mad. But it wasn't like that. Well, anyway, God's wrath is a part of his gospel.

The word *wrath* in verse 19 is *thumos* again, the boiling rage of God. The vines were cast into the great winepress of the boiling rage of God. The winepress was trodden outside the city, and the blood came out of the winepress even up to the horses' bridles. And the space of it—well in our figures it would be about 260 miles. Obviously, it's symbolism. At the same time notice that it's not grapejuice but blood which came out of the winepress—judgment.

The Final Interlude

In chapter 15 John saw another sign in heaven, seven angels having the seven last plagues. And they filled up the wrath (*thumos*) of God; the words *filled up* translate the Greek word that Jesus used when he said, "It is finished" (*teleo*). Well this word in 15:1 means that God's wrath is *filled up*. In other words the Lord says, "I've had it up to here. I'm just full up to the brim. I've had it!" Thus the boiling rage of God is to be poured out fully in the last series of seven. "I saw as it were a sea of glass mingled with fire" (v. 2).

Remember the sea of glass in chapter 4 that separated God from man? Well, now John sees a sea of glass mingled with fire. Did you ever stand on the seashore or on a ship out at sea and see the sunset? It looks like the sea is fire. This sea of glass is like the sea with the sun setting; the late afternoon sun makes the sea seem to be on fire. Now this may be imagination, but I hope it's holy imagination. The suggestion is that the end is drawing near. God has had his fill.

This is not dealing with time but with principle. There may come a time in our own generation, for instance, when God will say to communism, "I've had it up to here, and you're gone!" We worry about communism today, about what it's doing to our world and to our generation, and well we should. But it is not going to have the last word in history. Some of us can remember when Mussolini would speak from his balcony in Rome, and the whole world trembled. That balcony is still there. Likewise, when Hitler screamed his hatred for hours, the whole world trembled. But we don't tremble at Hitler and Mussolini anymore. We may tremble at somebody else.

In 1937, Dr. Ralph W. Sockman wrote a book in which he said that Christ has survived by over 1,900 years the empire that destroyed him, and he will survive the dictators who defy him now. We can look back on that and say *tetelestai*, it is finished.

But as we look ahead we ask, "What about communism?" What about all these other isms over the world? If the Lord delays his coming, they're all going to go the same way. I don't know when, how, or where; but it's going to happen.

God's going to have the last word. The whole theme of this book is the victory of Christ. So the sun is setting, and the sea reflects the fire as if it were afire. And those that have gotten the victory over the beast, and over the image, and over his mark, stand on the glass sea (v. 2). They're approaching God, in a sense. And they sing the song of Moses and of the Lamb (vv. 3–4). Victory is theirs!

One of the four beasts [living creatures] gave unto the seven angels seven vials or bowls of wrath (vv. 6–7). Now that's the boiling rage of God *(thumos)*. We've always been taught to think of love and grace coming out of the holy of holies. That is very true. But here is wrath coming out of that holy of holies. Where God is, there also is his wrath against sin. The holy of holies was filled with smoke as symbolic of God's presence. John heard a great voice, the voice of God, out of the *naos*.

The Seven Vials

Only God dwells in there, so it has to be his voice. He says to the seven angels, "Go your ways and pour out the vials of the wrath of God upon the earth" (16:1). This was done in quick order. Remember the partial destruction of the first two sevens, first a fourth and then a third? They started out affecting nature and then man. Here wrath starts out with man.

When the first angel poured out his vial, "there fell a noisome and grievous sore upon the men which had the mark of the beast" (v. 2). This series starts out afflicting the bodies of men. In the plagues in Egypt you'll see a similarity. Do not equate the two. John is simply drawing upon the information, events, and history which would be familiar to his readers.

The second angel poured out his vial upon the sea (v. 3). It became as the blood of a dead man, and every living thing that had life died in the sea. Here is total destruction. No more fish; no more commerce. Rome was dependent upon both for life. Then the third angel did the same (v. 4). The clear water, fresh water, drinking water became blood. Out of heaven voices are heard saying this is the thing which should be done (vv. 5–7). God has judged them appropriately. They have shed the blood of saints and prophets, and God gives them blood to drink. "For they are worthy" (v. 6).

The Greek word for "worthy" has in it the idea of scales or balances. I am fortunate enough to have in my library a nine-volume set of works edited by Dr. Kittel. I suppose that it is the most exhaustive work on the Greek language that we have today. And in the article on this word for "worthy," he talks about the idea of striking a balance. Recall the old scales we used to have in a store. You asked for five pounds of sugar. The groceryman would put a five-pound weight on one side of the scales. Then he would fill up a sack on the other side with sugar until it balanced the weight. That's the idea in this word *worthy*. So here the idea is that they're getting what they deserve. They poured out the blood of the saints. Now they're getting the punishment that fits the crime. They liked blood so much that God gave them blood to drink. Let them have a binge on blood.

When the fourth angel poured out his vial upon the sun, the power was given to scorch men with fire (vv. 8–9). The sun is the source of life. I'm told that the earth is set at exactly the proper angle for us to get the warm, life-giving rays of the sun. If that angle were upset by a very small degree, the earth would be burned to a charred ember. So all that God would have to do, if he wanted to do it literally, would be to change the degree of inclination of the earth a little bit. But even so, the idea is a total destruction of the very source of life in the solar system.

Then the fifth angel poured out his vial (vv. 10–11). Notice that it says "and they repented not." Suffering doesn't bring repentance, as we said before. The fifth angel poured out his bowl on the city of Rome itself. You kill the heart and the body dies. It was poured out on the seat of the beast, and his kingdom was full of darkness. That could be evil or it could be *confusion*. One of the things that was involved in the fall of the Roman Empire was confusion in government and everything else.

The sixth angel poured out his wrath upon the great river Euphrates (vv. 12–14). The river was dried up so as to make way for the kings (and their armies) to come across the river Euphrates. This is another reference to the Roman dread of the Parthians.

John saw "three unclean spirits like frogs come out of the mouth of the dragon, and out of the mouth of the beast, and out of the mouth of the false prophet." Dr. Dana says that they were vomited out. The false prophet represented the enforcers of emperor worship. The beast, of course, was Domitian or the emperor. And the dragon was Satan. Coming out of the mouth suggests that this was false propaganda to be used to raise an army against the Lord (v. 14).

Dr. Dana says in his book on Revelation that if you insist upon a literal interpretation of this, then you have to say that three frogs led this army or this army was commanded by three frogs. They were gathered together to a place called in the Hebrew tongue, *Armageddon*. *Armageddon* translates two Hebrew words *Har*, meaning mountain, and *Megiddo*, or the mount of Megiddo. The mount of Megiddo is surrounded by about a half circle, or perhaps a three-quarter circle with the plains of Esdraelon. This is some of the most fertile soil in the world. It was the favorite place of battle for ancient armies. It was flat, so chariots and cavalry could maneuver. Soldiers could maneuver. Perhaps there's been more human blood shed on that spot of ground than on any other spot that size on the face of the earth. Naturally, the Hebrew mind thought of the last great battle of the age as being fought on the plains of Esdraelon around Mount Megiddo, so Armageddon. We'll come back to this in chapter 19.

The seventh angel poured out his bowl into the air (vv. 17–21). A person can live a long time without water, and live even longer without bread. But how long can he live without air? We must breathe. This climaxes the symbolism that the sources of life were destroyed. "And there came a great voice out of the temple of heaven, saying it is done (v. 17). "It has happened" (Greek). Then in verse 18 we see again the symbols of judgment: voices from the throne (sounds), thunderings and lightnings, and a great earthquake. The great city (Rome) was divided into three parts; three being the divine number, this suggests divine judgment. Also other cities fell (v. 19). In the latter part of verse 19 we see Babylon's (Rome's) sins remembered before God. This "gave unto her the cup of the wine of the fierceness of his wrath," or the *thumos* of his *orgē*, as the Greek text reads. Even the islands and the mountains disappeared. Mountains and islands were great places to build defense positions in the Roman Empire. Heavy hail fell upon men, and they blasphemed God because of it. So, we see again that evil men weren't purged from their sufferings.

The Great Whore

Now chapter 17 deals with the woman that sat on many waters. They called her the great whore, the prostitute (v. 1). Now we've heard earlier, "Babylon is fallen, is fallen." Babylon is used in the book of Revelation for Rome. To the Jewish mind Babylon was a symbol of persecution, suffering, and captivity. Historically, Babylon had a vast interlacing series of canals, suggesting the many waters. The angel noted that the kings of the earth have committed fornication with this woman (v. 2). They had entered into this idolatrous system in worship.

Then John says that he was in the spirit carried into the wilderness. He saw a woman who sat upon the scarlet-colored beast, full of names of blasphemy and having seven heads and ten horns. The woman was arrayed in purple, a scarlet color. So there is the whore decked with gold, precious stones, pearls, and having "a golden cup in her hand full of abominations and filthiness of her fornication" (v. 4). Upon her was written the name "MYSTERY, BABYLON THE GREAT, THE MOTHER OF HARLOTS AND ABOMINATIONS OF THE EARTH." This alone tells us that John is not talking about the Babylon in Mesopotamia. To the Christians of that day this would only mean Rome. "I saw the woman drunken with the blood of the saints" (v. 6). She was on a constant binge with the blood of the saints and martyrs. And he says, although the King James Version reads: "I wondered with great admiration," the Greek reads, "I wondered a great wonder." He was amazed.

Then the angel explained the mystery of the woman: "The beast that thou sawest was, and is not; and shall ascend out of the bottomless pit [the abyss], and go into perdition" (v. 8). Continuing, he said that the seven heads are seven mountains, on which the woman sitteth." Everybody knows Rome was built on seven hills. "There are seven kings: five are fallen, [he deliberately didn't say emperors], and one is, and the other is not yet come; and when he cometh, he must continue a short space. And the beast that was, and is not, even he is the eighth, and is of the seven, and goeth into perdition" (vv. 10–11). Isn't that as clear as mud.

In order to understand it, we must look at the Roman emperors. Julius Caesar never allowed himself to be called an emperor. Augustus was the first Caesar who was called emperor. He reigned from 27 B.C. to A.D. 14. Tiberius was the second, reigning from A.D. 14 to 37. Caligula reigned A.D. 37–41; Claudius, 41–54; Nero, 54–68; Vespasian, 69–79; Titus, 79–81; and Domitian,

81–96. Now with that information let's go back.

There are seven kings, but you have eight names here. Five are fallen: Augustus, Tiberius, Caligula, Claudius, and Nero. Nero committed suicide in June of A.D. 68. But there was in the Roman Empire a superstitious belief that Nero was not really dead but had gone to live with the Parthians and one day would lead the Parthians in an invasion to destroy the empire. He was a crazy man and hated the Roman Empire. He said once that he wished that all Romans had just one neck so that he could cut off all their heads with one stroke.

Looking at these kings—five are fallen, and one is, and the other is not yet come. Now five are fallen. That would be Augustus through Nero. One *is*, which would be Vespasian. And the other is not yet come, and when he comes, he must continue a short space. That would be Titus who reigned only two years, 79–81. Now the beast that was, and is not, even he is the eighth, and is of the seven. But he's the eighth in number. Recall that the Romans had a belief that Nero was not really dead. But even if he were dead, he would come back to life again and lead in the destruction of the empire. Actually the angel is saying that Domitian is Nero come to life again. Nero was the first Roman emperor to persecute Christians as a policy of state. Domitian was the second. Now you'll notice if you read this carefully that "the beast that was, and is not, even he is the eighth, and is of the seven, and goeth into the abyss" (v. 11). Apparently the angel referred to Vespasian deliberately so that if the Romans got hold of this writing, they would not realize that he was actually identifying Domitian.

"The ten horns which thou sawest are ten kings" (v. 12). When Roman armies conquered a kingdom, its king was not killed. He continued to rule as a vassal. So the ten horns are symbols of the power of the ten kings which have received no kingdom as yet. Although they had no authority of their own, they "receive power as kings one hour with the beast." They had no mind of their own; they did what Rome told them. As you read interbiblical history you find that Herod the Great kept the road hot between Jerusalem and Rome, trying to keep in good with the powers that were in Rome.

So the only power such kings had was what the Roman Empire gave them. They gave their power and strength to the beast. In other words, the power they had over their people they used to carry out the orders of Rome. "These shall make war with the Lamb, and the Lamb shall overcome them: for he is Lord of lords, and Kings of kings" (17:14).

Rome's Final Destruction

In chapter 18 we have the picture of the final destruction of Rome. Now the fact that Rome did not actually fall as an empire until much later doesn't in any sense change what is said here. This is symbolism, and it is laying down principles. They applied in the first century, and they apply any time in history where a nation or a people rebels against God.

After reading chapters 18—20 you might want to turn back and read the second Psalm. "He that sitteth in the heavens shall laugh: the Lord shall have them in derision" (v. 4). And whether it's in the first century or in our present century, the principles still hold.

Again we have in 18:2 the announcement that Babylon the great is fallen. It has become the habitation of demons, foul spirits, and every unclean bird. Quite a pleasant place to live! Verse 3 says that the nations are drunk with the wine of the wrath of her fornication. Kings and merchants have committed fornication with her. Kings and nations are drunk with the wine of the wrath (*thumos*, boiling rage) of her fornication. Merchants have become rich trading with Rome. All these were involved in the Roman system.

Then in verse 4 John heard another voice from heaven saying, "Come out of her, my people, that ye be not partakers of her sins, and that you receive not of her plagues" (v. 4). In other words, complete separation. Be separated from her, because God's final and complete judgment is about to fall on the wicked. "For her sins have reached unto heaven, and God hath remembered her iniquities" (v. 5). The idea here is that you glue one piece on top of another. You glue another one on top of another. Finally it gets up to where it leads you right on up to the throne of God. Rome had done this with her sins. And God has seen it, he's known about it all the time, but that, of course, is a figure of speech.

Now "reward her even as she rewarded you, and double unto her double according to her works: in the cup which she hath filled fill to her double" (v. 6). Rome is going to get more than she has dished out. The prayers of the martyrs are being answered (v. 12).

This prostitute says, "I sit a queen, and am no widow, and shall see no sorrow" (v. 7). Like people are saying today, "It can't happen here." "It can't happen now." We look at the big cities and say, "It can't happen in America." But go look at Rome!

Whenever I go to Rome I visit the Roman Forum, and look in the direction of the Arch of Titus. It was erected to celebrate his victory over the Jews in A.D. 66–70. Then I look to the left to see the Colosseum where the gladiators fought to the death with wild animals and where Christians were fed to hungry lions. To the right I see Palatine Hill where the palaces of the Caesars once stood. Then looking down, right in front of the remains of the Temple to the Vestal Virgins, I see the little marble marker showing where Julius Caesar was assassinated. Over on the right is the little marble monument where once there was a golden milestone, measuring the distances in the Roman Empire from Rome to the rest of the Empire. To the left stands the Senate building—they tell me it is the only building that was in the forum which still stands intact. The Romans had an emperor and also a senate, which balanced one another like the executive, judicial, and legislative branches of our government balance each other.

Well, I look at all of that, and I recall at one time that was the center of the power of the Western World. Yet today it's just an attraction for tourists. One day Mrs. Hobbs and I went up on Palatine Hill. There we saw the ruins of Augustus' palace. There were stone masons repairing the ruins! At first, it seemed humorous. But I recalled that if they didn't do that, the ruins would have been gone a long time ago.

Yes, it can happen here! The whore said that it could not happen to her, but it did. And it can happen to us. It will unless we repent and turn to the Lord. We're traveling down the road to ruin as fast as we can go as a nation. I'm not a pessimist, I'm an optimist. But I am also a realist.

Now as the judgment came upon Rome, the kings of the earth who have committed fornication with her and lived deliciously with her, would bewail her when they see the smoke of her burning (vv. 9–10). The merchants of the earth would weep and mourn over her (vv. 11–16). Every shipmaster would mourn (v. 17). You see, the kings have lost their central power, the merchants have lost their best customer, and the shipmasters have lost their source of trade, the Roman Empire. The luxuries of ancient Rome were almost beyond belief. One banquet is said to have cost $500,000. On the menu they had peacock's tongues. Oh, she lived deliciously, and was no widow, and it couldn't happen to her. But it did!

Now I want you to notice something in verse 21. "And a mighty angel took up a stone like a great millstone, and cast it into the sea. Thus with violence shall that great city Babylon be thrown down, and shall be found no more at all." Like throwing a big millstone into the sea—it makes a big splash, it sinks beneath the waves, and soon the water is calm. That stone is at the bottom of the sea. In that day it was an impossibility to raise it. The idea is that Rome is going to fall. She's going to make a big splash, but she'll be forgotten. We all think that we amount to something. But when we die, it doesn't take long for the world to move on without us. Even the greatest may make news for a day or two, and that's it.

Some interpreters hold to the idea that before the end of time the old Roman Empire will be reestablished. Well, let us look at that in the light of verses 21–23. "Thus with violence shall that great city Babylon [Rome] be thrown down and shall be found no more at all. And the voice of harpers, and musicians, and of pipers, and trumpeters, shall be heard no more at all in thee [no more at all, indeed]; and no craftsman, of whatever craft he be, shall be found any more in thee; and the sound of a mill-stone shall be heard no more at all in thee; and the light of a candle shall shine no more at all in thee; and the voice of the bridegroom and of the bride shall be heard no more at all in thee." In other words, there'll be no more banquets or enter-tainment in Rome; there'll be no more industry. These huge banquets are gone. Family life is gone. You don't hear the voice of the bride, no weddings, *no more at all indeed.* Now just go back and read again. Starting with verse 21 draw a line under those words, "No more at all." *No more at all.* The Roman Empire going to be reestablished? I don't know how it could be said with finality any stronger than *no more at all!*

In chapter 19 we find praise to God and to the Lamb. Then in verse 9 it says, "Blessed are they which are called unto the marriage supper of the lamb." This supper is never presented in the book. In chapter 21 we can imagine it.

The Battle of Armageddon

"I saw heaven opened, and behold a white horse; and he that

sat upon him was called Faithful and True" (v. 11). Obviously this was Christ riding on the white horse of victory. We're coming to the battle of Armageddon. It's before the battle, and yet he's riding a white horse. He knows he's going to win. In fact, he won when he came out of the grave, but he knows the victory is going to be his. "His eyes were as a flame of fire." This reminds us of the description we find in the first chapter. He was wearing "many crowns." Domitian wore one crown; Christ wears "many crowns." And he had a name that no man knew but himself.

He was clothed with "a vesture dipped in blood: and his name is called The Word of God." I think that's the name. Some say that this blood is the blood of his enemies, but he hasn't fought the battle yet. Some say it's his own blood, the redemptive work and purpose of Christ. This latter is probably true. The armies which were in heaven followed him upon white horses, symbols of victory. Now they've been persecuted on earth, but look at what's happening up in heaven. They're wearing fine linen white and clean. To victory is added vindication and purity. But they don't wear any armor. Do you notice that? They have no breastplates, no shields, no swords. The only weapon is one out of Christ's mouth, that is the mouth of the one that's sitting on the first white horse. "Out of his mouth goeth a sharp sword, that with it he should smite the nations: and he shall rule them with a rod of iron: and he treadeth the winepress of the fierceness [*thumos*] and wrath [the abiding *orgē*] of Almighty God" (v. 15). He has on his vesture and thigh a name written, "KING OF KINGS, AND LORD OF LORDS" (v. 16).

Whereas in verse 9 we have mention of the feast of the bride-groom, the marriage feast of the Lamb, now the invitation is sent out to all the birds to come and eat the flesh of men and horses that are going to perish in the battle of Armageddon (vv. 17–18, 21*b*). There's quite a difference in the kind of banquet. But notice, here's the battle of Armageddon.

"I saw the beast, and the kings of the earth, and their armies, gathered together to make war against him that sat on the horse, and against his army. And the beast was taken, and with him the false prophet [the Roman Empire, Domitian, and the Concilia]. . . . These both were cast alive [along with those that received the mark of the beast] into a lake of fire burning with brimstone. And the remnant were slain with the sword of him that sat upon the horse, which sword proceeded out of his mouth" (vv. 19–21).

Now that's the battle of Armageddon. Isn't it tame beside some of the descriptions you've heard of it? I've heard talk about chariots, screaming horses, wailing men, and the clanging of sword against shield. Nowadays you hear of atom bombs bursting and tanks rumbling. I don't see a bit of that in this, do you? If you do, you see something I can't see.

I don't see any armor, I don't see any fighting, I don't see any weapon except the sword that proceeds out of the mouth of Christ. Didn't Paul tell us in Ephesians about the sword of the Spirit which is the Word of God? In other words, God is destroying his enemies, through the Word, the sword that proceeds out of his mouth. It's not in his hand. He doesn't stick it through somebody's body. He proclaims it. You can't destroy Communism by killing communists. You can't destroy paganism by killing pagans. They are ideas, and you can only destroy those ideas with a better idea. We have that better idea in the gospel, we don't use it like we should. So here is the battle of Armageddon. I don't think I've been unfair about it. I've just let the Bible talk.

Millennium and Last Judgment

Now we come to chapter 20, that passage where we find the millennium and final judgment. "I saw an angel come down from heaven, having the key of the bottomless pit [the abyss] and a great chain in his hand. And he laid hold on the dragon, that old serpent, which is the Devil, and Satan, and bound him a thousand years" (vv. 1–2). How shall we understand this? Well, first, the devil is a spirit. Are you going to chain a spirit with a real chain? So we have to admit that we're dealing with symbolism, don't we? Then the devil was cast into the abyss for a thousand years. The Lord shut him up and sealed him there, so he could not deceive the nations for a thousand years. After that he must be loosed for a season.

And John saw the thrones occupied by those who were beheaded for the witness of Jesus. They were given the right to rule. This suggests victory for them. These martyrs lived and reigned with Christ a thousand years. "But the rest of the dead lived not again until the thousand years were finished. This is the first resurrection" (see vv. 4–6). When the thousand years have expired, Satan is loosed out of his prison, to go out and deceive the nations, Gog and Magog to gather them together to battle. The number of them is as the sand of the sea. They compassed the camp of the saints, and the beloved city. Whether this is in Jerusalem or in heaven depends on your outlook. I think it's in heaven. They surround the camp still trying to defeat the work of Christ. But fire came down from God out of heaven and devoured them. "And the devil . . . was cast into the lake of fire and brimstone, where the beast and the false prophet are, and shall be tormented day and night for ever and ever [unto the ages of the ages]" (v. 10).

Now lets look at the term *thousand*. In 2 Peter 3:8 Peter says that a day is with the Lord as a thousand years and a thousand years are as a day. Time is no element with God. We should not try to run God's business by our calendars but by his. The word *millennium* of course is the Latin derivative. The Greek word would be *chilia* or one thousand.

Now comes the $64,000-question. What position do I (or you) hold about the millennium? Am I a postmillennialist? No. Am I a premillennialist? I used to be a *pre without a program*. When I was in seminary, we used to talk about the *posts* and *pres*. I knew I wasn't a *post*, so I said, "Well I guess I'm a *pre*." Dr. A. T. Robertson used to say, "If they want to know whether I'm a *post* or a *pre*, I'm a *pro*. I'm for it whenever it happens." That was all he'd ever say about it. And the truth of the matter is that's about all anybody can say with any exactness.

Perhaps we should mention the three positions concerning the millennium. They are *post*, *pre*, and *a* pronounced "ah." *Postmillennials* believe that the gospel will so do its work as to usher in a thousand years of peace on earth. Christ will return at the end of that period. This view was very popular until World War I. To my knowledge it is scarcely held now.

Premillennials hold that Christ will return to bring in this thousand years of peace. This view is widely held today. It ranges from mild *pres* all the way to the extreme position of the dispensationalists, those who have worked out a detailed system of dates and events. In my judgment this latter group should be listed as a fourth view concerning the millennium.

Amillennials (the Greek *alpha* or *a* placed before a word to indicate the opposite idea) hold that the millennium is not literal but symbolic. It is a numerical symbol of a long but indefinite period of time, reaching from Jesus' resurrection or ascension to his second coming. Among most groups one's position on the millennium is not a test of orthodoxy.

One man said that he was an amillennial. Whenever it happened, he would say, "Ah!" A lady told me that her husband said that he is an "ah." "Ah don't know nothing about it." We may all be surprised about this by the time the Lord returns.

Through the years I have studied this matter. I definitely am not a postmillennialist. Many answers to questions I have found in the so-called amillennial position that I did not find in the premillennial one. I don't find all the answers even in the "a"

REVELATION: THREE VIEWPOINTS 137

position. This is the reason I don't like labels. I prefer to be known as one who believes the New Testament as I understand it. But in the light of the symbolic nature of the book, I see the thousand years as a symbol of a long but indefinite period of time. I see it as symbolizing the period from the time of the ascension of the Lord until he returns to earth again. I see one second coming, one resurrection, one judgment. In John 5:28–29 Jesus speaks of the resurrection of the just and unjust in one statement. When talking about the resurrection, Paul talked about the Christian. He did not refer to the others, but that doesn't mean that they will not be resurrected at the same time as the Christians. It just means that his emphasis was upon the Christians. He was writing to help them.

I see the *tribulation* as being suffering that the people of Christ endure during that entire period, as they try to proclaim the gospel and live for him. But some see a period of seven years of tribulation before the end of the age. But look at Jesus' use of the word: "In the world ye shall have tribulation [be in a tight place like grapes in a winepress with seemingly no way out]; but be of good cheer [courage]; I have overcome [have fully conquered] the world" (John 16:33). When he spoke of a "great tribulation" (Matt. 24:21), he was speaking of the fall of Jerusalem in A.D. 70. One needs only to read Josephus' account of that event to see what Jesus meant. And note that he says it will be "such as was not since the beginning of the world to this time [A.D. 30], no, nor ever shall be." This final phrase seems to rule out a "great tribulation" near the end of the age.

Why do I not like labels? If you say you're an amillennialist, to some that means you are a liberal, that you don't believe the Bible. In my case—and I speak only for myself, though it can apply to others—I believe the Bible, all of it. I believe that the Bible says a "thousand years." I believe that. But I believe what the Bible *means*, not what somebody else says it means. I try to let the Bible talk to me. I believe in the "thousand years," but I believe what I understand the Bible says for me. Dr. A. T. Robertson used to say, "Let the Bible say what it says." I think Dr. W. T. Conner was more to the point when he used to say, "Let the Bible say what it means." Sometimes the Bible doesn't mean what it *says*. When it says, "Behold the Lamb of God, which taketh away the sin of the world" (John 1:29), it doesn't mean that Christ is an animal with wool, running around on his four feet, saying, "Baa." No, the Bible says what it means. It means he's a sacrifice. So we have to get behind the words to the meaning. I don't know of anybody who takes the Bible literally all the way. Where the Bible speaks in symbols, as when Jesus said, "I am the door," we must determine the meaning of the symbol. And that is what the Bible *means*. When I get behind this *symbol* as I see it (thousand years), I come forth with this position—right or wrong.

Now as for the "first resurrection" (20:5), John has been talking about the martyrs. Some see the "first resurrection" as one dying to sin and being raised to a new life in Christ. But I think the first resurrection refers to the martyrs. They died, but they are living on in heaven. Now when you have a first, you also have a second. So, actually, I see the second resurrection as the final resurrection of which Christ spoke, and of which Paul spoke in 1 Corinthians 15 and 1 Thessalonians 4, and other places.

As for the final judgment itself, note that it includes all people (vv. 12–13*a*). This judgment will not determine whether one will go to heaven or hell. It only reveals the fact that one's final destination is fixed the moment he dies or when the Lord returns. Those whose names are in "the book of life" (v. 15) go to heaven. All others go to hell.

But note "the books" in verse 12. The other books are a record of every person's deeds, good and/or bad. This record will determine degrees of reward for the saved, and degrees of punishment for the lost (Matt. 25:14–46; Luke 12:47–48).

Heaven at Last

Revelation 21—22 presents heaven as a beautiful city and garden respectively. But here again we have symbolism. In 21:1 John says, "There was no sea." No more separation from God or from loved ones!

In chapter 21, we have this beautiful description of "the holy city, new Jerusalem" coming down, prepared as a bride adorned for her husband. The word *adorned* translates the Greek word *cosmeo*. We get our word *cosmetics* from it. She was cosmetized for her husband or was made beautiful (vv. 1–2).

"The tabernacle of God is with men" (v. 3). The tabernacle in the Old Testament wanderings symbolized God's presence, and this idea holds here. "God shall wipe away all tears from their eyes" (v. 4). Things that have been so heartbreaking on earth are gone: death, sorrow, and pain.

John says that an angel carried him away to a great and high mountain to show him "the Lamb's wife" (v. 9). He showed that great city, the holy Jerusalem, descending out of heaven from God (v. 10). Some may say that this is going to be on earth. But it doesn't say that here. Anyway, John describes a city that looked like a big diamond (v. 11). It had a wall great and high with twelve gates, symbolizing absolute protection from evil and from enemies. On these gates were the names of the twelve tribes of Israel, symbolizing all the people of God. Three gates on each side show accessability (v. 13). Because the wall had twelve foundations, it is secure and substantial. On the foundations were written the names of the twelve apostles (v. 14). "Twelve" is a perfect number. The measurements of the city are given (vv. 15–17). The length and the breadth and the height are equal—"twelve thousand furlongs" would be 1,500 miles each way. Fifteen hundred miles wide, long, and high. Now how are you going to get a city that big on a piece of ground the size of Palestine—about 40 miles wide and 75 miles long north and south?

One man suggested that heaven would be a big apartment house, with the base in Palestine, and would then spread out. No, actually, it's a cube. The holy of holies in the Temple was a cube. This is God's holy of holies. This is the key. Then John talks about the wall being as a jasper or diamond. The city was made of transparent gold (v. 18). Precious stones are inlayed in the foundations of the walls (vv. 19–20). The gates are made out of twelve big pearls (v. 21). The streets of the city are pure gold like transparent glass.

Now all of that has to do with the beauty of the city. But I get another point out of it. The things on earth for which men fight, die, steal, and kill are so cheap in heaven that they use them for building material. So why bother to try to accumulate it on earth? When you get up there, you can go out and pick up all you want.

There will be no Temple in heaven symbolizing God's presence for "the Lord God Almighty and the Lamb are the temple of it" (v. 22). There'll be no night there, no need of the light of the sun or moon because the glory of God and of the Lamb is the light thereof (v. 23). Since there is no night, the city's gates will never be closed (v. 25). The combined glory of the nations typify heaven's glory, only it will be infinitely so (v. 26). No evil will be there (v. 27).

In closing his discussion of Revelation Dr. W. A. Criswell says that in chapter 21 we are approaching the city of heaven. As we come nearer and nearer, we see more details of the stones in the walls, the gates made out of pearl, and other things described above. Then in chapter 22 he says that we enter the city. And behold we find it is a city like a big garden, the restored Garden of Eden.

We find the pure river of the water of life, and on either side of the river there is the tree of life (vv. 1–2). If there was a flood, you see, you might get caught on one side of the river with the tree of life on the other. You couldn't get to it to eat. It is just like the four walls on either side of the city. Many ancient cities had only one gate on one side. If you were on the back side and the enemy was coming, you might get caught trying to get around on the front side to get in the gate. But in the description here there is a gate on every side—absolute security. Likewise, the tree of life is available, and it yields its fruits every month.

"And there shall be no more curse" (v. 3). Now the curse on Adam was not work. A grandmother worked hard all her life. Somebody asked, "Grandma, when you get to heaven what are you going to do?" She said, "I'm going to get me a rocking chair, and sit down for 10,000 years. Then I'm going to start rocking just a little bit." Well, I have an idea that she started rocking pretty soon. Because, you see, if we didn't have anything to do in heaven we'd decide we'd gotten into the wrong place. But the curse on Adam was not work. He had work to do in the Garden of Eden. The curse was that he got tired doing it. And he had to do it in a hostile atmosphere with a hostile nature fighting him. In heaven with a redeemed universe and a redeemed humanity we'll still have work to do.

I don't know what I'll be doing. I guess the singers will have a job, but they won't need any preaching up there. They'll have us polishing stars or something. But we'll all have work to do. For "his servants shall serve him" (v. 3)—without getting tired. Kipling spoke of painting and never getting tired. That's pretty close to what I think John meant here.

Now notice verse 11. Some people talk about a second chance after death. I think this teaches clearly the other way. "He that is unjust, let him be unjust still: and he which is filthy, let him be filthy still: and he that is righteous, let him be righteous still: he that is holy, let him be holy still." In other words, we're not going

to get better in hell until we're qualified to go to heaven. We're
going to stay just like we are at death or at the Lord's return. So I
don't see any picture of a second chance in the Bible, and
certainly not in the book of Revelation.

Postlude

The drama has closed, and we find Christ talking about those
who are in heaven and those that are not there (vv. 12–15). In
verse 12 "I come quickly" could mean *quickly* in time or *certainly*, or it could mean *suddenly*, as we have said earlier. We are
to keep on the alert every second for the Lord may return before
I utter the next syllable. Some see certain things which must
happen before that event. These may involve five minutes, five
years, or 500 years. I say that he may come back before I utter
the next syllable. That's what he taught. And I'll take his word
over anybody's word.

Now notice in verses 12–16 that the performance of the *drama*
is ended. In such cases either the author, or the star, after the
curtain is drawn, will step through the curtain and say a few
words to the audience. I see that in 22:16. "I Jesus [the star of the
drama] have sent mine angel to testify unto you these things . . .
I am the root and the offspring of David, and the bright and
morning star." In other words he is authenticating Revelation.
There were so many apocalyptic writings in that general period.
The writers of such would borrow from other writings so that one
would not know whether a given writing was true or not. So the
Lord steps through the curtain and says, "Now don't mess with
this one. Don't you do with this what some are doing. This is the
real thing." Thus he puts his stamp of approval on it (vv. 18–19).
"The Spirit and the bride say, Come" (v. 17). This is the Lord's
last invitation in the Bible. It is his invitation through the Spirit,
the Holy Spirit, and the bride, Christ's church, calling people to
come. "Let him that is athirst come. And whosoever will [is

willing], let him take the water of life freely."

And note the word of warning about changing the book. Some say it just refers only to Revelation, others say it involves the entire Bible. Whether or not one sees it as intended only for this book, I think it can apply to the whole Bible. Then Christ only testifies to these things, saying "surely I come quickly. Amen." And for us John says, "Even so, come, Lord Jesus." Note that it is not "Lord Caesar" but "Lord Jesus." Amen!

Part III

Apocalyptic

Ray Frank Robbins

7

A Book of Imagery, Numbers, and Symbols

When I was a lad, my pastor was a very confirmed, strong, dispensational premillennialist and he convinced me that that was the only true interpretation. So I adopted it, learned it, and could repeat it. I knew the sequence and all the programs of it. Then when I went to college I had a teacher who had been greatly influenced by Dr. B. H. Carroll from Southwestern Baptist Theological Seminary, who was a very strong postmillennialist. And bless my teacher's dear memory he had a lot of patience with me because when he projected his postmillennialism on this little country boy, who was a confirmed premillennialist, we had some clashes. But he was patient and persistent, and he finally convinced me that I was wrong, so I became a postmillennialist.

Then when I got to Southern Baptist Theological Seminary, my professors, Dr. E. A. McDowell and Dr. William Hersey Davis were amillennialists. And bless their dear memory we had some clashes, but they finally convinced me that I was wrong and they were right, so I became an amillennialist. And then, after I was graduated from the seminary I started studying the book of Revelation for myself, and I came to my present position after many years of studying and teaching. But this position was finally confirmed in 1962. I was granted a leave of absence from the New Orleans Baptist Theological Seminary to study at Oxford University. In Oxford there is one of the largest collection of apocalyptic writings anywhere in the world. Out of this study I was confirmed in the position to which I had already come. So whatever you believe, I have believed it too. I am sympathetic with whatever position you have, and I love you and give you the right to be wrong.

As we begin the study of this marvelous book there are certain things that we ought to keep in mind. First of all, it is a difficult book to interpret. This is so, primarily, because it is written in a code language. It was written in a language with which you and I are no longer acquainted. The nearest thing to this that we have in our literary method today is our cartoons, and I can't always understand them either. But the purpose of the writer was to reveal and to conceal, so it is a code writing.

This code method flourished from about 200 B.C. to about A.D. 100. Hundreds of books written then are still extant, but we have only one complete apocalyptic work in our New Testament and that is the Revelation.

Our literary method today is primarily of two types, prose and poetry, and if we approach this book from either viewpoint, then we misinterpret it. It is not prose and it is not poetry. It is apocalyptic. Because of this method of writing, the book of Revelation is a much-debated book. I am glad, however, that Southern Baptists have at least come to the place where we are willing to look at it even though we disagree upon its interpretation.

Apocalyptic writings were produced in times of persecution. In fact, they are usually called "tracts for hard times." In the last 1900 years whenever we have had times of depression or crisis, times of difficulty, interest in Revelation has increased.

We need to keep in mind the difference between the prophetic and the apocalyptic view of history. This will help us to interpret, I think, what this writer is saying. The prophetic view of history was that God and people work together. God and people work together to bring history to an end, to a goal. This was the prophetic view that we find in the former prophets. The Hebrews called the books of Joshua, Judges, Samuel, and Kings, the former prophets. In these books God and his people are represented as working together to bring history to its desired end. After the return from exile, and especially during the reign of Antiochus Epiphanes (175–163 B.C.), it looked like the more pious, the more godly, the more righteous the people were, the less they succeeded and the more they suffered. And so, there grew up a different view of history. This was known as the apocalyptic view. This view held that the world would become so evil and corrupt that God would intervene in history from without. He would break into history from without and would accomplish his purpose dramatically without the help of man. Now these two views of history were different in emphases.

The writer of Revelation combines the apocalyptic view and the prophetic view. We are not going to get into the argument about who wrote Revelation. This is a very difficult problem and we do not know. We shall call him John; that is what he calls himself, and we shall leave it at that. John combines the apocalyptic and the prophetic views. The first Greek word that he uses in the book is *apocalupsis*, that is apocalyptic, revelation, uncovering, or revealing. But he never uses this word in the writing again. It is obvious from his literary method that that is the type of writing he is doing. After the first word he refers to his writing as a prophecy (1:3; 22:7,10,18–19). He also associates himself with the prophets (10:7; 11:18; 22:9). He combines these two methods. He and Paul agree upon this, and of course, all the other New Testament writers agree.

The Jews divided time into two periods: The present evil age and the age to come. In the book of Revelation John sees the present evil age as having been broken into by Jesus Christ. When our Lord came, he brought the new age, and we are now living in both ages simultaneously. So we are citizens of this age but also citizens of the age to come. So in John's idea, God broke into this evil age with our Lord. This was the dramatic, apocalyptic breaking into history from without. Now when Christ came, he defeated Satan in his own life and released for the church a new power. So, Satan is bound; he also is unbound. He is bound in the lives of Christians. There is no way, no reason whatever, for Satan ever to be victorious in the life of the child of God. But he is still loose in the world, in this present evil age. He is bound in the life of a Christian. No one can ever say "I *had* to sin; I could not overcome it." Paul said, as did several other New Testament writers, that we do not *have* to sin as Christians. He is bound for us and yet he is loose.

This is what John is dealing with here: the apocalyptic, Christ breaking into history from without; and prophetic, Christ working with the church, with his people, to bring history to its victorious end. So it is both apocalyptic and prophetic. This is the reason he never talks about its being apocalyptic after his first word. The apocalyptic has occurred. Christ has broken in, and now he is working with his people in the church.

There is one other thing about this that we need to keep in mind in our interpretation of Revelation. We need to understand his use of numbers. In about 500 B.C. a man named Pythagoras, whom we usually think of as a mathematician, even though he never thought of himself as one, started a system of religion. He expressed his religious ideas with numbers and this system spread over the Eastern world. It went as far as China and India, and the Jews also adopted this system. Numbers were used to express religious ideas because vocabularies were limited. For instance, the number 1 was used to represent unity, unique, alone, independent, self-existent.

The number 2 meant companionship, added courage, increased strength, added power, etc.

The number 3 was the divine number, not only in Judiasm, but in other religions as well. When they wanted to speak of the deity, they would use a 3 instead of trying to write out the name of god. It was the divine number.

The cosmic number was 4. It referred to the world as we would call it today. When they wanted to speak of the universe or the created world they would simply use a 4, and we find this in the book of Revelation many, many times.

Then 7 was the number of completion. It was 4 and 3 added; the divine and the world. This is everything. This is spirit and matter—everything. This is the predominant number in Revelation and it occurs fifty-four times.

Another favorite number was 10. It developed so because it represented a human being. If a human being had ten fingers and ten toes, then he was complete, he was not maimed. So 10 came to symbolize the human completion and the multiplying of this was used in several ways.

Next to 7 in frequency in Revelation is 12. Twelve was the number for organized religion. It was 3 times 4. And we find reflections of this many times in the Old Testament and in the New Testament. Why were there twelve tribes instead of thirteen? Why did Jesus want twelve apostles instead of eleven? These symbols meant much to these people in their ideas and in their expressions. Multiples of all of these numbers are frequent, not only in the Revelation, but in other apocalyptic writings.

There also was some breaking up of these numbers. Three and one half was an insidious number. It was a breaking of the complete number, the 7. And also 6 fell short of the perfect number, 7.

So, numbers in the Revelation and in other apocalyptic writings meant something different from what they do to us. When we see a 5 or an 8 or a 10, we think of mathematics but they thought of ideas. If we are going to understand what John is saying, then we must listen to what *he* says and not what we think when *we* read these numbers. John is an inspired writer, not a mathematician.

There are at least seven truths in this Revelation that we want to keep in mind.

First, the sovereignty of God.

Second, the lordship of Jesus Christ.

Third, the centrality of the community of saints in the long story of mankind.

Fourth, the divine meaning of history. It is *his-story*.

Fifth, the continuing crisis of the world; that is, the struggle between good and evil.

Sixth, the perennial and final judgment of God. And here we ought to keep in mind John's concept of judgment. John did not limit judgment to any one aspect or period. The final judgment was simply the consummation of the judgment that is going on right now.

John doesn't separate the judgment of the future from the judgment of the present. In his Gospel and in Revelation they are the same. What is going on now is the same principle that will operate at the end. In the Gospel he says the ones who are believing have passed out of judgment, but the ones who do not have faith have come into judgment. They are being judged right now. The same principle of judgment that operates right now in a person's life is the principle that will operate in the future. The ones who have faith have passed out of judgment into life, but the ones who have not believed have already been judged because they have not faith in the only begotten Son of God.

Seventh, the sure goal of history. Robert L. McCan named his book on Revelation *A Vision of Victory*, and this is just about as good a title as you can have for it. John had a profound faith that God was going to be victorious in his church with his people. The church had two problems. One was intense persecution from without. Domitian had said this movement must stop, and Rome never placed its stamp of disapproval upon any movement that it did not stop. The second problem, an insidious heresy called gnosticism, had invaded the church and had almost taken it over. It almost destroyed the church from within. In fact, some scholars feel that gnosticism was the only problem. But it seems that there were two problems, persecution from without and heresy from within.

It looked like the Christian movement was going to come to nought. It looked like the church was going to fail. So John was answering these questions: Is God going to fail in his church? Is the church going to be defeated? And John's answer is no. God has released his power in his people, and God has given them the assurance that he would lead them to victory. If the question that he was answering was, "Is God going to fail in his church?" then my interpretation of the book is correct. His answer to the question is no, and here are the reasons why.

This book is an epistle, an apocalypse, and a prophecy. It has qualities of all three of these and we must keep these in mind as we go along.

Revelation is dependent upon the Old Testament for its imagery and its ideas. In fact, no other book in the New Testament is so infused with the concepts, ideas, images, and figures of the Old Testament as this one. One commentator, the writer in the "Torch Bible Commentaries" series counted 518 Old Testament references in the 404 verses.

The Old Testament books that are primarily involved in the background of this book are Psalms, Isaiah, Ezekiel, and Daniel. Most of the interpreters agree upon the meaning of the symbols because these symbols had become almost stereotyped. Anyone who has read any of the other apocalyptic writings soon sees this. These symbols had become idioms that were widespread and were almost universally used to express ideas. So the problem is not what these symbols mean, but the problem deals with time.

The legacy of time is the most difficult part of the book. To what time do the symbols refer? And this is where, of course, the battles take place. Does the symbol refer to the past? Does it refer to the present? Does it refer to the future and if so, when?

Let us turn now to the book itself. In the first chapter, verses 1–20 John gives his introduction. The first word that he uses is the Greek word *apocalupsis*, meaning a revealing, an uncovering, an unveiling. We are supposed to see what it is. He says that is why he wrote. He is supposed to uncover something, to reveal something. Now what is it that he hopes to reveal? Is it a plan for the ages? Is it the future, the end of time? What does he say that he is going to uncover? He says that it is a revelation of Jesus Christ. Whether this is a subjective or an objective genitive in the Greek, we do not know. That is, is he revealing Jesus Christ or is it Jesus Christ who is doing the revealing? Dr. Hobbs has said that it probably is both and that is what I think.

What is being revealed is Jesus Christ. But it is also Jesus Christ that does the revealing. There are five gradations in this opening statement. The primary agent, the one who does the revealing, is God. The secondary agent is Jesus Christ. It is given through Jesus Christ. The instrument of the revelation is the angel, a messenger. In Greek the word for angel, *angelos*, means messenger. In Hebrew the word *malāk* means messenger, and there is no way we can definitely determine whether these two words, the one in Hebrew and the one in Greek, mean heavenly messenger or earthly messenger. Whether he flies around with wings or whether he drives a Ford, only the context can determine.

The primary recipient was John. Who this John was we do not know. We shall leave it as John. (He identifies himself many times as in John 1:1; 1:4; 1:9; 22:8.)

The secondary agents were the servants, all of God's people. So, this is a revelation from God to the church through these different steps.

In verses 4–8 John gives the address and greeting. He writes it to seven churches which are in the Roman province of Asia. He wants the church to be the church in reality in the approaching trial that is before them. So to this end he scrutinizes seven churches. Since there were more than seven churches in Asia Minor, why did he select only seven? He could have mentioned all of them. From the third century it has been recognized that these seven churches represent the church. So these churches are both historical and prophetical. We will use this phrase over and over.

Judgments of praise and blame, in varying degrees, are passed on the churches. Undoubtedly, these churches are meant to stand in their diverse conditions for the Christian church as a whole. After chapter 5 there is no further contrast between the ideal and the actual church. Through chapter 4 the actual church and the ideal church are contrasted. But after chapter 5 the contrast is between the church and the world, the ungodly and the unredeemed. So John writes to seven churches that are in Asia.

In verses 7–8 John gives a summary and a prelude. It is difficult to determine the exact connection of these two verses with what precedes and what follows. It seems best to take verse 7 as a conclusion of what he said in the preceding verses and verse 8 as a prelude to the whole book.

Now John is ready to tell who Jesus is and to show what relationship he has to the church. So he gives the introductory or inaugural vision in verses 9–20. He identifies himself with the people. This always is a good thing to do in any situation when one tries to minister.

John said that he was with them in their problem, in the tribulation and in the patient endurance. He was on the Isle of Patmos. Why he was there is ambiguous in the Greek. He may have been there because of the opportunity to preach. He may have gone as a missionary to preach the word, but tradition says he was there because he had been imprisoned and this probably is a correct tradition.

Verse 10 says, "I came to be in the spirit on the Lord's day." This is the only place in the New Testament where the term "Lord's day" is used. He was prepared to receive the vision. It was the Lord's day, the day of worship, the day of so many memories. He says, "I heard behind me a loud voice like a trumpet." Always the trumpet was used in Jewish usage to indicate a loud, clear message. The trumpet was used to give a clear message of warning, or a challenge, or a summons to something. So what he says here is that he got this message clearly. There is no doubt as to its meaning.

Twelve times in the book John reminds us that he is commanded to write what he hears (1:11,19; 2:1,8,12,18; 3:1,7,14; 14:13; 19:9; 21:5). John says, "Turning to see the voice." I wonder what it looked like! This is a common idiom in apocalyptic writing. You remember when the committee went to see John the Baptist. They said, Who are you? Are you Elijah, a prophet, or somebody else, and what did he reply? "I am a voice." What is it emphasizing? John the Baptist was saying that who he was was not the important thing, but what he was saying. So this was what John was emphasizing here. He turned to see the voice. That is, he wanted to get the message. Turning to see was an indication of his receptivity on the revelation about to be given.

Turning around, he saw a dramatic scene. He did not see the one who was speaking so much as he saw some lampstands. When the King James translators translated the New Testament, the English people did not know what lamps were. Most of them had never seen a lamp. If the translators were going to communicate with the people, they had to use the instruments of lighting which the people knew. So they translated the word *candlesticks*.

But the Jewish people in the first century never had seen a candlestick. John wrote the word *lampstand*. These little lampstands looked like little cream pitchers.

In the Temple the Jews had seven-pronged lampstands that were significant. The number 7 also was significant to the Jews. The lampstands had three prongs on each side and one in the middle. At the top of each prong was a little lamp. When John turned, he saw the seven lampstands. Whether they all are joined together as they were in the Temple or whether they are separate is not clear. But the significant thing is that among these lampstands there was one like unto the Son of man. What is John saying here? In the midst of the church Jesus Christ is to be found. The church has Jesus Christ within it. The significant things about his essential being, and also his qualities or characteristics, are indicated by his clothing; these are symbolic representations of the Son of man. The sevenfold character of Christ is shown here. There are seven points of perfection indicated for the execution of his office.

First, he has snow-white head and hair. The white hair and the white head are symbols of purity and eternity. The whiteness is the revelation of the essential perfection and glory of Christ's character.

Second, his eyes were like a flame of fire. Please do not try to draw a picture. I have seen several books on Revelation where the writer drew a picture of this. This is not picture language. There is a big difference between the symbol and picture.

The symbolism "his eyes like a flame of fire," suggests his power to search the hearts of man and to judge aright. His eyes penetrate. They pierce the outer surface of things and get down to inner realities. He has infinite insight and infallible knowledge. Nothing is hidden from him.

Third, "his feet were like burnished bronze or brass refined as in a furnace." This symbol suggests his strength and his stability.

They symbolize progression and advancement. He has the ability, the strength to lead, to proceed. He moves as the head, the leader, of his churches in the march to victory.

Fourth, "his voice is as the sound of many waters." This was the symbol of majesty, authority. The irresistible power of his voice is stressed.

Fifth, "in his right hand he held seven stars." In Jewish apocalyptic writings the right hand was always the hand of power, of strength. So in his right hand he held seven stars. In many places we do not know the meaning of John's symbolism; and most of the time, when he uses symbols that were not stereotyped and known, he explains what he means and here is one of them.

Stars were used in apocalyptic writings for several things. Instead of leaving us to guess, he tells us what he means. The seven stars are the seven messengers, or angels. All true messengers of the churches are held in the powerful hand of Christ.

Sixth, "from his mouth issued a sharp, two-edged sword." Now do not draw a picture of this. It would be grotesque. This represents his sword of speech. It suggests the penetrativeness of his divine truth. The sword of his mouth is what he uses in the warfare against evil.

Seventh, "and his face was like the sun shining in full strength." This is the revelation of the essential deity of Christ. None could gaze upon his heavenly glory and majesty. When the Jews wanted to express something that was absolutely impossible to look at directly, they would talk about the sun when it was directly overhead. So, this is what he says, no one can really penetrate or see or look at Jesus in his glory.

At this point the Son of man commissions John to write. He says in verses 17–20, "When I saw him, I fell at his feet as one dead!" This is a reaction of a human being in the presence of deity. So John simply reacts because he sees Jesus Christ as God revealed, as God manifested. After this John tells what he means by the stars and the lampstands.

In chapters 2 and 3 he writes what are usually called "letters." Now these "letters" are actually not letters. They are "literary compositions" and they are built in the most exact literary style. They are masterpieces. These letters (we will still call them letters) to the seven churches are both historical and prophetical. They refer to the actual condition of the churches in the writer's day, and they are intended for instruction, encouragement, and warning for the church or churches throughout time. The church, or any one local church, will at any period find itself reflected in one or more of these seven churches.

For two churches, Smyrna and Philadelphia, there is nothing but praise. For two churches, Sardis and Laodicea, there is nothing but blame. For three churches, Ephesus, Pergamum, and Thyatira, praise and blame are intermingled. Each letter consists of seven parts. Now that is significant.

First, there is a superscription to the church addressed.

Second, there is a description of the divine author. Most of the time the descriptions are taken from the inaugural vision of Christ in the midst of the church.

Third, an account is given of the spiritual condition of the church.

Fourth, he gives an appropriate message of praise or censure.

Fifth, he gives an exhortation in view of the special need.

Sixth, he gives a promise to him that overcomes. That is, a promise to those that are morally victorious in the struggle.

Seventh, attention is commanded to the voice of the Spirit. He that hath an ear let him hear what the Spirit says to the churches. Not to this particular church, but to all the churches. It always is in the plural.

The only apparent interruption to this symmetry is in the summons to attention. In each of the first three letters the summons precedes the promise to the overcomers. In the last four, it follows the promise. However, this is in accordance with the largest symmetry of the writer. He always breaks his 7s into 4 and 3 or 3 and 4.

Time will not permit us to look at these letters. Let us look at the first one only. Dr. Hobbs has done a marvelous job of getting through the Revelation.

Notice what he says in the letter to the church in Ephesus. To the "angel." Now what this means we do not know. My guess is, and this seems to be the consensus of scholarship, that when he uses the word *angelos* here he is talking about the pastor or pastors. If John tells me when I see him, that I was mistaken, I am not going to argue with him about it. If he tells me that was exactly what he had in mind, I'm not going to be surprised. I think he is talking about the pastors of the church.

In 2:2–3 there is the commendation of the church. Jesus (the Son of man) wants them to know that he knows everything about them. And in these two verses he says that he knew seven things about them. He knew their work, their toil, their patient endurance, their fidelity in fellowship, their orthodoxy in doctrine, their purity in motive, and their unwearied exertion. In other words, he simply says, "I know all about you."

And then, in verse 4, he gives the Son of man's complaint against the church. The King James translators slipped in the little word *somewhat*, but it is not in the Greek. He says, "I have this against you. You have left your first love." What was their real problem? They had become so concerned about orthodoxy that they were hating that which Christ hated but were failing to love those whom Christ loved. They had become so concerned about hating false doctrines, false ideas, and false teachings that they had included the ones who held these in their hatred. They had left the one thing that characterizes a community as a church. The only distinctive of a Christian community is love. Jesus gives the remedy for the problem in three verbs: remember, repent, return. Unless they do these three things, he says, he will come and remove the lampstand. The inaugural vision of Jesus in the church in chapter 1 is a night scene. The stars and the lamps indicate this. The church is in a dark world, morally dark world, and the only light shining in this dark world is the church. But the church gets its light from the one who is in the midst of the church. When a church ceases to give moral light in a community which is motivated and activated by love, it ceases to be a church. The Son of man says to the church in Ephesus that unless they love, their lampstand will be removed. He is not saying that he will come and snatch it out or get it when they are not looking. He is saying that this is the moral retribution for not shining. If a church does not shine, it is not a lampstand.

In verse 7 the promise is given. John does this with all of these seven letters. The definitive work on these seven letters was done by Sir William Ramsay, a British scholar of a generation ago who spent his life in the area of Asia Minor. I recommend his marvelous book, *The Letters to the Seven Churches*. Nearly everything since that time that has been written on these letters goes back to Ramsay. Barclay's little book is a summary of what Ramsay says. We are going to pass over these other six letters, but each one of them is built in the same kind of literary structure and each one is important.

In chapter 4 there is a call to the church upon the eve of conflict. This is a call to believe in God. This chapter does not go beyond the Old Testament revelation of God. It shows God as creator, stressing his power. In the rabbinical writings when God's power was emphasized the writers referred to his creative activity. So this chapter stresses one thing, God's omnipotence. The central teaching of this chapter is the sovereignty of God. He is the creator over all the universe. In *The Meaning and the Message of the Book of Revelation* Dr. E. A. McDowell points out seven attributes of God that are revealed in this chapter.

John begins chapter 4 with the word meaning "after this."
There is no justification whatever in assigning what follows to a
time after this world. The phrase "after this" is used over and
over by this writer in the ordinary, natural sense. After having
seen what he had just seen, he said, I saw something else. This is
the normal use of this phrase. It is used to express a new phase or
a new variety of the spectacle. After seeing the seven churches he
saw an opened door in heaven. He did not see the door as it
opened; he saw the door as it stood open, stood ajar, and this is
significant. What he saw was available for anyone who had eyes
to see. He could gaze through the open door. The voice which he
heard is the same one which he mentioned in 1:10. The voice
tells him that he is to receive yet greater insight into spiritual
things. He is in the spirit. He does not mean literally that he is
taken out of his body and taken off like some disembodied spirit
apart from a body, but he is in a condition where he can receive
greater insight.

The prophet does not see heaven but rather God on the
throne. This word *throne* occurs seventeen times in chapters 4
and 5, stressed especially in chapter 4. The point is that God is the
sovereign of this universe. Domitian is not sovereign, but God is.
The power of the sovereign God is available to the church. The
command to "come up hither," is to get enlightened. He was to
receive greater insights and learn what must take place. Now,
when John wrote this, he did not put down any chapter divisions or
verse divisions and it is quite arbitrary where we put these. The
chapter divisions were made in the thirteenth century. The verse
divisions were made in 1551.

Where did John intend verse 1 to end and verse 2 to begin? The editors of the Greek text, the textual critics, disagree.
Westcott and Hort put this phrase, *meta tauta* (after these
things), with verse 2, and I am convinced that this is the correct

place. Verse 1 should end with "Come up hither, and I will show you what must take place." They begin verse 2 with "after these things I was in the Spirit." I believe that is what John says. If he corrects me when I see him I am not going to argue with him, but I believe that is what he says. And Westcott and Hort believed this. Since you cannot disprove it and I cannot prove it, we shall leave it until we see John. I have 1,492 questions listed that I want to talk to John about as soon as I see him and this is one of them.

Most of the time John puts this little phrase *meta tauta* at the beginning of a statement and not at the end. Because of this practice I think this is where it ought to go. John says, "After these things I was in the Spirit, and lo a throne situated in heaven." No actual placing the throne is given, but when he looked through this opening he saw the throne already situated and one sitting upon it.

What he saw here is a dramatic presentation in symbolic language of God reigning in the world. He does not describe God. In no place in the Bible is God ever described, but John uses two precious stones here. He sees the jasper, probably the diamond, and the carnelian or sardius, a red stone. The diamond apparently symbolized God's holiness, righteousness, and glory. The carnelian may have symbolized his justice, judgment, and wrath.

Also around this throne there were twenty-four elders. The number 12 was the number of organized religion and there were two covenants or two people of God, the old and the new. The twenty-four elders symbolize the whole redeemed community of God.

From the throne issued flashes of lightnings and voices of thunder. These are apocalyptic symbols which are used to indicate God's power. Throughout the apocalyptic writings these convulsions of nature, like hail, thunderstorms, and lightning are used to indicate the deity. Not just God's deity, but if they were in other religions they indicated the god's power. So here it simply stresses one thing, the power of God.

Then around the throne there was a glass-like sea. Now a sea often is used to indicate separateness. Apparently he is saying this God is alone, he is supreme, and no one is like him. All others are separated from him.

Four living creatures are around the throne in this symbolic picture. You remember that four represented the creation, the cosmos, the world. So here he seems to be referring to creation. Now the Greek word here is not *beast;* really it is the word for life. Living beings or creatures is the best that can be done in translating this word. This seems to represent inanimate and animate creation apart from man.

Next, the living creatures continue to say that this one is holy. So two things are stressed about the one on the throne. He is powerful and he is holy. He is the God of power and he is the God of holiness.

In 4:9–11 the creatures are shown as worshiping the creator. All creation should worship the Creator. There is as much difference between the lowest creature and God as there is between the highest creature and God because these are in different realms. God is the creator and all others are creatures. When my three boys were small, I took them out one night to give them their first lesson in astronomy. They were about two, three, and four years of age. I was pointing out the different constellations and different stars, and the oldest little boy was beginning to catch on as I was pointing them out. Finally, the youngest boy who was about two and a half pulled my leg and said, "Daddy, you can almost reach them, can't you?" Now from his vantage point he thought the end of my finger was going up pretty close to the stars, but from my vantage point I knew that the difference between his finger point and mine was infinitesimally small as far as the distance was concerned between our finger tips and those stars.

So, the vast difference between the best and the worst is so infinitesimally small as contrasted with the creator. This is what he is saying; this one on the throne is different. He is different from all of his creatures. He is the creator and all the others are creatures.

The creator and all the creatures are manifested in chapter 4, but is that all that there is to creation? Did God have no purpose in creation? Is that all that creation is about? If it is, creation is one great mistake. If God did not have a purpose or goal or plan for his creatures why create us? One rabbi said, God's purpose for creating Gentiles was to have fuel for hell. What did God have in view? Did God create all these creatures just so he would have something to burn in hell? Now the answer to that question is given in chapter 5.

In chapter 4 God is revealed as the Creator, but that is not all God is. God is also the Redeemer. That is, he seeks to enter into the life of his creatures, those who have come to moral shipwreck, and help them. Supremely, of course, he does this in Christ Jesus. But he did not start this in Bethlehem. Jesus Christ did not change God, he revealed God. These two chapters should be read together to get the complete picture that John is trying to show us.

John then saw upon *(epi)* the outstretched hand of the one who sat upon the throne a scroll. This scroll, this piece of paper we would call it today, was rolled up on his hand. It was rolled up and his hand was outreached. He did not have it clasped, he was holding it so one could get it. It was available for anyone to take and read it. But when God held it out, John saw that no one was worthy to open the scroll and break the seals. This scroll was sealed with seven seals, that is, seven drops of wax along its edge. It was completely sealed. Letters were sealed when the scroll was rolled up and the writer put drops of wax on the edge and then pushed his signet ring into the wax. Then if it were broken it could never be put back unless one had his signet ring.

God's purpose for creation was completely sealed. No one understood. No one knew.

God was seated on the throne with the scroll sealed with seven seals. Next John saw a strong angel proclaiming with a loud voice "who is worthy to open the scroll and break the seal." No one in heaven, on earth, or under the earth was worthy to open the scroll. This is the symbolic way of saying no one anywhere was able to open the scroll or look into it.

John now becomes a participant in the vision. He weeps because no one was able to open the scroll. Then one of the elders spoke to him. Why does the elder speak to him? The elder represents the redeemed. Why does the elder do the talking? Because only the redeemed know the redemptive power of God in Christ Jesus. He is the one who does the talking. So, one of the elders said to John, "Stop weeping." Here is a mixture of metaphors which John uses often throughout the book. The lion of the tribe of Judah has conquered so he can open the scroll with the seven seals.

Between the throne and the four living beings or creatures, and among the elders John saw a lamb. So Christ is in his church; He is in creation *and* in his church. How is Christ in the world? The Jesus of history is in his people and in the world. He is present in his Spirit. In fact, Paul identifies Jesus and the Holy Spirit. In 2 Corinthians 3:17 he says the Lord is the Spirit. At least 164 times Paul uses the phrase "Christ in you," or a similar phrase and he says being filled with the Spirit. That is practically the same thing. So the Spirit of God who was in Jesus one hundred percent was released through his death, burial and resurrection experience and is now made available to the believers. Christ is in us.

John saw among the four living creatures and among the elders that Christ is present in the church and in the world. He saw a lamb standing. These two figures of speech *lion* and *lamb* are both important. He has the strength, the characteristics of a lion, and yet he accomplishes his victory through suffering as the lamb. But notice this lamb. He is standing. He is standing up, he is alive, as though he had been dead. Now these mutually antagonistic metaphors are important. He is standing up; he is alive; but he had been dead.

The Lion-Lamb has seven horns. Horns are symbolic in all apocalyptic writings for power and if the Lion-Lamb has seven horns then he has complete power. He has seven horns and seven eyes. Eyes are used as symbols for knowledge. He has seven eyes which are the seven spirits of God. That means that God's Spirit is in him completely. This is God's Spirit, in other words, personified in the human Jesus.

The Lion-Lamb went and took the scroll from the hand of the one on the throne. "Went" is in the aorist tense. He went one time and took the scroll. "Took" is in the perfect tense. Now it is almost impossible to translate a Greek perfect into English. A Greek perfect indicates an act that took place in the past, and the consequences of the act remain until the present. So, John changes the tenses here. That is, the Lion-Lamb picked up the scroll and he still has it.

In other words, Jesus Christ in his death, burial and resurrection experience is the only one who can give meaning and purpose to creation. He did it at the cross and he is the only one who does it right now. And this is significant in the change of tenses here.

When he had taken the scroll, the four living creatures and the twenty-four elders fell down before the lamb. What is he saying here? All of creation, inanimate, animate, and the church all recognize that he is the only one who can give meaning and purpose to their being, their creation.

They all fell down before the lamb, each holding a harp and golden bowls of incense. These items are trappings of worship. The incense represents the prayers of the saints. They all sang a new song. The new song is not the old song of creation that is mentioned in 4:8–11. This is a new song of redemption. It is a praise for the Redeemer and redemption.

In this song the Lion-Lamb was praised because he was worthy to take the scroll and to open its seals. He had been slain and by his blood did ransom men for God from every tribe, tongue, people and nation. Now, why this fourfold enumeration? All creation, all people are involved. And the redeemed reign on earth. The manuscripts are about evenly divided between the present tense and the future tense in translating the verb to reign. They already have been made a kingdom so the present tense better suits the sentence. That is, they reign now. During the time of this present evil age overlapping the age to come, God is reigning now through his people. In the first chapter we are told that he made believers into a kingdom of priests, that is the best translation.

In 5:11–14, the redeemed worship the Redeemer. Then John saw around the throne and the living creatures and the elders a great innumerable host. The Lion-Lamb is worthy to receive power, and wealth, and wisdom, and might, and honor, and glory and blessing. Why this sevenfold description of praise? He is worthy to receive all praise. The 7 indicates complete. He is worthy to receive all the praise because of his redemptive effort. He was slain; he gave his life.

To the New Testament writers the word *blood* and the word *death* and the word *cross* all meant practically the same thing. They are figures of speech stressing one essential truth, that is, life given all the way. When a Hebrew committed a sin, he knew that only God could deal with the sin. However, he knew that

God could deal with the sin only if he gave it to God. Just killing a lamb would not help. The prophets castigated their people for thinking that sacrifices pleased God (Isa. 1:10–17; 66:3; Jer. 6:20; Mal. 1:10). Isaiah said "away with this slaughterhouse business." God does not want people to kill lambs. God wants people to give their lives to him. Now the sacrificial system was a way, a method, a symbol, or a ceremony by which the person could express that which he previously had done in his own life. He had given his life to God. When a Hebrew brought an animal and laid his hand on the head of the animal, he was identifying himself with the animal. He was identifying his life with the animal life. As Dr. Smith so beautifully said, when the animal was killed and the blood came out, the life came out, because the life was in the blood. And when the life came out, it went to God where all life comes from in Hebrew thought. And when it went to God it not only carried the animal life to God, but it took man's life to God, including his sin.

Our Lord made one major change in the interpretation of the whole sacrificial system. Over and over again he insisted during his ministry that no one was going to take his life as they did the animals' lives. Jesus was going to give his life. It was a free volitional choice and he was going to lay it down himself. When a Hebrew committed a sin, he knew that he could not bribe God and that he could not get rid of the sin himself. The only one who could get rid of sin was God, but God could not deal with it unless the person gave it to God, and the killing of the animal after identifying himelf with it indicated that he is giving his life to God.

When Jesus comes into a person, he identifies himself with him, that is, he unites with him. The verb to believe, *pisteuo*, comes from a little root which literally means "to unite." It is a Sanskrit root which is developed by George Curtis in his two-volume work, *Principles of Greek Etymology*. He traces this root back to a Sanskrit root which means to unite life and it was used for hundreds of years, according to Curtis, to express the uniting of human life. The only way that life can be changed is for life to enter into it from without. A human being cannot effect change in his selfhood, no matter what he does. He cannot make himself better and he cannot make himself worse. He can only express what he is. No one can help himself by what he does any more than he can help himself by giving himself a blood transfusion.

If life that is evil flows into a person from without, then it makes him more evil. If life that is good flows into a person from without it makes him better. And the best life is God's life. God's life was demonstrated in Jesus Christ. And if God's life flows into a person it makes him better. The word *faith*, the word *believe*, the word *trust*, and the word *faithful* all come from this root, which means to unite life.

Jesus Christ's death, then, was the giving of his life to God. He gave his life all the way. When anyone allows Christ into his life, then when he sins, Christ enables him to give his life, including his sin, to God. The only solution to the sin problem is God, but God cannot deal with sin unless it is given to him.

In 1 John 1:7 the writer says that if we continue to walk in the light as he is in the light then two things accrue to us. One, we are having fellowship one with another. If you are in the light and I am in the light, then you and I are sharing together the light. And the second thing, the blood of Jesus Christ, the life of Jesus Christ given to God, is cleansing us from every act of sin. Every time we sin, the only solution to that sin is God, but God cannot deal with it unless we give it to him. But we will not unless we have some help. We cling to it, we deny it, we rationalize it, we excuse it, we blame somebody else. But if Christ is in us, he enables us to give it to God. How do you know he can give a life to God? He gave his own. How far did he go in giving his own life? He went all the way to the end. Now, when Jesus uses these metaphors, blood, death, and cross, he means life given to God all the way. He must enact this same thing in us or it is not effective. Salvation is something that is real and personal in each life. When we sin, there is a solution: the blood of Christ. This is the only solution to the sin problem that man knows.

Why is it that Jesus Christ is worthy of this sevenfold adoration? Because he is the one who has given his life and made it available for man so that man can have the life of God. He shared God's life with us. So, in verse twelve a sevenfold adoration, all praise, is given to the Lion-Lamb. Every creature joins in the worship of God and the Lion-Lamb.

8
A Vision of God's Judgment on Evil

In chapter 6 the difficult part of the Revelation begins. Up to this point most interpreters agree as to its meaning, but here the multitudinous interpretations begin. In this chapter the dramatic movements of the apocalypse begin. This is a drama as Dr. Hobbs has so wonderfully pointed out in his book. All the preceding chapters have been somewhat introductory.

The first cycle of visions here shows a series of events which follow the successive opening of the seals on the scroll. This scroll that the Lion-Lamb took is now broken in 6:1 to 8:1.

The writer pictures the breaking of each seal as revealing the *means* of the divine judgment. During the period when the present evil age overlaps the age to come, evil and good are intermingled. We are living in both the good and evil ages and we have both good and evil in our being. God is now judging the evil age by the age to come. John depicts the means of this judgment in the breaking of the seals.

This vision shows the conflicts and struggles of the church, the judgment of God upon her enemies, and how her victory is to be won. When the Lion-Lamb broke the first seal, out galloped a horse. Now this is dramatic. Out of the scroll came a white horse and a rider who had a bow and wore a victory crown. Now this is not a crown of reigning. There are two words in the Greek for crown and this is the victory crown. He went out conquering and to conquer. There are many different interpretations to this horse

172

and rider that I have gathered. Without trying to go into all of these and refute them I simply shall give you what I think. I believe this refers to the Antichrist. My good friend Dr. E. A. McDowell thought it referred to conquest, but I can see very little difference between war and conquest. Many of the commentators take this as the gospel or as Christ, or a lot of other good things, but I cannot see this as something good because of two reasons: One is that John's symmetry would be broken in the first series if he depicts good. John usually breaks his sevens into 4 and 3. If this is good then he has 1, 3, and 3, and that is different from all of his others in his book. The other reason is that evil always tries to emulate good. Evil never comes and says I am evil. Evil never says follow me and I will destroy you. Evil always comes and tries to imitate good and claims that evil is better than good. So, because of these two reasons I am convinced that with the first horse and rider there is the personification of evil. This is evil at its worst. Only John uses the term *Antichrist*, and in his first epistle he says there are many Antichrists (1 John 2:18; 4:1,3).

Later on John uses a similar figure to the horse and rider in this book, that is, the Christ, so I am convinced that this is the Antichrist. This is the personification of evil that tries to destroy the church and Christ.

When the Lion-Lamb broke the second seal or wax drop, out came another horse and rider. This was a red horse. This horse and rider symbolize warfare. God is now using these instruments as means of judgment. Though they are themselves evil God uses them in his judgment against evil. God is still sovereign and everything in this universe is under his control, even evil. He never surrenders his sovereignty to anything.

When the third seal was broken, a black horse and his rider came from the scroll. In the wake of the blood shed there follows dearth and scarcity, hence, the third rider is famine, bringing prices of wheat and barley many times the normal cost. This is famine. Not of oil and wine, but of the necessities of life, wheat and barley. Black is the color of gloom and mourning. The mourning is caused by the famine and scarcity.

When the fourth seal is broken, out comes a fourth horse and rider. And if you have in your translations "come and see" just scratch out the "see" as Dr. Hobbs said earlier. There is no "see" there. Some late scribe put in "see." He misunderstood what John wrote. The command is to the horse and the rider. Come! So out comes the fourth horse and the rider. He was a pale horse. A horse with the pale color of a corpse ridden by death with the grave running along beside him. This is a gruesome picture. Death comes riding out on a horse and the grave comes along beside him. As death kills the people the grave picks up the corpse. What do these four horses and riders represent? They represent the various phases of the judgments which are permitted by God to afflict all mankind.

When are these things happening? When did they happen? They are happening all the time. As the church is in the world these occurrences are being used by God to judge sinful humanity: Antichrist, war, famine, and death.

Now, while these first four seals have to do primarily with the material world, the last three have to do more specifically with the spiritual world.

The fifth seal was then opened. Here the martyred souls under the altar could be seen. Now how could he see souls? What does a soul look like? He is talking about people. He is not speaking in the Greek sense of soul. From the biblical perspective people do not have souls. They are souls. In fact, man is a total being. There are nine different words used in the New Testament to refer to a human being, but these are used in synecdoche, that is they all refer to the human being, the total being from different aspects. You do not have a part of you that is spirit and a part that is soul and a part that is body and a part that is something else. You are a

human being. But what is a person? What is a human being? He
is a living soul, he is a spirit, he is a body, he is life, he is flesh.
What is a human being? No where does any biblical writer ever
try to tell us what a person is. The disciplines of psychiatry,
psychology, anthropology, sociology never attempt to tell what a
human being is.

What does the word *person* mean? *Persona* is a Latin word
which means an actor's mask. What one sees is not the real
person. In the Greek New Testament the word *prosōpon* that is
usually translated person means around the eye, that is, the face.
No where do the Bible writers ever attempt to tell us what a
human being is. He is a creature. He is not God. He is a creature
that is created with need and capacity for God, for other persons,
and for things. That is what the Bible is about.

Nine words are used in the Greek New Testament to refer to a
person. This mysterious being is not an animal, yet he is. He is
not God, but he has capacity for God-like life. He is a strange,
mysterious, miraculous creature. He will never cease to be, and
yet, he is not complete unless he has God in his life. He is never
complete unless he shares life with others. He is never complete
in this realm unless he has things and shares things. That is all
that life is about. That is all the Bible is about. But when John
says he saw souls under the altar he is simply talking about
human beings, not disembodied spirits like the Greeks thought.

Under the altar where the blood of the sacrifice was collected
(Lev. 4:7), John saw these people. Martyrs were crying out like
the blood of Abel. The cry of the martyrs here is not a cry for
personal revenge: "God get even with them!" This is a cry for the
vindication of justice. It looked as if good was failing. It looked as
if that for which they had lived and died was not going to
succeed. God says, "Do not get discouraged. Do not get impa-
tient. My program is not in a time schedule. Just be patient. I am
going to work out good over evil. I am going to vindicate what

you lived and died for. Just be patient."

The sixth seal portrays a worldwide cataclysm showing the confusion of the foes of Christ. The enumeration here of seven calamities seems to denote the all-extending nature of God's judgment. There are seven calamities that are enumerated in verses 12 ff. Why does he say seven? The foes of Christ's church are now being judged. This is the wrath of God that Paul develops in Romans. It is the natural law of sin and retribution. God is against evil and the way by which he counteracts evil is that he lets evil produce its results. And the worst thing that God can do to one of his creatures is to turn him loose to sin. Sin is its own punishment. Nothing is more devastating and more terrible for sin than sin itself. Sin carries its own consequence in the sinner.

Here John shows God's way of dealing with those who oppress his church. This shows the universality and the completeness of this judgment. These forms are not to be taken literally, they are apocalyptic. They are almost stereotyped. Every one of these is found in other apocalyptic writings. In fact, many of these same figures are found in Peter's quotation of Joel 2 at Pentecost (Acts 2:16–21). You remember when the Spirit came in power the people concluded that the disciples were drunk on fresh new wine, not fermented or completely ripened wine. Peter said, "Oh, no, we are not drunk. It is too early in the morning to get drunk. But, this is that which was spoken by the prophet Joel." Then he quoted Joel: "In the latter days I will pour out my Spirit upon all flesh." Then he says there shall be all kinds of convulsions in nature: earthquakes, falling stars, the moon turning to blood, and the sun being darkened. Now did these things happen at Pentecost? Or was Peter mistaken? He is interpreting the experience in apocalyptic language. Surely what Joel said took place, and Peter understood it. What Joel and Peter meant was that which had happened was not the ordinary course of events. This event was a dramatic intervention by God, which was apocalyptic. You remember the difference between prophetic and apocalyptic. The prophetic view was that God works with his people to bring the end that he has in view. But the apocalyptic view is that God intervenes from without. So, what John was saying here was that God had intervened from without in a dramatic, spectacular way and this could not be explained as the normal course of events in nature or anything else. John uses these figures of speech to emphasize that this is apocalyptic.

There are seven calamities mentioned here. These symbolize the overturning of all that up to this time has been considered unshakable and firm. If sin brings evil consequences as it must in any moral-ordered universe, and if God's nature is revealed fully in Christ, then those who are sinning are sinning against Christ, and the consequences are inevitable. Horrified at the results of their own action, men seek to escape from God. The sting of a guilty conscience, the torment of remorse, the dread of meeting a holy God, and the face of a rejected Savior, these give more terror to the human soul than all the tumult of crashing empires, the approach of death, and the most startling commotions that could be in nature like earthquakes and so on.

So, the sixth seal has portrayed a worldwide cataclysm showing the confusion of the foes of Christ. He concludes this broken seal with the question, who can stand before this? Who can stand during these judgments that God uses against evil? Why is not the whole human race destroyed? John has an answer.

In each of the series of judgments between 6 and 7 John has an interlude. Chapter 7 is the first interlude. This depicts God's care for the faithful. This is a complement of the incidents that are recorded in the preceding chapter, which takes up the question "who is able to stand?" In verses 1–8 the church militant is depicted. The church is safe in the midst of these judgments. The church is in the world, but the church is not of the world. Our Lord's recorded prayer in John 17 indicates this. Jesus did not pray that he would take us out of the world, but he would keep us from the evil, or from the evil one, however it should be translated.

During this time the church is safe. The church is viewed by John as being a whole. God's people constitute one whole, the old and the new. There are some on earth and there are some in heaven. However, the church constitutes one people. Verses 1–8 deal with the church on the earth. Those who are in the struggle, of the great tribulation, right now—how are they safe from this terrible judgment which he has just discussed in the preceding chapter?

After this John saw four angels. Why four? Because of the four corners of the earth. While in Great Britain, I attended a society meeting of people who are dedicated to the proposition that the earth is flat. These people use this as their major Scripture to prove it. If you want to, you can prove anything, as Dr. Hobbs has said. Dr. Hobbs said that if one uses the proof-text method that he could prove that Eve was the mother of possums. Because an opossum is alive and the Scripture says that Eve is the mother of all living things.

The Jews believed that the earth was flat. They believed that evil winds came from the four corners of the earth. Dr. McDowell discusses this at great length in his book, *The Meaning and Message of the Book of Revelation*.

Let us come back to the Revelation now. The winds from the four corners of the earth, that is, the winds that did not come from the north, east, south, and west were thought to be evil winds. So here John depicted a restraining influence. John says that God's judgments are tempered with mercy. God holds back his judgments. Then John saw another angel descending from the rising of the sun, that is from the east. No individual angel is particularized though an archangel may be intended since he has authority over these other four, but he does not say this. This fifth angel's mission was to render secure the servants of God, the church.

This angel from the east had the seal of the living God. According to tradition in the rabbinical writings, when the Hebrews left Egypt, when they came across on the dry land at the Red Sea, God imprinted on their foreheads a sign and this sign stayed on them until they got into Palestine. It even preceded the manna. God gave each one a sign. Now this is the background for this. God gives a print, a sign, on his people. In actuality what is the sign? God has now shared his life with his people and that makes them different. They have a different kind of life and that is what is symbolized here.

The angel called with a loud voice, do not hurt the earth, the sea, or the trees until I have sealed the servants of God upon their foreheads. John heard the number that were sealed, 144,000. The number here is a multiple of twelve times twelve times one thousand. Any number multipled by itself was a completion of that number, so if 12 symbolizes the people of God, then he is simply saying every person of God is set apart; he is sealed, he is protected. The 1,000 designated the people in the messianic reign. God's people have something in this world which sets them apart from the world. They have the seal of the living God.

There are problems here with John's listing of these tribes. Some that are included ordinarily are not included in lists of the Old Testament. Of course, the Old Testament lists are not always the same. Also, there are two tribes, Dan and Ephraim, that are omitted. We do not know why they were omitted. We will not go into that here. But the tribes symbolize that God's people are safe. They are sealed with the seal of the living God.

Verses 9–17 depict the church triumphant. This is the church, the members who have come out of the struggle on earth. They are still God's people but they are now in heaven. In verses 9–10 the redeemed in heaven are described as a great multitude which no man could number from every nation, tribe, people, and tongue. Where are these from? Every where! The fourfold enumeration stresses the universality of the group. They are standing before the Lamb, clothed in white robes. They are victorious.

In apocalyptic writings clothing was often used to designate the character, the kind of life the person had. So if they have white robes, they are now clean; they are pure; they are righteous. The palm branches were used during the Feast of Tabernacles by the Jews as part of the victory celebration commemorating their release from Egyptian bondage. In his Gospel, 12:13, John sees the victorious saints with palm branches in their hands, and they are crying out, present tense, with a loud voice. They are in this condition of release, the condition of heaven. They know they are in heaven because of what? Salvation belongs to God who sits upon the throne and to the Lamb! God through Christ has shared his life with them and they are in heaven because of that.

Next the angels and the elders and the living creatures join in this praise that the saints are giving. All the angels stood around about the throne, the elders and the four living creatures and they fell on their faces before God and worshiped God saying, "Amen, blessing and glory and wisdom and thanksgiving, and honor and power and might." How many of these are there? Seven! This sevenfold enumeration or ascription of praise denotes its universal and all-embracing character. God and the Christ are to receive all glory and power and worship.

In verses 13–17 John discusses the glorious state of the redeemed. The elder speaks because he is typical of the church. In the Revelation when an explanation is made of visions which refer to the church, the active part is taken by an elder. Angels, however, introduce visions which have significance which are unexplained. But anytime that a vision deals with the church it is the elder who explains it because he is the one who understands this. So, one of the elders addressed John saying, "Who are these in the white robes?" Where did they come from? And John says, "You know, sir." Why does he know? Because he is one of them! These are they who have come out of the great tribulation. Here we have one of our words that we are going to battle over. When is the great tribulation?

According to the way that I see it, the great tribulation began when our Lord came, and the great tribulation is going on now, and the great tribulation will continue until our Lord comes back. This is the struggle of the church against evil and the persecution of the church by evil in the world. Now, do not shoot me yet. Wait just a little while. The ones in heaven are the ones who have been in the struggle on earth. The great tribulation is the conflict in the world between good and evil. When a saint dies, he moves out of the great tribulation. However, he is still a part of the church.

Dr. McDowell points out that there are four things that those who have washed their robes and made them white in the blood of the Lamb are promised. First, in verse 15 they are given the privilege of living and serving forever in the presence of God. Second, in verse 16, they shall suffer no more from hardship imposed by nature. Third, in the first part of verse 17, they shall enjoy contact forever with the source of life. That is, the Lamb will be the shepherd to guide them always. Fourth, God himself will serve as their great Comforter; that is in the latter part of verse 17.

So, here we have four rewards promised to those who have washed their robes in the blood of the Lamb.

The interlude has been completed, John now tells about the seventh seal.

Revelation 8:1 says that when the Lamb opened the seventh seal there was silence in heaven for about a half an hour. Now I have eleven different interpretations listed here that I have gleaned through the years about this. I like Dr. Hobbs's interpretation of this very much and I am indebted to him greatly in many places, not only in Revelation, but in Hebrews. I think his book *How to Follow Jesus* is the best work that I have ever read on Hebrews and I would recommend it highly.

Many times in the Old Testament the going forth of God in judgment is introduced by a reference to silence (Hab. 2:20; Zeph. 1:7; Zech. 2:13). And in other apocalyptic writings this usage was customary. So, I am convinced that this is a silence of trembling suspense, a dramatic pause, a silence of expectation of judgment which is customary in apocalyptic writing. Why does he not tell us what happens? Nowhere in the Revelation, I am convinced, does John ever describe heaven and he never describes hell. He always stops short of this. Now, if that shocks you, when we get to the last few chapters we shall explain what we mean.

The events narrated under the trumpets are not expositions of the seventh seal, but a separate vision supplementing what has been set forth in the seventh seal. Now this is John's customary literary procedure. In his first epistle he writes and says, "I write these things that you may know that you have eternal life." In that little book he wants the people to know that God is in their life, that Christ has entered in, has shared his life with them, that they are Christian. In 1 John he has three tests. First, he gives the test of obedience. Next, he gives the test of love. He then gives the test of faith. He goes around this, one, two, three, and of course, he goes over and over the same thing again.

Now, he does a similar thing in his Gospel. He gives seven signs. As Dr. Hobbs said, John never uses the word *miracle* in his Gospel. In the King James translation the word is miracle, but the Greek word is not miracle. The Greek New Testament has three words: miracle, wonder, and sign. A "miracle" was the divine intervention in the natural order. A "wonder" was the results produced upon those who saw it or heard about it or read it, the results in their lives. A "sign" was what the miracle was supposed to teach. Now the same event could be, and was interpreted many times to be, a miracle, a wonder, or a sign. But John never uses the word *miracle*. He is not interested in the event per se, he is interested in what it teaches. That is what he does in his Gospel. Seven times he selects these events and he says here are some signs, some teachings, to show you that Jesus Christ is the Son of God. That is what his purpose is in the Gospel (John 20:30–31). Now he does the same thing in Revelation. He has three cycles dealing with the same thing, that is, God's judgment upon the world, and God's protection of his church in this struggle. One is the seals, one is the trumpets, and one is the bowls.

When the Lion-Lamb opened the seventh seal, there was silence in heaven for about a half an hour. This is a brief period. Then John saw the seven angels who stand before God with seven trumpets. Trumpets were used, as we have already said, to indicate a clear, understandable message. John sees seven messengers representing the judge of men to each of whom is given a trumpet. Before they are made ready to sound, verse 6 says that another messenger came and stood at the altar. There is given to him much incense that he should add it to the prayers of all the saints. The time for the answering of the prayers of saints for God's judgment upon sin has come. In 6:10 the martyrs prayed, "Lord, how long are you going to wait?" John is now told that God will vindicate the cause of his people.

Another angel came and stood at the altar and to him was given much incense to mingle with the prayers of all the saints. The background of this symbolism is to be found in the practice of the Jews praying in the Temple. When the people fell on their knees in prayer, the priest put some incense on the altar and burned it.

As the smoke of the incense went up it was held that the prayers of the people were going to God. This is John's symbolism.

Of course, the smoke did not carry the people's prayers to God any more than the animals killed took the lives of the people to God. A person could kill an animal and not give his life to God. A person can kneel and not pray. It is much easier to go through the ritual and not have the reality. This is what the prophets continually called the people back to, because the people decided that if they would do the ritual this accomplished the reality. But the people who crucified our Lord, God Incarnate, God personified in a human being, killed animals day by day. They made their sacrifices and they said their prayers and the smoke of their incense went up; but they were not praying, they were not in touch with God. So, the greatest danger to organized religion is confusing means and ends. The greatest danger to your own life and to my life is confusing means and ends. It is easy to conclude that if we do something, if we perform something, this is reality, this gets us in touch with God; but no symbolism, no ritual, no performance gets us in touch with God. It must be the expression and not the means to it.

Now the Jews started out as God's people. But gradually and insidiously they confused means and ends, and they came to the conclusion that if they killed animals, if they said prayers, if they read the Scripture, if they kept the sabbath, if they paid the tithe, if they did all that the law said, this made them good people. Jesus came and said, "Fellows, you have got it mixed up. Only God can make you good. But God can make you good only if you let him into your life. If you 'faith' him, he will give you his qualitative life. If he shares his life with you, then he will enable you to do these performances as expressions of this qualitative life." But if you try to make yourself good by doing these things then you do not need God, and that is exactly the place where the Jews were. When he came and said, "Here is what you need, let

God into your life like he is in mine," they said, "We will kill you. We do not need God, we are getting along fine without him." And they killed him.

God does listen to his people in this struggle. We can share this tribulation with him. He is interested in us. He is in us and we need always to keep this in mind about understanding God. God is in us. This is stated by nearly all the writers in the New Testament. God is in us. He shares his Spirit with us, but he is not confined to us. He is in me and he is in you, and he is beyond both of us. Now he was in Jesus 100 percent. Jesus was just as much a human being as you are. He was no docetic Christ. The first heresy of the Christian movement was that Jesus was God. That sounds like good Baptist preaching, but it was a heresy at the very beginning. That is a half-truth and a half-truth is a whole lie.

Jesus is God-man. He is just as much human being as you are, yet he was a human being who shared God's life 100 percent, totally, completely. He is the God-man. He is fully man and he is fully God. That is, the divine and human life were shared totally and completely. Jesus was aware of the fact that God was in him. He said that if you have seen me you have seen the Father. He said, I and the Father are one. He was aware that God's life was in him completely and yet he was always aware that God was not confined to him. There was God beyond his experience, his life, because he prayed to God. He did not pray to himself! He always was aware that God was in him and that God was beyond him. God cannot be confined to any experience or to any place or in any way. He is always beyond anything that we conceive or experience. Even our Lord who had God in his life completely was aware that there was God beyond him.

So, John said the prayers of these people were going to God, yet God was in their lives. Then the angel took the censer and filled it with fire of the altar and threw it on the earth and there were peals of thunder, loud noises, lightnings, and earthquakes. These symbols indicate that God has heard the prayers of the saints. This is apocalyptic language simply meaning that God has heard what they have been praying.

The seven trumpets were made ready to sound in verse 6. It may help us to understand the judgments announced by the trumpet if several facts regarding them are taken into consideration. First, the destruction produced is partial: one third. The destruction produced by the seals was one fourth. Second, the trumpet visions are calls to repentance. The word at the conclusion of the final plague in 9:20 indicates this. It says "the rest repented not." These are calls to repentance of the unrepenting, ungodly world. And then third, as in the case of the seven seals, the seven trumpets are divided into two distinct groups of four and three. There is also a parenthesis or an interlude between the sixth and seventh trumpets.

The first four trumpets introduce judgments that affect nature in the four realms classified in John's day, the earth, the sea, fresh water, and heavenly bodies. And then the last three trumpets are concerned more especially with the inhabitants of the earth. Because of their great severity they are designated by John as woes. Much of the symbolism is derived from the plagues in Egypt. Now these visions of the plagues of the seven trumpets indicate calamity that will occur again and again and again. Not as single and separate events, but woes that may be seen every day in one form or another throughout the world. Let us look now at these.

The first trumpet was hail and fire mingled. John is not a chemist or scientist in the laboratory; he has hail and fire mingled with blood. This first trumpet seems to indicate blight upon the earth. The second trumpet, a great burning mountain is cast into the sea. The third trumpet, a blazing star falls on the waters. In symbolism he is saying that sin of the world carries moral and spiritual poison to the springs of life. With the fourth trumpet there is the darkening of the sun and the moon and the stars. Like the ninth plague in Egypt even the heavenly bodies are used as warnings to those who do not serve God.

The sounding of the fifth trumpet is preceded by a vision in which the prophet sees an eagle. The King James Version has the word *angel* here. There are some very late manuscripts that do have *angel*, but the oldest and best manuscripts overwhelmingly have *eagle* here. This prophet sees an eagle flying in midheaven screeching three coming woes. This is a prelude to the remaining three trumpet blasts. In the last three of these blasts not nature, but the souls of men are ravished. The eagle is a symbol of what is swift and unerring in sweeping upon its prey and it often is used in the Old Testament and in the intertestamental period to symbolize this.

Now this eagle announces the swiftness and certainty of the coming woes. The inhabitants of the earth are the ungodly, the worldly, those on whom God's wrath has been invoked by the saints whose prayers are now answered. The triple denunciation renders the threatened judgments more emphatic and terrible.

These three woes now are described: the first one in 9:1–11; the second one in verses 12–21; then the third one in 11:15–19.

The fifth trumpet is given in 9:1–12. With the sounding of the fifth trumpet, swarms of locusts more terrible than those of Egypt appear. John pictures a hole or shaft in the earth and out of this hole comes a great belching smoke stream and after the smoke gets up it becomes locusts. The locusts are loosed by one who has fallen from heaven known in Hebrew and Greek as "destroyer." In both the fifth and the sixth trumpets the attackers, though in animal form, are in reality demonic powers. As Christ has the key of hades and of death, Satan has the key to this hole, this shaft of the bottomless pit. The locusts do not consume vegetation but they attack men for five months, the normal length of a locust plague. They are described in terrible words and they fill the hearts of people with terror, dread, and hopelessness. These people seek to find death but cannot find it. These judgments fall upon the wicked persecuting world, yet they do not harm believers. The vision well may symbolize the rottenness of the world from inner decay, but no harm can come to those who have been sealed for they are secure from the devastation. Now, this is not automatic or something that is superficial. The people in the church do not receive the consequences of sin. Why? Because they have found a way to escape the sins. Sin bears its consequence in the Christian as well as in the non-Christian. The moral law of sin and retribution operates in the moral order. And when the Christian sins, he reaps the consequences just like the unredeemed man does. Suppose I decided that I wanted to start drinking and I really reveled in it. I drank and drank and burned up my stomach, then I repented and asked the Lord to forgive me. Would he forgive me? Oh, yes, he would forgive me, but what about my stomach? John is talking here about the inevitable results of sin and retribution. These who have God in their lives have learned to abstain from, they have the power of God to keep them from engaging in the sins that produce the retribution. He is dealing with the moral law here. He is dealing with something that is alive and vital in the world, not something that is superficial. God's moral order is not changed, but it is overcome when one allows God in his life to enable him to abstain from these causes that produce these effects.

From some theological legalists, we have inherited a terrible tradition in the Christian community that makes salvation a kind of transaction. Now the Bible knows no such idea. How do you effect change in your selfhood? How do you become more Christlike? Only one way, Paul says in Galatians and in Colossians. The same way you started it, by "faithing." If you get a little of God's life when you begin it, you get more of it the same way.

If you get this kind of life by letting God share his life with you, you get more of it the same way.

These locusts are not real locusts, and all the description of them is intended simply to enhance their gruesomeness. This plague lasts for five months and the people long for extinction. The moral consequences of evil bring people to despair and they have no desire to live. Evil is a devastating master. It destroys the desire to live.

The locusts are described in verses 7–10. This description is simply to enhance the gruesomeness of the principle of evil, of this demonic power in people's lives. The description is taken from several different sources. Notice that in appearance the locusts were like horses arrayed for battle. Their heads looked like crowns of gold, their faces were like human faces, their hair like women's hair, and their teeth like lion's teeth, and on and on. This is given to enhance the gruesomeness and the terrible demonic power of evil in people's lives.

Two instruments for oppressing the oppressors of God's people have been set forth, natural calamity and internal decay (9:1–12). Now a third instrument is mentioned. This instrument of judgment is external invasion. These are three instruments of judgment that God uses against the world.

Then the sixth angel blew his trumpet and I heard a voice from the four horns of the golden altar. This voice is interpreting the desires and expressing the prayers of the saints. That is the reason it came from the four horns of the golden altar. This is where the saints pray. In Exodus 30:2 the four horns of the corners of the altar were symbols of strength. Here he is simply expressing the potency of prayer.

A voice from the golden altar told the sixth angel who had the trumpet to release the four angels who are bound at the river Euphrates. Now Euphrates was the natural boundary of Palestine. In the history of Israel, invasions usually came from the northeast and when an invader got across the Euphrates there was nothing else to stop him, no natural boundary. In the Roman Empire this was the boundary line, and across the river was Parthia. The Romans were constantly afraid that the Parthians would cross over and invade the Empire. The loosing of the angels signifies that God's permission is given for the avenging hordes to rush in. God's restraint is removed and destruction overflows the land. The third part of mankind means that the judgment is partial, it is a warning.

John sees a large army in the field. Two hundred million horsemen! What does he mean by this? Did John get out and count them? No, he just means a great enumerable host. Horses, to the prophets, were symbols of destruction, strength, and ruthless conquests. War is described as a punishment and warning for unbelievers.

The appearance of the riders is terrifying, however, the attention centers not upon the riders but upon the horses.

In verses 20–21 John gives the response of the stubborn, ungodly people to these judgments. The rest of mankind who were not killed by these plagues did not repent of the works. God's reason in his judgments is always redemptive. He loves his creatures, even the ones who are in rebellion, the ones who are disobedient, the ones who are not saved. He loves them just as much as he does the ones who are saved. God's love is not conditioned by the character of the one being loved.

He loves the most ungodly, the most uncouth, the most uncultured man in the United States, as much as he does Dr. Hobbs. That is what *agapē* really means. All of God's judgments are remedial. God is trying to help us, even the church. In fact, his law of sin and retribution is always remedial. The judgments that come into the Christian's life as the consequence of sin are his ways of saying, don't do these things.

In these six trumpets, three instruments of judgments are

given: natural calamity, internal decay, the external invasions. These visions were given to bring reassurance to the saints that the world will never triumph permanently over the church. God hasn't forgotten his world. He is working in his world. He is using these methods to bring judgments to bear upon the disobedient, the unfaithful ones, the ones who are persecuting the church.

Apparently these plagues depict the continuous operation in history of the effects of sin and retribution. They show how man forever suffers from disobedience to God and yet how, in his blindness and rebellion, he will not recognize the tragic results of his sin. He refuses to repent. As the terrors of judgment fall, people grow more reckless. When people reject the warnings of judgment, they are left to their fate that they have chosen. The persecuting world then becomes the impenitent world with nothing to await but still heavier judgments of God. God does not change his method because we refuse. The farther we go, the heavier the judgments are in our disobedience.

Revelation 10:1 to 11:14 records the second interlude. As an interlude was inserted between the opening of the sixth and seventh seal, so there is one introduced between the sixth and seventh trumpet. Both of these are intended to comfort the people of God.

John saw a mighty angel coming down from heaven. The description of the angel shows the celestial dignity of the messenger. In John's writings, in fact in the whole Bible, God's glory is reflected in his messenger, in the same way it was reflected in Moses. This angel is a messenger from God. He was coming down from heaven wrapped in a cloud, with a rainbow over his head and face like the sun and legs like a pillar of fire. All of these are indications that he has a mission from God. He has dignity. He has a little scroll.

The angel set his right foot upon the sea and his left foot on the land. This message is intended for all sea and land, everywhere.

The angel cried out with a loud voice like a lion roaring. Seven thunders then sounded. John heard a voice from heaven saying, "Seal up what the seven thunders have said." These seven thunders symbolize the wrath of God which has been so forcibly impressed upon the author in the vision of the trumpets. God's judgments can be revealed only in symbol. They cannot be explained or understood. There is something about the operation of God's judgment in the world that we cannot fathom. Some evil people seem to prosper. Some good people seem to suffer and God seems to punish some more than others. There is some mystery about God's operation in the world that we cannot fathom. So God says, "Don't try that, John. You are not supposed to understand all of it." And we would learn a lot if we would listen to what God says here. About many things we have to say "We don't know."

"The angel whom I saw standing on sea and land lifted up his right hand to heaven and swore by him who lives for ever and ever." Two characteristics of God, his eternity and his omnipotence, are referred to in order to demonstrate the certainty of the fulfillment of the prophecy which follows.

The visions of the first six trumpets have shown that in the world the ungodly do not escape judicial retribution, but the six trumpets did not bring repentance. Therefore, there can be no longer delay. God's judgment operates. If people do not repent, do not turn to God, God does not change his method of retribution.

In the days of the voice of the seventh angel, when he shall begin to sound, the mystery of God should be finished. Now *mystery* in the New Testament means that which man does not understand unless it is revealed to him by God. Actually, the word *mystery* to us has a different meaning. Mystery in the New Testament means that we cannot know unless it is revealed by God, but God is trying to make it known. And the problem in understanding the mystery is not God's willingness for us to know it, but our unresponsiveness to what he is trying to tell us.

John again becomes a participant in the vision. The voice which John had heard from heaven spoke to him saying, "Go take the scroll." This symbolism here of taking the scroll is taken from Ezekiel 2:9 through 3:3. The taking of the scroll represents the deliberate acceptance of John as he now becomes a partaker in the vision.

The scroll in chapter 5 represents the whole counsel of God as it was made effective by Christ. So the little scroll here represents that part which is made effective through the witness of the church. The eating of the scroll was a common apocalyptic figure. The figure is used many times in other apocalyptic writings. The eating of the scroll indicates that the person assimilates, takes into his being, the message to such an extent that the messenger and the message cannot be separated. One never refuses truth and remains the same. You judge every person who listens to you and rejects the truth, or God judges him through your message. And this judgment is a bitter experience for any prophet. John is now a participant in this message that he has given.

The mercies of God and the judgments of God go together. In fact, they are inseparable; in some ways they are the same. The wrath of God and the love of God are the same thing. God is trying to share the divine life with his creatures. If we make a positive response to this, it is love, it is salvation. If we respond negatively, it is judgment.

Several years ago I went to a church where I was serving as interim pastor, and when I arrived one of the deacons met me. I had known the family for more than twenty years. The deacon said he wanted me to go to the jail with him to see his son. On the way, this good, godly man told me about the week's experiences. Soon after I had left from the previous weekend, this man's two teenage boys had committed some act, some misdemeanor, and the dad had felt compelled to punish them. He gave both of them the same punishment. They both did the same thing together and he gave them the same punishment. The younger of these two boys, after the punishment, came to his dad and said, he appreciated what his dad had done. He said he knew that he did it out of love. He realized that his dad was trying to help him and he appreciated it. He appreciated his dad's love and interest.

The older of these two boys had an entirely different reaction. In a spirit of rebellion he went out and did something far worse, a real crime, for which he was in jail. I tried to talk to him. I had known him since he was a small child, and I tried to talk with him. His dad was sitting there. And from this son's mouth there spewed a stream of violence, of judgment, of condemnation against his dad. He said, "My dad doesn't love me," "He has disgraced me," "He hates me," and on and on and on.

Now, from that dear dad's viewpoint, he acted in one way. He acted with one motive. He was trying to help these two boys. His energy went out for one reason, to try to help. But they responded in two entirely different ways. One interpreted it as love, the other interpreted it as wrath.

In a similar way, God's divine energy goes out to his people to try to help them. He is trying to help the saved and the lost. If we respond in obedience, we see it as love. If we respond in disobedience, we see it as wrath. But from God's viewpoint it is just one way. He is trying to share his life. He is trying to help us. Sometimes we understand an action of God as wrath and then later on when we get a better viewpoint of it, we change our minds, and we see it as love. But God hasn't changed. He is the same. God's divine life is eagerly shared. He comes with his divine energy to help his creatures. If we respond in the right way, we see it as love. If we respond in the wrong way, we see it as wrath. But in our anthropomorphic terms we end up contradicting what the Bible teaches. Malachi says explicitly that God never changes (Mal. 3:6). So we get in a dilemma. Maybe God is loving me now, at another time he is mad with me. No. Our response to God's divine energy determines whether it is love or wrath.

9

A Picture of Deliverance and Victory for God's People

In 10:1 through 11:14 John gives the second interlude. First he saw the strong angel; then he saw the little scroll that he was told to eat. This means that the mercies and judgments of God go together. This is a figurative way of saying that the message, when first received, seemed like honey in the mouth, but becomes bitter when it is interpreted or becomes judgment on those who hear.

Then in chapter 11 is depicted the measuring of the Temple and the two witnesses. Nowhere else (if they do here) in Revelation do Jerusalem and the Temple signify the earthly place. It seems that the command was given to measure the Temple in order to direct the prophet's attention to the size of the church of God. The six trumpets have spoken of the large portions of mankind against whom they were directed, but men did not repent. The seventh trumpet is about to sound which will announce more terrible woes upon the world.

It seems probable that the Temple must be interpreted to mean the dwelling place of God, or the church. Of course, this is the *naos*. There are two words in Greek for Temple. This is the one which means the holy of holies, or the Temple, the place where God dwells.

So, God dwells in his people. John said this. Paul said it, and many others. In fact, Paul found this out with a very sad experience on the road to Damascus. He learned that Christ so lives in his people and so identifies with them that what everyone does to his people, he does it to Christ. This seems to be the idea here.

John is told to measure the Temple, the altar, and all that worship there, the whole church of God, but not to measure the outside. The nations will trample over the holy city. Always in the Revelation the holy city is a type of the church. Therefore, the Temple and the holy city mean the same thing. John often mixes his metaphors. He portrayed the Lamb standing up, though dead, or slain. So here we've got the holy city and the Temple as the same reality.

John was told that the world was to trample under the holy city for forty-two months. This is an idiomatic statement that John is going to use over and over with several different lengths of time, always referring to the same period. Here it is forty-two months.

In Judaism two witnesses were required to confirm a verdict. So here the two witnesses seems to signify the church, the old and the new. The church in its double or complete witness.

The nations will trample under God's two witnesses for forty-two months. But during that forty-two months I will grant my two witnesses power to prophesy. The 1,260 days is the same as forty-two months, or three and a half years. The beginning of this forty-two months was when the Lord came and the forty-two months will continue until he comes back. This is an indefinite period, uncertain and no one knows when. Three and a half is half of seven. No one knows how long it is.

During this time, the two witnesses are clothed in sackcloth. This symbolically expresses the same truth that is stated in verse 2, that is, they are trampled under foot. During this time the church is despised. It is trampled under foot by the world.

In verse 4 the two olive trees and the two lampstands are not identical. The background for this is Zechariah 4 where only one lampstand is mentioned. The two olive trees which supply the oil for the lampstands are emblems of the old and the new covenants, God's supply of life to his people. So the lampstands typify the Jewish and Christian churches, all of God's people.

These two witnesses are symbols of the church, the witnesses of God. And the picture, or background, for these are taken from the experiences of Elijah and Moses. The most probable reference in verse 5 is to the act of Elijah as recorded in 2 Kings 1:10. It's the fire of their witness which refines and purifies and convinces some. It is also the fire of condemnation which follows those who reject their testimony, as Jeremiah 5:14 says. Fire throughout the Scriptures is used to symbolize two things: a purifying agent and a punishing agent. So the witness of the church either purifies or it condemns.

In verses 7–14 of chapter 11 is depicted the witnesses' temporary defeat, but ultimate triumph. I wish we had time to go into every one of these statements. John says that after these two witnesses are killed in the great city which is symbolically, or allegorically, called Sodom and Egypt where our Lord was crucified—well, he was not crucified in Sodom or in Egypt—but these two names are used in apocalyptic writings throughout to symbolize two things. *Sodom* was the name for evil, and *Egypt* was the name for oppression. So the oppressive, evil world tries to destroy the witnesses and apparently does. From an outward viewpoint it seems that the church is destroyed, but it was the same way with our Lord. His apparent defeat was his most signal victory. At the time it seems the church reaches its lowest, it is then raised up by God to be its best.

Notice the way in which the ungodly, those who dwell on the earth, after they have killed the two witnesses will make merry over them and exchange presents. These are simply trappings for a joyful occasion. It looks as if the evil world had destroyed the church. The evil world says, "Hallelujah!" But why does the world hate the church? Two reasons are given here. They have been a torment. The church is a constant reminder to the ungodly world of what God wants them to be. God uses the church to convict, to convince, to persuade, to witness to his saving way for them.

In this paragraph the evil world is symbolized as defeating or trying to defeat the church.

Then the seventh trumpet announced the reign of God. This is found in verses 15–19. At the opening of the seventh seal, you remember, there was silence in heaven. Here at the sounding of the seventh trumpet, voices are heard in heaven but there is silence as to the fate of the wicked with whom the trumpet visions have been chiefly concerned.

In the Revelation, the fate of the church as well as the doom awarded the ungodly always stops short of describing the circumstances after death. That is not what John is concerned with.

The seventh angel blew his trumpet and there was a loud voice in heaven announcing the reign of God. It is important to get exactly what John says here. The Greek can be literally rendered: "The rule over the world became our Lord's and his Christ's and he shall reign forever and ever."

John is reaffirming the great eternal reign of God in Christ. So the elders join in this song of praise. The elders are peculiarly indebted to God since the establishment of his kingdom is the victory of the church. The elders say we give thanks to thee, Lord God Almighty, who art and who was. Now in the Greek text there is no future here. Some late scribe put in "are to come," but it is not in the Greek. Only two, *who art* and *who was*. The future is purposely omitted since God's coming is now an established fact. God's coming took place in our Lord, in the incarnation. It is an established fact.

"And thou hast taken thy great power and did reign." God never ceased to reign, though for a time he reigns through Jesus Christ.

And then God's response is given. The open Temple and the

ark are portrayed. God's dwelling place now is open. God's Temple in heaven was opened and the ark of the covenant was seen, that is, God's purpose and plan are now revealed. They can be seen by anyone. And God's dwelling place is in his church. His purpose and plan are now being revealed and shown in his church, in his people.

In the first eleven chapters God's sovereignty over the world in Jesus Christ has been proclaimed. Now it remains to portray the manner in which the rule of God in Christ precipitates a reaction from evil, or from Satan. The development of Revelation from this point on is the account of the conflict between the sovereignty of God in Christ Jesus and the pretended sovereignty of Satan expressed through the rulers of the world.

In 12:1 through 14:20, a war is depicted between the woman which represents the church and the dragon which represents Satan. From here on the conflict is described as between the powers between heaven and hell, rather than between the individual Christian and the oppressors.

Here a dragon seeks to destroy the child. This woman here with the sun, moon, and stars, represents the church or that part of Israel from which the Messiah came, the true Israel. The garments that she wears, which are ornaments, are emblems of light. Her child is a son of light. This portrays the birth of Christ in apocalyptic fashion. So, a great sign appeared in heaven. A woman clothed with the sun, the moon under her feet and on her head a crown of twelve stars. All of these emblems are important.

She was with child. The eager, expectant waiting of those devout souls, who, before the coming of Christ, were longing for the consolation of Israel, is fittingly symbolized here by the figure of this expectant mother. There is also the suggestion that for the redemption of the race a new and divine force had to be born into the world. That's what John says in his Gospel in 1:1 and 1:14.

Then appeared a red dragon. This is, no doubt, to enhance its terrible appearance, with seven heads. The concept of seven heads suggests completeness of his wisdom and cunning for the execution of his plans; that of ten horns suggests human power. The diadem, or crown, suggests authority, not victory. John identifies the red dragon a little better further on as Satan and the devil, and so on. Where did he come from? No one knows. The Bible never tells us. No where in the Bible does it tell the origin of Satan. The poet, John Milton does, but the Bible doesn't.

When the curtain rises in the Scripture, evil is there. Satan is present. How he got there the biblical writers never attempt to tell us. Now if you read Isaiah 14 you will see that the prophet is writing about a king, not Satan. There is nothing in that chapter about the devil. I had a seminar with a Jewish rabbi on Jewish literature at the University of Edinburgh. This rabbi wrote his thesis on the origin of the evil impulse and the good impulse in man. Our professor, Dr. O. S. Rankin, was always late for the seminar, so I always received from this Jewish rabbi what he had learned in his research during the previous week. He told me that there was absolutely no attempt in any Jewish writing, canonical or noncanonical, of anybody ever attempting to say where evil came from. They all acknowledge the fact that evil exists, but where it comes from no one ever attempts to say. Now Milton helps us out with his beautiful epic poem about a war. According to Milton, God sent his forces under the leadership of Michael and they had a big war. Michael defeated Satan and threw him out of heaven, and Satan is now down here. But that is not biblical. Nowhere in the Bible is there any such idea. How Satan got to be Satan we don't know. The Bible doesn't tell us. The Bible writers are not interested in this. There is only one ultimate and that is God.

When this man-child was born, when she brought him forth, the devil or this dragon tried to kill him. She brought forth the male child who is to rule all the nations with a rod of iron. This goes back to Psalm 2:9. But her child was caught up to God and to his throne. Now, verse 5 passes over the whole incarnation experience of our Lord. This one verse summarizes his birth, his life, death, burial, resurrection, and ascension. That is all he is going to tell us about the incarnation. God caught him up to his throne.

The woman (i.e., the church) fled into the wilderness. The wilderness in apocalyptic writing indicates a place on the way to, but yet not in. It is taken from the motif of the wilderness experience. When the Hebrews got out of Egypt, they were not yet where God wanted them. They were on the way. God protected them in the wilderness, so the wilderness is on the way to becoming what God has in store for his people. The woman fled into the wilderness. God prepared a place for her there. She is nourished for 1,260 days. How long is that? It is three and one half years or forty-two months.

Verses 7–12 seem to be a parenthesis to account for the implacable hostility of Satan. Why is evil so hostile to good? Why is Satan so hostile to Christ? Because Satan is a defeated power. The incarnation of our Lord assured the defeat of Satan. He completed the victory in his own life and assured the completion in the church. So, this paragraph is put in to account for the hostility of Satan.

Failing to destroy the child, God took him up, the dragon persecuted the woman who brought forth the child. When the dragon saw that he had been thrown down to the earth, and of course, this movement from heaven to earth is not spatial, it is spiritual. Heaven in the Bible is not just a place up in space. Heaven is a condition as well as a place. In fact, in Ephesians five times Paul says "in the heavenlies" (1:3, 20; 2:6; 3:10; 6:12), and then he tells us where he is talking about. Where? In the heavenlies, in Christ Jesus. The translators put in a noun. Paul used an adjective only—in the heavenly—realm, condition, place, what-

ever. In the heavenlies—in Christ Jesus. That is, when one lets
God share his life with him in Christ Jesus, he enters right then
into the heavenly life, in the heavenly realm, heavenly condition.
So the church is the condition of heaven while one is passing
through this world.

So when the dragon was thrown down to the earth, he pursued
the woman, that is, the church. But the church is now protected.
She was given two wings of a great eagle that she might fly into
the wilderness. The wilderness now is the place of protection,
the place on the way to, but not yet in, where she is to be
nourished for time and time and half a time. What is that? It is
forty-two months or three and a half years. This is the time
between the first coming and the second coming of our Lord.

In the wilderness, that is in the world now, on the way to, but
not yet complete, the serpent poured out water like a river after
the woman. Satan is trying to destroy her, but the earth swallows
up the river. This is a beautiful figure which seems to indicate
that the efforts of Satan to destroy the church becomes a way of
protecting the church. The early Christians, in fact, every
member of the church was at one time a member of the world. As
one church father said, the blood of the martyrs became the seed
of the church. So it seems here that in the world as Satan tries to
destroy through his agents, through evil people, these evil
people become saved. They actually protect and become the
church. There is a strange condition in which it seems that
the thing that is trying to destroy the church actually saves the
church, because every member of the church was at one time
hostile to and antagonistic to the church. So this river that the
dragon tries to drown the church with sinks down and protects
the church. But the earth came to the help of the woman. The
earth opened its mouth and swallowed the river which poured
out of his mouth. The male child was saved and now the church is
being protected.

The dragon was angry with the woman. When he couldn't destroy the child, or Christ, and he couldn't destroy the church, then the dragon went after the children. Who are they? The individual church members.

The method by which he endeavors to destroy the individual church member is related in the following chapters. Now the first method that he uses in chapter 13 is the beast out of the sea. John saw a beast rising up out of the sea. This beast seems to symbolize world power. In John's writings he has several antagonists to the church: the world, the flesh, and the devil. Now the world is John's word for the aggregate of evil society. It is human society organized independently of God, in antagonism to God, and in hostility to God. It is evil society trying to destroy the church.

Now this beast out of the sea gets its authority from whom? From Satan. So Satan now uses world power, organized evil, trying to destroy Christ's church.

Notice verse 7. An authority was given it over every tribe and people and tongue and nations, all who dwell on the earth. That is, there is something about organized world power that makes people think that they must cooperate. They must fall in line. They must abide by its rules. If they are going to survive, then they have got to follow the world and its program.

All of the authority and all of the cunning that this beast out of the sea gets is from the dragon. World power is an instrument of the dragon.

"Everyone whose name has not been written"—how John wrote this, of couse, is not clear. How should it be? The translators put this in two or three different ways. What is before "the foundation of the world"? Slain or written? Why did the translators get it confused? It is not clear in the Greek. It is ambiguous. It can be "every one whose name has not been written in the Lamb's book of life before the foundation of the world." It can be "the one who was slain before the foundation of the world." Now, my own guess is, and if John tells me I am wrong I am not going to argue with him, but I think that he is going to say, "That is exactly what I had in mind, Ray." I think this "before the foundation of the world" refers to the one slain. Jesus Christ's death on the cross was an expression in time of the eternal character of God in self-giving of himself to help his creatures. The cross expressed what God had always been in regard to his creatures, giving of himself to us in order to help us. I believe that is what he says.

Verse 10 is very difficult. There is a problem of the text and there is a problem of understanding what it means. Notice, if anyone is to be taken captive, to captivity he goes; and if anyone slays with a sword, with a sword must he be slain. This kind of statement calls for two things: endurance or patience and faith. John seems to say that the warfare of the saints is spiritual. They are not to seek to defend the gospel or themselves with a sword in their loyalty to the gospel. He says captivity produces captivity for him who seeks to take others captive. He who takes the sword shall perish by the sword. John sees war being made upon the saints by the evil world, but does not think that they are to retaliate with like kind. The first beast is met and destroyed, vanquished, by two things, patience and faith.

John then saw another beast, a beast out of the earth. Notice its description. It had two horns like a lamb. We said when we saw the first rider come out of the broken seal that evil always tried to imitate good. Here this second beast has all of these figures of speech representing good. He tries to imitate Christianity or the church or the lamb. This beast out of the earth had two horns like a lamb, yet its message was like the message of the dragon, the devil. It had a voice like a lamb, pretending to be what is best for people; God's message for people is always for our best, but it had the nature of the dragon. That is, its real message was the dragon's message. It exercises all the authority of the first beast, that is, the world power, and makes the earth and inhabitants to worship the first beast. What does this beast out of the earth represent? I am convinced that it is false religion.

In John's day this principle had its expression in emperor worship, like the first beast out of the sea had its expression in the Roman Empire, but I am convinced that these two beasts didn't start with Rome and they didn't end with Rome. World power has been with us ever since the world started. It is the aggregate of evil, and for the Bible writers it was personified in Babylon, Assyria, Persia, Greece, and Rome. In modern America, world power is the aggregate of evil society in opposition to God. And false religion didn't start with emperor worship and it didn't stop when emperor worship stopped. This principle is always with us. In fact, in our own country there are a lot of false religions.

Now, these two beasts are allied with, or work for, whom? Satan. All of these details about this second beast that he gives are simply false religion's attempt to try to deceive the people. False religion tries to emulate, imitate, and duplicate that which God does through his people. False religion doesn't come and say, "I'm evil, you worship me and I will destroy you." False religion comes and says, "I'm a lot better than that good. You follow me and I will give you a lot more than good will." World power and false religion are allied and they go together.

In verse 18 John says the interpretation of this second beast calls for wisdom.

Let him who has understanding reckon the number of the beast, for it is a human number. John didn't say it is a number of a man. That's a mistranslation. It is a human number. It is something that is characteristic of all humanity. Man is incurably religious and left to himself alone he will build him a humanistic religion in which he is the god. Everywhere you ever see a human being he is giving devotion to some god. Archaeologists tell us that as far back as they can go in their digs and find evidence of a human being, they also find evidence of a god. But all the gods that man makes are humanistic gods. That is, man is his own god in some form or another.

So worship is common to humanity. Its number is 666. Ingenious attempts have been made from the second century to work out some person.

Six in the Jewish law of numbers had the hiss of the serpent. It fell short of perfection, fell sort of the complete number. So, 666 simply says imperfection, or the perfecting of imperfection. False religion is the height of man's imperfection. He is trying to create a religion in which he can be his own god. Man is a creature, not the creator. Man was created for God and he has got to have God in his life if life has any meaning or purpose to it. And only God can give life to man. It is a human trait or characteristic, to try to be his own god.

John has shown three enemies of the church, the dragon and the two beasts; that is, the devil or world power and false religion.

In chapter 14 John depicts the other side in the struggle, the church. Here the church is led by the lamb. There are 144,000 led by a lamb! The 144,000 represent the church militant, the church down here. Over on one hill John pictures a dragon and two beasts and their followers. Over on another hill depicts a lamb and 144,000 and they are ready to go into battle. John doesn't describe a battle, but he simply says that they are ready for warfare. The church and evil are locked in a struggle between good and evil and John is representing it here.

How long and when is this to take place? From the time of our Lord's coming until he comes back. It is going on right now.

The redeemed on earth are pictured in close communion with heaven. All the details here in the first five verses picture the redeemed on earth as in close harmony and in close touch with heaven.

In verses 6–7 John begins to show the consequences of this struggle between Christ and his church with the dragon and the two beasts. The first angel in verses 6–7 proclaims the final triumph of the gospel. John saw another angel flying in midheaven with an eternal gospel. What is the gospel? Last year Dr. Jesse Fletcher, then with the Foreign Mission Board, spoke in our chapel on missionary day, and as he was preaching he used the word *gospel*. Then he stopped and looked at us for several seconds and said, "By the way, what does gospel mean?" He let us think for a few moments. Then he said, "If someone comes rushing up to you and says, 'I've got some gospel, some good news,' and you said, 'Wonderful, tell me what is the good news.' He looked you straight in the eye and said, 'You ought to brush your teeth.'" And then he waited for several seconds. He said, "No, that is not good news, that is good advice." He said, "Any dentist will tell you that that is good advice. But that is not good news. We often confuse good news and good advice."

The gospel is not the historical fact of Jesus' death, burial, and resurrection. That is not good news to a lot of people. The gospel, the good news, is the fact that in this experience of death, burial, and resurrection God has done something for us that we cannot do for ourselves. Left to ourselves alone we can never help ourselves. We are in such a condition that we have got to have help and he has brought the help to us in Christ Jesus. In Christ he has done something for us that we cannot do for ourselves. That is good news. Not just the fact that he lived and was crucified and died and was resurrected. But the fact that I am helpless and hopeless and that God in Christ comes to me and does what I can't do, that's good news. Because if I don't have some help I am forever lost. But it is good news that he comes to me to help me.

Then John heard another angel flying in midheaven with an

eternal gospel. The gospel is eternal in its nature and in contrast to the power of the dragon and the beasts which are set for destruction. And this gospel is to be proclaimed to whom? Nation, tribe, and tongue and people. Who are they? What does this fourfold enumeration mean? Everybody! This is the gospel to be given to all people.

This angel proclaims the gospel, in verse 7, in opposition to the second beast who bids people who dwell on the earth to make an image of the first beast. You remember that the second beast said to make an image to the first beast. That is, if you want to get along in the world, false religion says that you had better worship world power. False religion says that if you want to get along in the world then make a compromise, worship evil or world power. That insidious idea can creep into Christianity. If you want to get along, you had better worship the first beast. So the first angel proclaims the final triumph of the gospel.

Then the second angel announces the fall of Babylon. Here John mixes his metaphors, as he does many times. Babylon is the same as the first beast. In its oppression of the Jewish nation, Babylon became the type of the world power which persecutes the church. Of course, at the time of the writing of Revelation, Rome was the personification of this, but never think that world power fell when Rome fell. World power is still persecuting the church. It is applicable to the persecuting world in any age.

Then the third angel proclaims the doom of those worshiping the beasts, in verses 9–12. Here those who worship the beasts and those who worship his image are regarded as one people. This is the fornication referred to in verse 8. Fornication and adultery, are used throughout the Old Testament as signs of unfaithfulness to God.

The first angel proclaims the triumph of the gospel, the second angel announces the fall of Babylon, and now the third angel proclaims the doom of those worshiping Babylon or the beast.

But what about the church in these judgments? Verse 12 gives a call for endurance of the saints, those who keep the commandments of God and the faith of Jesus. The church is to be faithful to God during these judgments.

John heard a voice from heaven saying, write, blessed are the dead who die in the Lord. That is, the ones who are faithful during this struggle are safe. Even though they lose their life in the struggle they are safe. "Blessed indeed," said the Spirit, "for they rest from their labors and their deeds follow them."

In verses 14–16 we have a dramatic picture of the harvest of the church. This is pictured as a wheat harvest. Here are the redeemed during this time of the church. God is gathering to himself the members of the church from the world.

Then in verses 17–20 we have a graphic picture of the vintage of grapes. This is a graphic apocalyptic picture of what happens to people during this time without Christ. The redeemed are gathered to the Lord; the ungodly, the unconverted, are destroyed.

Now, the stage is set for the resumption of the action involving the great conflict between Christ and the dragon. The two beasts have made their appearance and are ready for the war. In chapter 14 the third interlude is given.

Chapter 15 introduces seven plagues which are the last. These plagues are representations of the wrath of God. They are similar to the visions of the seals and the trumpets, but there is progression. They are not just a recapitulation; there is development and progression.

This is a vision of seven bowls. These bowl-judgments are the last in that they finish, they complete, God's method of dealing with evil. In the first vision, how many were affected? One fourth. In the second vision one third, and in this, all. This is God's ultimate method in dealing with evil. There is no restriction, no holding back. God's wrath is completed. The ultimate expression of his wrath is against world power.

Chapter 15 is a summary or an introductory chapter to that which follows. John saw another sign in heaven, great and wonderful, seven angels with seven plagues which are the last. For the wrath of God is in them.

And John saw what appeared to be a sea of glass mingled with fire. And then, in this chapter, he discusses three things: the seven angels with the seven plagues, then the overcomers, or the church, praise God for his justice in judgment—the church sees that God's program of judgment is just and right. The church sees that and they are claiming it. And finally, in verses 5–8, the seven bowls are given to the seven angels.

In chapter 16 the first hour bowls are in the sphere of the physical. The first bowl, evil sores upon men (vv. 1–2). The second bowl, sealike blood of a dead man. The third bowl, rivers become blood. And then the fourth, the sun's scorching heat.

These first four bowls seem to represent man's misuse of earth's natural resources. The last three bowls are in the realm of the spiritual.

With the fifth bowl the kingdom of the beast is darkened (vv. 10–11). That is, his very seat and authority is turned to evil, darkened.

With the sixth bowl the drying up of the Euphrates and the gathering of the kings of the earth are depicted. This is a close parallel to the previous vision. Look carefully at verses 12–16 because one of the debated words is found here. Notice that in this graphic illustration the sixth angel poured out his bowl on the great river Euphrates and its waters dried up to prepare the way for the kings of the east. God's restraint is removed. And John saw unclean spirits issuing from the mouth of the dragon and from the mouth of the beast and from the mouth of the false prophets. So here John identifies these three. All of these are in reality the same. The three foul spirits are like frogs in their unclean nature. Frogs, to Jews, were unclean. John says the frogs are unclean and he says they are demonic spirits. These frogs become unclean spirits like the locusts. They also perform signs and go abroad to the kings of the whole world to assemble them for the war on the great day of God the Almighty.

John then quotes the same words that he had quoted to the churches in Sardis (3:3). "Lo, I am coming like a thief! Blessed is he who is awake, keeping his garments that he may not go naked and be seen exposed." And the evil spirits assembled the kings at the place which is called in Hebrew "Armageddon." The word means simply mountain of Megiddo. In all probability this is the Plain of Esdraelon around which is Carmel or Megiddo. This was the battlefield of Israel. Many of the battles recorded in the Old Testament took place in this Plain of Esdraelon (Zech. 12:11; 2 Kings 23:29; 2 Chron. 35:22–24; Judg. 5:19; 2 Kings 9:27; etc.).

So Armageddon is used many times in apocalyptic writing. It came to symbolize struggle, warfare, destruction, conflict. It was used almost in the same way as the word *Waterloo* is used in the English-speaking world today. If we say "somebody met his Waterloo," we do not mean that he goes over to Belgium and encounters Napoleon there. This word has become symbolic of defeat in the English-speaking world. He met his Waterloo, he was defeated.

So John says this struggle between good and evil is a warfare. It is going on. Where is it located? Nowhere, and everywhere.

As Dr. Ray Summers says, "You can't find Armageddon on a map." This takes place in the heart and life of every person. It takes place in the life of every church. It takes place in the world between good and evil. The church and the Christian are in a struggle with evil.

The contents of the seventh bowl is poured out into the air. This is the special sphere of Satan. According to Paul, Satan is in the air (Eph. 2:2). And what is John symbolizing by this? In

Greek the word *pneuma* that we translate spirit was used in three ways. The same word was used to refer to spirit, wind, and breath. All three of these are unseen forces. Satan is an unseen force around us. Just like the Holy Spirit is an unseen force. He cannot be seen but you know that he is operating because he operates through your life. So the seventh bowl is poured out into the air, the special sphere of Satan. That goes from 16:17 to 19:10.

In verses 17–21 we have the earthquake and the hail that follows.

In 17:1–18 is depicted the nature and history of the great harlot Babylon. But before we look at that, let's look at the four enemies of the church which John has delineated up to this point. The dragon, in 12:3 ff., is Satan. The second one: the beast out of the sea or the harlot Babylon is world power. They are the same. You'll find those in 13:1 and 14:8, respectively.

Third, the beast out of the earth or the false prophet is false religion. You find that in 13:11 and 16:13.

Fourth, the ones who worship the beast. That is, the people of the world.

So, we've got four enemies now against the church in John's dramatic presentation: Satan, world power, false religion, and ungodly individuals.

In chapters 17—19 John shows us by symbolic pictures what befalls three of these enemies: Babylon, the beast out of the sea, and the false prophets.

The first one, in 17:1–18, is the great harlot, or Babylon. He doesn't call it the beast out of the sea, but it is the same thing. He describes this harlot Babylon in verses 1–6. This is world power. Then, he relates the mystery of this harlot which is the beast. He identifies them and says that these two mean the same thing. In fact, he is going to make that direct statement (17:18). So he explains in verses 7–14 the mystery of the woman and the beast.

When John saw her, he marveled greatly. There is something about evil's intentional destruction of good that is simply amazing.

But the angel told John not to marvel because he would tell him the mystery of the woman and the beast with seven heads and ten horns that carries her. The beast was and is not. The reason evil is so antagonistic to good is that evil is a defeated power. Evil is on the way out. God is going to be victorious. The church is going to prevail and evil is going to be destroyed.

John continues the discussion about these kings. To understand this calls for a mind of wisdom. It surely does. The seven heads are seven hills. Because there are seven hills upon which Rome was built, this must refer to Rome. No. Hills in all apocalyptic literature are symbols of strength, and 7 is the symbol of completion. So world power personifies itself and seems to be saying, "I'm fully powerful. I'm all strength." Now in that day maybe Rome did personify world power, but Rome didn't end world power. When the Roman Empire fell, world power did not fall. This truth is still applicable and is still present today in the organized evil of the world against the church.

Seven heads are seven hills on which the woman is seated. There are also seven kings, five of which have fallen, one is and the other is yet to come. Not literally, but John says the majority. This "little while" here is another synonym for "three and a half years" or "forty-two months." This struggle will not last forever, it is going to be ended. It will go on for only a little time.

Now in 17:15–18 the harlot is destroyed. That is, evil power is depicted as being destroyed. Destruction of this evil power, Babylon, is depicted in chapter 18 and in Old Testament taunt songs, doom songs. The angel announces and justifies the fall of Babylon in verses 1–3. In verse 2 the three phrases express the same idea, the low and hateful state to which Babylon is reduced.

"He called out with a mighty voice, 'Fallen, fallen is Babylon the great! It has become a dwelling place of demons, a haunt of every foul spirit, a haunt of every foul and hateful bird.' "

Then a voice from heaven summoned God's people to separate themselves from her. This is the prophets' message throughout the Bible: God's people, though they live in the world, are to separate themselves from the world. This challenge was not issued during the Roman Empire only. It was issued during the Babylonian Empire. It was issued during the Persian Empire. It has been issued at all times. God's people are constantly summoned to depart, to get away, and not to become a part of the world kingdom, that is, of evil. So in verses 4–8 the people of God are summoned to separate themselves from evil power.

Then the lamentations that follow are given to express one thing, the total and complete destruction of evil world power. He uses three groups to lament the fall of this world power: first, the kings, then the merchants, and then the sea masters and seamen. Now the lamentation here is not because of the sad fate that has befallen world power. These three groups are sad over the destruction of evil in the world because they have lost their goods. They have lost their way of enhancing themselves. Evil men lament defeat of evil because it cuts off their source of income, their source of wealth.

Chapter 19:1–10 depicts the judgments. First, John gives the four hallelujahs. Then he heard what seemed to be the mighty voice of a great multitude in heaven. The final pronouncement upon the wicked city of earth issues from heaven. As usual, at the termination of a judgment in Revelation comes the triumphant song of the heavenly hosts. The triumphant church now rejoices. The four great hallelujahs are found in verses 1–6. This is where Händel got his inspiration for his great masterpiece.

In verses 7–9 there is a beautiful symbol of the marriage of the Lamb. This is a figure under which is depicted the complete union between Christ and his church. It stands in contrast to the fornication of the harlot and the worshipers of the beast. There it is the union of the world worshipers with world power under the symbol of fornication. Here it is a figure of a marriage feast of the Lamb, and this is often used in apocalyptic writings and even in the Old and New Testament.

John is again tempted to worship the angel but he is told not to do this. Then follows the vision of the victorious Christ.

In 19:11–16 is depicted the appearance of Christ for the battle as King of kings and Lord of lords. This is a symbol of the victorious Christ as he comes forth in his conquest. On his garments and on his body his name is written. The Greek has it written that part of the name was on his garment and part on his thigh. This seems to symbolize that his righteousness, what he was and what he did were identical. In apocalyptic writings the garments symbolized righteousness. Now his righteousness is not just what he does, but what he is. And he is the word of God. He is God's truth going out. From his mouth issues a sharp sword. His method of overcoming evil is the truth, the Word of God with which he is to smite the nations. And he (*he* is emphatic in the Greek) will rule them with a rod of iron. The symbolism here in the latter part of verse 15 is descriptive of warfare and victory and judgment. He shall rule; no longer the kings of the earth; he is the one in control. He is Lord of lords and King of kings.

Then an invitation is extended, because of his victory, to a great feast. Now this is in contrast to the feast that is described in verses 7–9. There it was the feast of the church with the Lamb. Here is an invitation to birds when the ungodly people will be eaten. In Jewish thought if three things happened to a body after death there was no hope of resurrection: if the body was lost at sea, if the body was eaten by birds or animals, or if the body was burned. If a human body was eaten by birds it was the most disgraceful thing that could happen. So the summons goes out to the birds, the vultures, to come and devour these people who are destroyed. Now this is gruesome, but symbolic. It is a symbol of total and complete defeat. When the battle is over in this graphic symbolism, only one is left on the battlefield. The evil city has been destroyed. The beast has been destroyed. The followers of Satan have all been destroyed. Only one is left: Satan, the dragon. He stands alone like a deserted general on a battlefield with every troop gone. What is John depicting? God's complete victory over evil.

In chapter 20 John tells what happens to Satan. Then John saw an angel coming down from heaven holding the key to the bottomless pit, the shaft in the earth. And the angel took this old dragon from the battlefield and bound him. When was Satan bound? At the cross! Every Christian's life could be completely free from the encroachment, the temptation, the destruction of Satan. Christ has released in the Christian's life a power that assures victory over Satan. Satan is not destroyed, he is restrained. He is limited. This same figure of binding a strong man is used by Jesus (Mark 3:27; Matt. 12:29). Jesus said that if you are going to spoil a man's house and he is a strong man, you must first bind the strong man and he says he was doing this. He was binding Satan.

Satan was bound when our Lord came. As far as the Christian is concerned Satan is absolutely bound. There is strength given to the Christian to keep Satan completely restrained in his life.

But Satan is not bound completely. In the world he is not bound. Satan is bound and he is loosed for a thousand years. The thousand years is the same as the three and a half years. What is the origin of the millennium? Did John use the word first? No. The word *millennium* is used many times in the interbiblical writings. There are three numbers that are used in these writings to refer to the reign of the Messiah. The numbers are 40, 400, and 1,000. But these three numbers are used over and over. The reign of the Messiah would be 40 years, 400 years, and 1,000 years. However, these writers were not talking about how long the messianic reign would be. They were talking about what kind it would be.

When Jews used the multiple of 4 in their writings, they referred to the place. Where it would be. Where would the messianic reign be located? The 4 stressed the whole world. If a Jew used a thousand, he was emphasizing all humanity. A thousand is ten times ten times ten. It was the cube of ten. Any number raised to its third dimension brought it to its completion. One thousand stressed who was to be involved in this reign? Everybody, for either salvation or judgment. God's reign through his Messiah will be everywhere and all will be involved. One doesn't have to read much in these writings to find this. This is the only place in the Bible where we have the Greek word that we translate *millennium*, which means a thousand years. But it is not the beginning of this idea. This idea went back at least a hundred years and maybe a hundred and twenty-five years in Jewish writings. And they used these numbers over and over to refer to the reign of the coming Messiah. Now if Jesus was the Messiah, if he ushered in the reign of God, then God's messianic reign started when he came, and it will continue until he comes again. During this time, everybody everywhere will be judged according to God's rule and reign through him.

The coming of Christ bound Satan and threw him into a pit for a thousand years. During this time he is bound. After this? What is the antecedent of this? After this has started, or after this has ended? Which? After this has started. After this has started, not after this has ended. After this has started he must be loosed. How long? For a little time. The little time is the same as the thousand years. In other words, he is bound and he is loosed simultaneously. With the Christian he is bound. There is no way in the world for Satan to get at a Christian if the Christian will let God keep Satan bound. So the binding and the loosing are simultaneous. So often we say "after this" and we mean after this ended, but that is not what John is saying. After this started he must be loosed. He's bound and he is loosed simultaneously.

John then portrays the reign of the martyrs and the saints. This is the first resurrection. Then John saw thrones and seated on them were those to whom judgment was committed. During this time, the thousand years, God reigns through his church. God's people, the church, reign with him. Jesus said the same thing to the apostles. They shall sit on twelve thrones judging the twelve tribes of Israel (Matt. 19:28; Luke 22:30). God is now judging the world through his church. This is where the world gets its judgment. If the church were what it ought to be, we would see a reaction from the world. Nothing condemns a bad person more effectively than a good person. The good person doesn't have to say a word, he just needs to be what God intended him to be. Here is the judgment of the world.

Look at verse 4 because we need to translate it correctly. The Greek says, "And they lived and reigned with Christ a thousand years." There is no "again" in the Greek. They lived and reigned with Christ during all of this time. From the time of our Lord's coming until he comes back, the church is living and reigning with him. And the rest of the dead are the unredeemed. The literal rendering of the Greek is: "the rest of the dead lived not even to the end of the thousand years." All during this time the ones who do not accept Christ really never live at all. This is a figure of speech that is used by Paul and other New Testament writers. People without God are dead in trespasses and sins (Eph. 2:1). The people without Christ never know what it means to be alive. The rest of the dead lived not even to the end of the thousand years. This is the first resurrection. The first resurrection takes place when one who is dead in trespasses and sins comes to life. When he accepts Christ, he comes to life. He is quickened, he comes to life. This is the only way dead people are made the people of God. This is the first resurrection.

Blessed and holy is he who shares in the first resurrection. Those who have this first resurrection have complete power. The second death has no power over them. Those who come to life here live forever. The second death has no power over them. That's what Jesus told Martha when she was weeping over Lazarus. "I am the resurrection and the life." The one who "faiths" me though he were dead, he will come to life, and the one who lives in me shall never die (John 11:25). The second death has no power over the ones who share God's life in Christ.

During this thousand years these redeemed ones are suppose to be serving as priests. That is exactly what God saved Israel for. Now that is what the church is supposed to be doing.

Satan is cast in the lake of fire and brimstone. This struggle between Satan and Christ isn't going on forever. The binding and loosening is not going to continue forever. Satan is going to be destroyed. This is shown in verses 7–10. In verse 7 John says, "And when the thousand years may be perfected." A passive in Greek indicates that the action is done to the subject. This is a first aorist passive subjunctive. John says that when God has made history come to the conclusion that he originally intended, Satan will still be loosed. The conclusion that God had in mind is personified, completed, totally fulfilled in Jesus. We do not know the order of the words when he was on the cross, but possibly the last word that Jesus said was this word *teleios*, "it is finished." Here was God's purpose for his people. In Jesus' own life, he personified, he demonstrated what God had in mind for human beings.

Now, when he accomplished this in our Lord he did not completely bind Satan in the world. But Christ's experience of victory must be shared by the church. God is going to completely overcome Satan. John shows this in great apocalyptic figures.

In Ezekiel 38 Gog and Magog are names for a ruler and for the nations over which they rule, so this is evil and evil people. In verses 7–10 John shows the complete victory over Satan. Satan is thrown into the lake of fire and brimstone.

Then John depicts the destiny of the unredeemed. Complete victory has been won over the dragon (Satan), the beast out of the sea, the beast out of the earth, now there is only one group left. These are the unredeemed.

In chapters 21 and 22 we have a picture of the blessedness of the church, the new Jerusalem. If all the enemies of the church have been now destroyed, this struggle between good and evil leaves the church victorious. Here we have a glorified picture of the saints of God, or the church. John is not talking about heaven. He is talking about God's victory in his people. John saw a new heaven and a new earth. The word here is *kainos* not *neos*. In Greek *kainos* means something that is rejuvenated, something that is made over. God has been working in this struggle to bring good out of evil and he has completed it here. This is a vision of victory in the church.

John saw a new heaven and a new earth for the first earth and the first heaven had passed away and the sea is no more. He saw a new city. The old city, Babylon, had been destroyed and the new city comes down out of heaven. This is an apocalyptic figure that is used hundreds of times. To come down out of heaven simply means this is what God does. It is not what man has worked up. It is what God has achieved. God is going to give victory in the church. John is saying to the struggling persecuted little group of Christians, do not despair, God is with you, he is in you, Christ is in the midst of you and he is going to lead you to victory. John envisions the blessedness of the church and he does so in very beautiful figures. These figures include fellowship with God in the Holy City, all things made new, God dwelling with his people. The church is God dwelling with his people. And John uses the city here of a perfect cube which was a duplication of the holy of holies, and the holy of holies was a symbolic abiding of God with his people. So the church is the place where God dwells with his people always. The beautiful figures about this city: its radiance, its security, its glories, and so on are symbols of the victorious church.

Then John concludes by saying that this prophecy is sure. It has the attestation of God, of Christ, and the angel. This prophecy, this vision of victory, is sure. God is not going to be defeated. Heresy, gnosticism, the Roman Empire, and persecution are not going to destroy the church. God, through Christ Jesus living in his people, is going to bring them to victory.

10
Summary

David C. George

The kind of study undertaken in this symposium proved to have some unique values, especially an intensive and comprehensive study of the text itself. Most books or conferences would do well to cover a book like Revelation one time through, but the experience of going completely through the book three times results in a much greater familiarity with content and awareness of detail. Repetition and review are old learning techniques, but they are still indispensable for mastering the content of a complex document.

Besides learning what the book says, one also begins to notice what the book does not say. There is, after all, no mention of any "rapture" in Revelation, although it is often mentioned by people who talk about the book. There are also surprisingly few details about the return of Christ, the battle of Armageddon, or the nature of heaven—things we have come to think of as major teachings of Revelation.

Also much can be gained from taking several tours of the same territory with different guides. It is helpful in studying Revelation to observe how wise, honest, devout men differ as they interpret the same Scriptures. As you come to know them and their viewpoints, you come to love and appreciate them in spite of variations in interpretation. You also become more independent of them and freer to develop your own view.

This comparative study of interpretations points up the fact that every interpreter brings certain presuppositions with him to the study of the Bible. It is right and good to be committed to a viewpoint, but it is also necessary to be able to stand back and be objective at the right time. Those who are completely absorbed in one viewpoint need the discipline of critical study to gain some detachment. Only then will they be able to proceed with a more creative and constructive interpretation. This is the pathway to growth, Christian fellowship, and a clearer knowledge of the Scriptures.

This threefold study also helps to dispel controversy and misunderstanding. Those who know only one interpretation of Revelation often have a distorted idea of what others believe. Hearing an alternative view from one of its best representatives can change the caricatures and prejudices we have built up from secondhand reports. For this reason it would have been helpful if the dispensational view could have been included in this symposium.

The following discussion will attempt first to put the three viewpoints in historical and denominational perspective, then to summarize and compare the three, and finally to describe some insights as to the value of the study of Revelation.

Putting the Views in Perspective

Southern Baptist treatment of Revelation has generally taken two directions, one popular and the other scholarly. Popular interpretation has tended to be premillennial and has been strongly influenced by the dispensational theories of the *Scofield Reference Bible*. This widely used work, first published in 1909, followed the views of John Nelson Darby, a British teacher of the Plymouth Brethren denomination. Darby joined the Plymouth Brethren in 1827 and began his innovative system of Bible teaching about this time. He visited America six times between 1859 and 1874 and was well received (see George E. Ladd, *The*

Blessed Hope, Eerdmans, 1964, pp. 40–43). His influence came
at a time when American Christians were reacting against postmillennialism and rising modernism. A series of prophetic Bible
conferences brought together many earnest Christians who were
seeking a positive interpretation of the Bible.

Both Darby and Scofield held that God deals with man in
different ways in different time periods called dispensations. This
in itself does not separate dispensationalism from other systems
of theology. What is distinctive about the dispensationalists is
their insistence on a future literal fulfillment of all the promises
made to literal Israel. This makes it important to assign each
biblical statement to its proper dispensation and leads to a sharp
distinction between Israel and the church as two different
peoples of God. Revelation is assigned largely to a time when the
church will be raptured (caught up) into heaven and God will
continue his purpose on earth with the restored nation of Israel.

Premillennialism is not new. It is as old as the church. Dispensational premillennialism, however, did not appear until after
1830. Only then was this strong emphasis placed on a separate
future plan for Israel and the secret coming of Christ to rapture
the church away from the earth before the tribulation.

Dispensationalism was adopted by such influential leaders as
H. A. Ironside and R. A. Torrey. The *Scofield Bible* made it
available to anyone wishing to purchase a Bible with extensive
notes. The printing and format of the volume made it much more
readable and attractive than other Bibles then available. Schools
like Moody Bible Institute, the Bible Institute of Los Angeles,
and later, the Dallas Theological Seminary, provided dispensational training for church workers.

The Dallas Theological Seminary, a nondenominational school
founded in 1934, is today the leading center of dispensationalism.
The first president, Lewis Sperry Chafer, elaborated the view in
his eight-volume *Systematic Theology.* The current president,

John F. Walvoord, has produced the definitive dispensational commentary on Revelation, *The Revelation of Jesus Christ* (Moody Press, 1965). Theology Professor Charles Caldwell Ryrie has given a modern apologetic for the view in his *Dispensationalism Today* (Moody Press, 1965). Thus, dispensationalism has some able scholarly advocates.

The real impact of dispensationalism has come through popular expressions of the view. It received a new popular appeal in the early seventies through the writings of Hal Lindsey, a Dallas Theological Seminary graduate. His *Late Great Planet Earth* (Zondervan, 1970) became a best seller. It presented the dispensational view of prophecy and world history in sensational journalistic style. He presented his view of Revelation in the same popular style in *There's a New World Coming* (Vision House, 1973). Lindsey's writings coincided with the so-called Jesus Movement of the early seventies and had wide influence on many young people as well as adults.

Because dispensationalism offered a systematic, literal interpretation of the Bible and because it was readily available, it has appealed to many devout Southern Baptists, including many pastors. The best-known among these, and the most widely published, is Dr. W. A. Criswell, pastor of the First Baptist Church of Dallas, Texas (see his *Expository Sermons on Revelation*, Zondervan, 1969).

Southern Baptist scholars have usually taken a different direction. Before 1916 they generally shared the prevailing postmillennial view and held that the world was experiencing a period of increasing Christian dominance—the millennium—after which Christ would return. Hence, the name postmillennial. World War I and other tragic events of the twentieth century refuted such optimistic views. More recently Baptist college and seminary teachers have tended to be amillennial, that is, they have not taught the occurrence of a millennium, or earthly kingdom, between the return of Christ and the final consummation. They have also rejected other features of popular, dispensational premillennialism.

Amillennialism among Baptists is partly due to the strong influence of Calvinism on early Baptist thought. The reformation theology of Calvin, following Augustine and Paul, saw the church as the new Israel, the people of the covenant, and did not look for literal fulfillment of the Old Testament promises to the Jewish nation. There are also historical and scholarly reasons for not accepting the dispensational variety of premillennialism. Students of church history knew that this was a new doctrine of the mid-1800s. It is also probably true that controversy with extreme dispensationalists tended to push Baptist scholars away from the premillennial view, especially when they encountered J. Frank Norris, a Fort Worth pastor who combined dispensationalism with antidenominationalism.

These categories certainly never encompassed all Baptists. Many, both scholars and laymen, simply ignored the issue and therefore gave little attention to Revelation. This was even true of the Sunday School Board. Its literature and programs had generally avoided extended studies of Revelation, confining its use of the book to a few of the less disputed passages. Two significant exceptions to this which prepared the way for later developments were the inclusion of sessions on Revelation at the Nationwide Bible Conference in March, 1971, in Dallas, Texas (see George R. Beasley-Murray's lectures from that conference in *Highlights of the Book of Revelation*, Broadman, 1972), and an adult Vacation Bible School unit, *Studies in Revelation*, published by Convention Press in 1974, with exposition by Herschel H. Hobbs. Thus the Revelation Bible Conference, out of which this volume came, was the climax of a new willingness to deal with the book in Sunday School Board programs.

It is interesting and instructive to note that eschatology has never been a test of fellowship among Southern Baptists even though there have been sharp differences at this point. The basic reason for this is that the Bible does not make eschatology a test of fellowship, and Baptists have resisted the establishment of any creeds which would add such a requirement to biblical faith. There have been personal and local efforts to enforce eschatological orthodoxy, of course, but no one view has been so predominant that its adherents could effectively censure those who held different views. It is basic Baptist policy to unite around the basics of Scripture, Savior, evangelism, and missions and to permit diversity in nonessential matters. The right of individual interpretation has been zealously guarded.

Southern Baptists were also spared the experience of intense conflict with modernism which drove many conservative Christians in other sections to rally around the banner of premillennialism as a defense against the modernistic rejection of literal exegesis. The strength and relative isolation of Southern Baptists during formative years sheltered them from many trends that affected other groups. This meant that there was not as much pressure to conform in eschatology as there was in some other evangelical quarters.

In recent times, new options have developed which have encouraged a new look at Revelation. On the world scene, World War II and the onset of the nuclear age made apocalyptic themes seem very real. At the same time intense activity in biblical studies in the twentieth century has resulted in a new appreciation for all parts of the Bible, particularly those that deal with eschatology. New insights into interpretation have enabled scholars to be more objective about what the original writers meant and what their writings mean to us today. In the study of Revelation this has meant more and more agreement by scholars of different views, as George Beasley-Murray points out in his introductory remarks.

REVELATION: THREE VIEWPOINTS 229

The whole field of theology has taken a primary interest in eschatology since 1960 as young European theologians like Jürgen Moltmann and Wolfhart Pannenburg have addressed the Christian message to modern man's need for future hope.

In evangelical circles this growing interest in the future has been accompanied by a rediscovery and revision of the premillennial view. Some scholars have espoused a view usually called historic premillennialism because it reasserts the view of early Christians who believed in an earthly millennium without distinguishing sharply between Israel and the church. These interpreters point out that there is no specific teaching of the rapture of the church out of the scene before the tribulation in Revelation.

Historic premillennialists emphasize that it is not necessary to be a dispensationalist in order to be a premillennialist. George Beasley-Murray, now on the faculty of Southern Baptist Theological Seminary, and George Eldon Ladd of Fuller Seminary, have been the leaders in writing from this viewpoint. Dale Moody, also of Southern Baptist Seminary, has taken this position in *The Hope of Glory* (Eerdmans, 1964).

The developments at Fuller Seminary in California are of special interest because Charles E. Fuller, radio evangelist and founder of the school, was a dispensationalist trained at the Bible Institute of Los Angeles. His son, Daniel Fuller, wrote a doctoral dissertation on "The Hermeneutics of Dispensationalism," in which he argues convincingly for the historic premillennial view and against dispensationalism. Daniel Fuller, Ladd, and others have led the school in a move away from extreme literalism and have encountered opposition within fundamentalist circles.

Against this background the three views of this volume may be seen in perspective. Herschel Hobbs presents the classic amillennial view of scholarly Baptist interpreters. Ray Robbins shares the basic amillennial outlook, but his studies in apocalyptic literature and New Testament theology have led him to stress the theological significance for the Christian in the present instead of past historical references or future events. George Beasley-Murray elaborates the historic premillennial position. The dispensational view is not represented in this series, and the conference sponsors made no attempt to include every possible view.

Three Views in Summary

This chapter is a report by one conference participant who found much of value in each of the three views without subscribing totally to any one of them. But here is a brief summary of each view.

Beasley-Murray's Premillennial View

The view of George Beasley-Murray stands in sharp contrast to those of Hobbs and Robbins in at least two respects. First, he places more emphasis on eschatological events as future occurrences which will take place in the last days. Second, he believes Revelation points to a fulfillment of the kingdom of God on earth. In preparing his conference material for publication, he has focused attention on three areas: (1) principles of approach, (2) the second coming, and (3) the kingdom of God.

He approaches the book in terms of three literary functions. Revelation is apocalypse, prophecy, and epistle. Although its nature as epistle is often overlooked, it is significant because it indicates a primary application to the life situation of its first readers. The great message of the book is its assurance for Christians of every age that the opposition of men cannot frustrate the purpose of God. In the light of this truth, God's people are challenged to be faithful. Revelation shows the true nature of world powers. For political power or other earthly power to be given the attributes of God is a work of Satan and will lead to destruction. The future of the world is with God and his people.

In contrast to Robbins, Beasley-Murray sees clear teaching of the second coming of Christ in Revelation. But he does not believe that Revelation is a handbook of last things. It does not give systematic information about the Lord's return. The second coming is not described in its relation to the church but in its relation to rebellious men. There is little detailed discussion of the event itself.

Beasley-Murray also insists that the second coming must not be seen as an isolated event. It is part of a whole which includes the death and resurrection of Christ. He sees chapters 4 and 5 as the central vision, the theological center of Revelation. Here the God of creation is the God of redemption. Salvation and the kingdom form one whole work of God in Christ.

Revelation presents a diversity of pictures of the second coming, not a single coherent picture. Pictures are necessary because the event transcends the mental capacity of man. The description of the future event has present significance. "The glory of the event has power to transform present living" (see p. 50).

Judgment is an inevitable accompaniment of Christ's return. At his coming he is revealed in power. He comes to fulfill his promise to overthrow evil. Satan and his followers must submit to his judgment. Beasley-Murray sees the descriptions of judgment in Revelation as equivalent to the Old Testament portrayal of the Day of the Lord, not as symbols of the destruction of the created order.

The result of the second coming and the goal of the book is the kingdom of God. Jesus Christ is exalted to a position of sovereignty because of his conquest. When he enters upon his reign, his people will reign with him.

Beasley-Murray urges that the account of the millennium in chapter 20 be read in context with the account of the victorious return in chapter 19. He sees clear evidence here of an earthly kingdom. The fact that anyone doubts this, he feels, is only due to misuse of the doctrine by millennialists and strong reaction by opponents. In support of his interpretation he points to the work of objective, critical scholars like Paul Althaus, who, even though he does not believe a millennium will occur, believes that John describes a millennium. "We take it as reasonably certain," Beasley-Murray says, "that John's vision is intended to teach that the coming of Christ will usher in the kingdom of God in history, and that at the last the kingdom in history will give place to the kingdom in the new creation" (see p. 58).

Beasley-Murray points to Old Testament parallels to clear up some of the questions about John's vision. He applies 20:4 to the whole church, not just the martyrs, appealing to Daniel 7. He interprets the releasing of Satan after the millennium in the light of Ezekiel 38—39, where the people of God are attacked after they are gathered. In the light of Genesis 3, he finds it appropriate that the one challenged paradise in the beginning should be found doing so in the end. This indicates that the fulness of God's rule is not attained in this world, even under the best conditions. The apocalyptic view is realistic about the unceasing possibilities of evil in this world.

Beasley-Murray's treatment of 21:9 to 22:5 is of special interest. Like Hobbs, he sees this as applying to the kingdom beyond this world. But, like Robbins, he thinks that it also applies to the kingdom in this world. (Robbins, of course, would not refer the kingdom in the world to the period of the millennium.) Beasley-Murray sees nothing in the description of the city of God that could not apply to the kingdom in this world. Again, Robbins would agree with the same difference. To Beasley-Murray, the city of God is to be present in the kingdom in both its interim and its final forms.

In summary, Beasley-Murray sees Revelation as a series of steps by which the purpose of God reaches its destined end. The millennium is an interregnum. The thousand years does not designate duration but quality. Jewish thought in John's day saw history as a week of years which would be followed by the sabbath of the Messiah's kingdom. The kingdom which will be revealed at the coming of Christ will not be something totally new. It will be the revelation of the kingdom which has been a power on the earth since the resurrection. It will be a Christian kingdom, according to Beasley-Murray, not a kingdom of the Jewish nation. There will be no reversal to old covenant religion in the earth. The Jews will have the same privilege others have to turn to Christ and find their place in his kingdom.

Hobbs's Amillennial View

Hobbs stresses the nature of Revelation as apocalyptic and therefore a writing in code language. He also sees it as a drama in which the stage setting ought not to distract us from the main message which is the victory of Christ in the cosmic struggle of good and evil. He gives special attention to the linguistic method of interpretation, using many word studies to illuminate his interpretation.

Hobbs also leans heavily on historical study as an aid to understanding. He believes that John the apostle wrote the book during a period of persecution under the Roman Emperor Domitian, and he stresses the first-century relevance. The symbolic language of the book is seen as a method of giving encouragement to persecuted believers. John presented his vision, Hobbs says, as an alternative way of looking at things in the province of Asia around A.D. 95.

Acknowledging a large measure of agreement with other views, Hobbs said upon the conclusion of the conference, "Take away a few thorny spots and we all agree." Outlining his own eschatological perspective, he expressed the belief that Christ's return could occur at any time, but he counseled against efforts to spell out the time or the details.

Concerning the time reference of the book, Hobbs points to the phrase, "things which must shortly come to pass" (1:1). This he interprets to mean the events described will certainly occur, and they will occur suddenly. The events anticipated are primarily events in the immediate future. Hobbs insists that any interpretation of the book must have relevance to first-century Christians before it is extended to believers in any later age. "It did speak to the first-century Christians. But the principles laid down are applicable in any age anywhere, anytime, to any people of God who suffer for their faith" (see p. 77). Pointing to the original setting he notes that what happened was the death of Domitian in A.D. 96 and the resulting decrease of persecution.

Hobbs believes that the term "signified," meaning "showed with signs," in 1:1, provides a key to interpreting the book. Revelation is symbolic, and it is inconsistent to take parts as symbolic and then choose to take some parts literally. He predicts trouble for those who opt for a consistently literal approach and chooses for himself the consistently symbolic approach.

Hobbs feels that the symbols of Revelation can be understood through a study of their spiritual significance elsewhere in the Bible or through a study of historical counterparts. Thus he sees the rainbow around the throne (4:3) as a symbol of hope like the rainbow following the flood (Gen. 9:13). Thunder he interprets as judgment. The rider on the white horse resembles ancient pictures of a Parthian soldier and so represents conquest. All of the symbols have meaning for today. The world is in crisis, but God is still on his throne. His intervention may seem to us to be delayed, but it is nonetheless certain.

The two groups portrayed in chapter 7 are the heavenly redeemed and the earthly redeemed. The great tribulation (7:14) is the whole period between the first and second comings. In describing it, Revelation uses events and ideas of the first century to express what is true in all times. Thus the sea beast is the Roman Empire and the earth beast is the local provincial council which enforces emperor worship.

The description of the battle of Armageddon uses the image of the warring nations of the first century gathering at the ancient battlefield of Megiddo. It points to the final conflict of the age, but it should not be taken literally in its details. Hobbs notes the lack of any details about the battle itself, the victory being accomplished by the power of Christ's word without physical struggle.

Hobbs also gives a symbolic interpretation to chapter 20. He acknowledges that amillennialism does not have all the answers, and he judges such labels to be misleading. Insofar as amillennialism is equated with liberalism by some, he does not wish to be labeled in such a way. The millennium, he believes, symbolizes the period from the ascension of Christ until his return. He sees one second coming, one resurrection, one judgment. The tribulation is concurrent with the millennium and describes the suffering of Christians during the same period.

Chapters 21—22, according to Hobbs, are a symbolic description of heaven. The rich imagery employed makes a literal interpretation unthinkable. The fact that the heavenly city is said to descend does not mean that the setting is intended to be on earth. The gates symbolize accessibility; the walls indicate security and stability. The precious materials describe the beauty of heaven, but they also suggest to Hobbs the transformation of values whereby things highly prized on earth are mere building materials in heaven. He cites W. A. Criswell's observation that heaven is a city as we approach, but a beautiful garden once we are inside.

The announcement in 22:12, "I come quickly," Hobbs interprets to mean that the Lord may return at any moment. The book ends with a personal word from Jesus. As the drama concludes, he and not Caesar is Lord.

Robbins' Apocalyptic View

It is perhaps unfortunate that the three views in this study had to be given concise labels. At least in the case of Robbins' view, the term apocalyptic could be misleading. Apocalyptic here does not mean that Robbins looks for the future occurrence of the climactic events commonly associated with the apocalyptic viewpoint. Rather, his study of apocalyptic writings has led him to conclude that the apocalyptic events have already occurred in the life and work of Jesus Christ.

Robbins defines apocalyptic as that view which holds that the world is so evil that God must intervene from without. Prophecy is that school of thought that holds that God and man work together to bring history to its goal. Revelation, Robbins says, combines both views. The apocalyptic has occurred with Christ's breaking into history. Now the prophetic process is taking place as God works in the church with his people. This means that Robbins sees Revelation as applying primarily to the church in the present time. This does not mean that Robbins does not believe in the future coming of Christ with its attendant events, simply that he does not see these clearly spelled out in Revelation. For those latter-day occurrences we must look to the Synoptic Gospels, Acts, and Paul.

Robbins, like Hobbs, sees Revelation as written in code language, but language that was familiar to the early readers. The purpose of the book is to reveal, not to conceal. Robbins' interpretation of the book views the language as highly symbolic. He emphasizes the basic truths of the book and stresses the main theme as the revelation of Jesus Christ, not the revelation of a plan or a series of future events.

The historical background of the book is significant, however. Robbins sees a situation of heresy within and persecution without which raises the question, Is God going to fail in his plan for his church? The answer is an emphatic no, accompanied by the reasons for this answer.

Like Beasley-Murray, Robbins sees the redemptive work of Christ as highly significant in Revelation. Unlike Beasley-Murray, he makes future historical events subordinate to the work of Christ in giving spiritual life to those united with him by faith. Salvation and the Christian life involve a real change in selfhood as men receive the life of Christ.

The events described throughout Revelation, Robbins feels, are stereotyped symbols of events that are happening all the time in our lives. Thus, the tribulation began when the Lord came, it is going on now, and it will continue until he comes back. The holy city is a symbol of the church. Heaven is a condition, not just a place. Armageddon is the continual struggle between good and evil. The judgments in Revelation are remedial. The wrath of God is simply the divine energy of God which is perceived as love by some and as wrath by those who oppose him.

Concerning the crucial passage in chapter 20, Robbins points to the fact that Satan was bound at the cross, but not completely bound. The thousand years is a symbol of the Messiah's kingdom in apocalyptic literature. It points to the quality of his rule, not the duration. The short time of Satan's loosing is concurrent with the thousand years. He is both bound and loosed at the same time. The phrase "after this" refers to the time after the kingdom begins, not to the time after it ends. The first resurrection takes place when one who is dead in sin comes to life.

Chapters 21 and 22 likewise refer to the condition of the church. The end of the book is the victory of the idealized church. This happens whenever the believer becomes Christlike.

Like Hobbs, Robbins sees no literal earthly reference in the fact that the new city comes down from heaven. This is simply apocalyptic symbolism meaning that it is God's doing, not man's.

He sees all the beautiful features of the new city to be ways of expressing God's abiding with his people, and the church is the place where this takes place. But unlike Hobbs, he relates the symbol to God's action in the church in every age instead of God's establishment of the eternal order in heaven.

By rigorously and consistently applying theological principles in interpretation, Robbins has produced an inspiring interpretation of Revelation. His work should help us to establish more continuity between Revelation and the rest of the New Testament. The force of his reasoning will open up many new insights for the serious student, even as it raises many questions. His is a noble effort to shift attention away from what it meant and what it may mean in the future to what it means here and now. This is a much needed contribution to hermeneutics in evangelical life.

Some Insights Gained from a Study of Revelation

Insights as to Interpretation

A comparative study of three different interpretations of Revelation is an instructive exercise in hermeneutics, the science of interpretation. We find our interpreters agreeing on some principles, disagreeing on others. Each of the three accepts the value of careful linguistic interpretation. Each stresses the literary nature of Revelation as apocalypse, prophecy, and epistle. All three agree that study of the historical situation is important, although Robbins places less emphasis on history. All agree that Revelation has great practical relevance for believers in every age. All three agree that Revelation is highly symbolic, but Beasley-Murray is more concerned than Hobbs or Robbins to insist that the symbols point to earthly and historical realities and not to spiritual truths only.

The crucial difference in interpretation comes at the point of theological principles. Every interpreter must ultimately set his exegesis in relation to his wider frame of thought. How he does this will depend on certain basic presuppositions. The great issue between Beasley-Murray, on the one hand, and Hobbs and Robbins, on the other, is the former's conviction that the Bible, and especially Revelation, points to a future realization of the kingdom of God in the realm of earthly temporal existence. Beasley-Murray stands with those who see God working through holy history, a connected series of historical events—past, present, and future—which accomplish his purpose in the world. He also feels that failure of the church to proclaim this hope leads to the loss of a vital element in the Christian message, one that has returned in secular form in the Communist vision of utopia. He sees an important apologetic value in the promise of an earthly hope (see *Highlights of the Book of Revelation,* pp. 74–77).

Hobbs takes a more devotional and homiletical approach, interpreting Revelation in terms of its symbolic significance for the believer now and for the eternal order to come.

Robbins starts with the conviction that the writer of Revelation is concerned, not with future events on earth or with the eternal heavenly order. He is primarily interested in how the eternal future reality has already been realized in those who are united with Christ by faith. Whereas Beasley-Murray views Revelation in the light of the prophets and the Synoptic Gospels with their emphasis on the kingdom of God, Robbins sees it in the manner of the Gospel of John with eternal life as the present experience of those who believe. The fact that both of these emphases are present in the Bible suggests that there is truth to be found in both interpretations.

Insights About God

One important value of a study of Revelation is its strong doctrine of God. This teaching of the book is often overlooked, in spite of, or perhaps because of, the fact that there is no controversy regarding the portrayal of God in the book. The New

Testament presupposes what the Old Testament teaches about God and usually offers little specific teaching about the first person of the Trinity. Revelation is a shining exception to that rule. In the very first verse, God is identified as the source of the visions. The portrayal of God is very exalted. His eternity, transcendence, and power are stressed. The book is also strongly trinitarian. In 1:4–5 God is the sovereign ruler of the universe, but he reveals himself through Jesus Christ the Son, and he is personally present with his people as Holy Spirit. The reference to seven spirits is an indication of the fulness and completeness of the Spirit of God.

Chapter 4 portrays the whole universe in praise and adoration of the Creator, a passage without equal in the whole New Testament. In spite of the prolific use of imagery, the writer is very reserved in describing his visions of God. He is the One seated on the throne, but his features are not described. His glory is symbolized by precious stones but not by likeness to any living creature. His throne is surrounded by a crystal sea, thunder, and lightning, suggesting that it is inaccessible. He receives the adoration of all created beings. With all his majesty he wills to be known and enjoyed by man. From his throne flows the river of the water of life, and his presence in the new Jerusalem provides light for his people (chaps. 21—22). He makes himself known not only through his Son, but also through angelic messengers and inspired men.

Throughout the book the mercy as well as the wrath of God are seen. Robbins discusses these as two ways of perceiving the one basic nature of God, depending on the attitude of the perceiver. At the end of the book, God's presence is all that is needed to satisfy man's longing for heaven (21:3; 22:1–5).

Insights About Christ

In the final, summary session of the conference, Beasley-

Murray pointed out that the most important teaching of the book is one that all three of the teachers agreed upon. Indeed, he pointed out, even the dispensationalists would agree with this statement of the theme: Christ is our hope.

Above all else the book is the revelation of Jesus Christ (1:1). His presence in the midst of his people is the point of chapters 1—3. Beasley-Murray agrees with Robbins and Hobbs that Christ comes to his people in every age and situation. The hope of the second coming should not cause us to overlook the continual coming of the Lord to his people.

Chapter 5 is central to the book. Both Robbins and Beasley-Murray, in different ways, give special emphasis to the fact that the doctrine of last things (eschatology) grows out of the saving work of Christ (soteriology). Beasley-Murray specifically describes the second coming as the closely connected fulfillment of the death and resurrection of Christ.

Chapter 19 is also vital for Christology. Instead of focusing on the details of the second coming, the picture focuses on the nature and function of the one who comes.

Insights as to Last Things

Both Robbins and Hobbs would agree that the thousand-year reign of Christ and his people is a symbolic reference to the time between the first coming of Christ and the second coming. Both feel that the tribulation and the chaining of Satan span the same period of time as the millennium.

Beasley-Murray would agree that the tribulation is characterized by the kind of trouble Christians experience in every age, but he seems to feel that there will be a specially intense tribulation in the last days which will match this description in the fullest possible sense.

Hobbs sees chapters 21 and 22 as a description of heaven, the eternal order beyond time. Beasley-Murray agrees, but points out that it has an additional reference to the millennium, the holy city being present in both the earthly and the heavenly orders. Robbins sees these chapters as applying to the church and the Christian life in every age.

In terms of contemporary schools of thought in eschatology, Robbins finds the concepts of Revelation closer to realized eschatology. The kingdom of God has come to men in the life, death, and resurrection of Jesus Christ. Any further fulfillment of the promise of the kingdom will come in the eternal order beyond time and that is not within the scope of the book of Revelation as he sees it.

Beasley-Murray would be closer to inaugurated eschatology. The kingdom of God was established in the world by the coming of Christ, but its complete fulfillment awaits the future action of God in the events of the end time. Hobbs would probably agree with this and would stand somewhere in between the two emphases.

In the background of these views of eschatology there are issues about the relation of time and eternity and the significance of earthly-temporal existence in God's future activity. These are beyond the scope of this study, but they need to be explored by anyone who wants to develop an interpretation of Revelation that will be true to the biblical text and true to the actual events of history as the future unfolds.

It should be emphasized again that all of these men believe in the second coming of Christ. Robbins simply feels that the evidence for this is found in the Synoptic Gospels, Acts, and Paul, and that Revelation does not speak specifically about the Lord's return.

All three interpreters in this volume differ from the currently popular preoccupation with eschatology, which tends to be extremely literal. All of these men are sufficiently versed in the intricacies of language that they recognize varying levels of symbolism in all forms of language. Popular interpretation almost invariably spills over into speculation, indulging the curiosity of people about the perplexing events of history and offering some explanation from Revelation. None of these scholars is willing to be sidetracked into setting dates or identifying today's evil powers in Revelation. Popular interpretation can hardly resist sensationalism. It gives audience appeal to sermons and sales appeal to books. None of our three teachers works on this level.

Perhaps the greatest appeal of popular eschatology is its simplicity. It uses graphic language and leaves no questions unanswered. A careful scholar cannot give answers to all questions. Perhaps this is a weakness in much scholarly interpretation which needs to be corrected. Biblical interpretation which does not communicate to the man in the pew, much less the man in the street, is certainly deficient. All three of our expositors communicate well, and a number of lay persons participated in the conference. It is to be hoped that others will share in reading the materials and engaging in further study. There is a great need for pastors who can share the wisdom of the professors with their congregations.

Insights About Salvation

In discussing the portrayal of Christ in Revelation we noted the importance of soteriology for eschatology. Whichever interpretation we follow, Revelation makes a valuable contribution to the understanding of salvation. This book puts salvation in a larger framework than simply the deliverance of the individual from sin. It envisions a state of being in which man and the creation enjoy fullness of life because they are in perfect fellowship with God and his life flows like a river into theirs (22:1–2).

Robbins, with his special emphasis on eternal life in present experience, gives particular attention to this in expounding 5:9. He equates blood with sacrificial death and interprets it as life given all the way. Understanding faith in terms of its root meaning of unite, he points out that in Christ, our lives are given to God and changed by the coming of his life into ours.

Insights Concerning the Christian Life

All three interpreters agree that Revelation had a message of assurance and help for its first readers and that it offers the same for us today. The primary intention of the book is pastoral, to encourage faithfulness under persecution. Its message for first-century Christians is also its chief value for twentieth-century Christians. Whether physically oppressed by authoritarian governments or spiritually assaulted by the secular deities of money, pleasure, and power, believers can draw strength to face tribulation. Physical suffering and death are confronted in Revelation, and the assurance is given that beyond these is the joy of the presence of God. Revelation tells us that the waves of troubles that sweep over us cannot destroy us if we remain loyal to Christ. The entire book is a commentary on John 16:33, "In the world you have tribulation; but be of good cheer, I have overcome the world."

Revelation reminds us of God's sovereignty, Christ's presence, evil's defeat, and the church's victory. Those who attended the Revelation Bible Conference testified to this as they went away. Those in church-related vocations found new insight for preaching and new encouragement for their work. The presence of many lay persons indicated the perennial interest of the public in the book of Revelation. This is partly due to popular expressions of apocalyptic hope in our day, but at a deeper level it is an indication of the fact that Revelation speaks to men's needs.

Insights About the Church

The three views in this study all see Revelation as a church book. All students agree that the church is at center stage in chapters 1—3. The dispensationalists hold that the church is out of the picture from 4:1 to 19:10. That view is not shared by any of the interpreters in this volume. The portrayal of the people of God in various forms throughout the book is of great value for the church today. It encourages us to be true to Christ and to each other even under the most difficult of circumstances. More than once during the conference mention was made of the oppressed churches in countries under authoritarian rule today.

A special area of help for the church is the rich tapestry of worship scenes in Revelation. Some of the songs of praise in the book such as those in chapters 4 and 5, may have been in use in the churches to which John wrote. The words of adoration in 19:6 inspired the "Hallelujah Chorus" in Handel's *Messiah*. The vision of God in his glory in chapter 4 and the beautiful prospectus of heaven in 21—22 can inspire Christians today to enter into his presence with singing.

Insights Concerning Evil

One of the enduring values of the book of Revelation is its realistic exposé of the evil nature of the anti-God forces in the world. All power that is not subservient to the purpose of God is ultimately satanic. Religious institutions as well as political institutions can become demonic. The social and economic processes of life are affected by idolatrous religion. The believer's running battle with evil in the world is seen to have its source in the basic opposition between universal evil and the righteous God.

Revelation leaves no doubt about God's attitude toward evil or the ultimate fate of the unrepentant. Judgment is certain. The book gives graphic detail to the plain statement of Paul, "The wrath of God is revealed from heaven against all ungodliness" (Rom. 1:18). Throughout the unfolding judgments in Revelation God wills repentance and offers mercy. But when repentance is lacking, God will not forever tolerate rebellion.

The message of victory over evil is vitally important for the twentieth-century world where millions live under authoritarian rule and even the free nations are overwhelmed with corruption. Revelation's vision of the defeat of evil by Christ in his atoning death and triumphal return offers hope for such a world.

Insights for Life in the World

Revelation is a survival manual for Christians in a troubled world. The problem is that some see it as an opportunity to escape from reality and to retreat into a dream world of imagined future bliss. This was not the case for the first readers. They earned the right to seek refuge in a future hope by their courageous involvement in this present world. It is a tragic irony, then, when comfortable, affluent Americans make the discussion of Revelation and the events of the last days into a hobby or a fantasy world and avoid involvement in mission and ministry in the present.

The promises of Revelation are conditioned upon being faithful unto death. Believers are to hold the power structures of this world in suspicion. They are to guard against compromise which would dilute their devotion to Christ. But they are not to give up on the world. The message of Revelation is that there is hope for life in the world, and believers are to continue to function in the world through the church. They are to continue to witness to God's mercy as well as to his judgment. Those who wave the apocalyptic banner in today's world need the perspective of Revelation. Our three interpreters agree that Revelation is prophecy and epistle as well as apocalyptic. The apocalyptic word of God's intervention in history needs to be balanced with the prophetic word of man's responsibility as co-worker with God and the epistolary word of the divine possibilities for constructive action through the church.

Useful Books on Revelation

ASHCRAFT, MORRIS. "Revelation," *The Broadman Bible Commentary*, Vol. 12. Nashville: Broadman Press, 1972.

BEASLEY-MURRAY, GEORGE R. *Revelation (The New Century Bible)*. London: Oliphants, 1974.

_____. *Highlights of the Book of Revelation*. Nashville: Broadman Press, 1972.

BRUCE, F. F. "The Revelation of John," *A New Testament Commentary*, G. C. Hawley et al., editors. Grand Rapids: Zondervan Publishing House, 1969.

CAIRD, G. B. *A Commentary on the Revelation of St. John the Divine* ("Harper's New Testament Commentaries"). New York: Harper and Row, 1968.

CHARLES, R. H. The Revelation of St. John ("The International Critical Commentary"). 2 vols. New York: Charles Scribner's Sons, 1920.

CRISWELL, W. A. *Expository Sermons on Revelation*. Five volumes in one. Grand Rapids: Zondervan Publishing Co., 1961–66.

DANA, H. E. *The Epistles and Apocalypse of John*. Kansas City: Central Seminary Press, 1947.

HOBBS, HERSCHEL H. *The Cosmic Drama*. Waco, Texas: Word Books, 1971.

_____. *Studies in Revelation*. Nashville: Convention Press, 1974.

FARRER, A. M. *The Revelation of St. John the Divine*. Oxford, 1964.

JONES, RUSSELL BRADLEY. *What, Where, and When Is the Millennium?* Grand Rapids: Baker Book House, 1975.

LADD, GEORGE E. *A Commentary on the Revelation of John*. Grand Rapids: William B. Eerdmans Publishing Co., 1972.

MCDOWELL, E. A. *The Meaning and Message of the Book of Revelation*. Nashville: Broadman Press, 1951.

MORRIS, LEON. *The Revelation of St. John* ("Tyndale Bible Commentaries"). Grand Rapids: William B. Eerdmans Publishing Co., 1969.

PRESTON, R. C. and HANSON, A. T. *The Revelation of St. John the Divine* ("Torch Bible Commentaries"). London: SCM Press, 1949.

RISSI, M. *Time and History: A Study of the Revelation*. Richmond: John Knox Press, 1966.

Robbins, Ray Frank. *The Revelation of Jesus Christ.* Nashville: Broadman Press, 1976.

Robertson, A. T. *Word Pictures in the New Testament,* Volume VI. Nashville: Broadman Press, 1933.

Summers, Ray. *Worthy Is the Lamb.* Nashville: Broadman Press, 1951.

Swete, Henry Barclay. *The Apocalypse of St. John.* London: Macmillan and Co. Ltd., 1909.